Spirituality and Ethics in Education

T0355424

To Shelley

"Wherever people gather,
her deeds speak her praise."

Proverbs 31:31

Spirituality and Ethics in Education

Philosophical, Theological and Radical Perspectives

Edited by
HANAN A. ALEXANDER

sussex
ACADEMIC
PRESS

BRIGHTON • *PORTLAND*

2 4 6 8 10 9 7 5 3 1

First published in 2004 in Great Britain by
SUSSEX ACADEMIC PRESS
P.O. Box 2950
Brighton BN2 5SP

and in the United States of America by
SUSSEX ACADEMIC PRESS
920 NE 58th Ave.   Suite 300
Portland, Oregon 97213-3786

British Library Cataloguing in Publication Data
A CIP catalogue record for this book is available from the British Library.

Library of Congress Cataloging-in-Publication Data
Spirituality and ethics in education : philosophical,
    theological, and radical perspectives / edited by
Hanan Alexander.
        p. cm.
    Includes bibliographical references and index.
    ISBN 1-903900-03-4 (alk. paper) — ISBN 1-903900-07-7
    (pbk. : alk. paper)
    1. Spiritual life. 2. Moral education. I. Alexander,
Hanan A., 1953–
BL624 .S687 2004
207'.5—dc22
                                                    2003022288
                                                    CIP

Typeset and designed by G&G Editorial, Brighton
Printed by MPG Books, Bodmin, Cornwall.
This book is printed on acid-free paper.

Contents

———

Preface

This book is about the connection between spirituality, ethics, and education. Until recently, schools had abandoned their spiritual connections. Today, however, there is a spiritual awakening in education that places the quest for a moral life at the heart of teaching and learning. In this volume, leading philosophers, theologians, and critical theorists from North America, Europe, and Israel explore both theoretical and practical aspects of how families, schools, and communities can become more spiritual and more moral.

The volume contains papers selected from the Second International Conference on Children's Spirituality sponsored by the University of Haifa's Center for Jewish Education in collaboration with the Children's Worldview Project of University College, Chichester. It is the second in a series of volumes on the topic of children's spirituality, following publication of the proceedings of the First International Conference in 2001 edited by Jane Erricker, Cathy Ota, and Clive Erricker under the title *Spiritual Education: Cultural, Religious, and Social Differences – New Perspectives for the 21st Century*.

As the editors of the first book in this series emphasized, these volumes represent more than the publication of conference proceedings. They also embody the coming of age of a new subject of scholarly inquiry and professional practice dealing with the impact of the recent spiritual awakening on children and education (Erricker, Ota and Erricker 2001: 1–3). The fact that these proceedings are being presented in a book series under the imprimatur of Sussex Academic Press promises a sustained, intense, and in-depth effort to explore and clarify the contours of this new academic field.

The term "spiritual" connects self and community to a glimpse of that which transcends the limits of space, time, and value (Heubner 1999). It embraces the optimistic view that there could always be another place, an alternative time, a better way (Phenix 1971/1974). Children's spirituality is concerned with the ways this transcendent view is experienced in childhood, such as in a child's natural sense of awe and wonder; the shapes that this childhood view has taken across persons, cultures, religions and historical epochs; the ways it has been suppressed, controlled, or manipulated by adult societies; and the potential it holds for educational renewal in the present day. Education in spirituality, then, is concerned with nurturing such as connection between self, collective, and transcendence across the generations (Alexander 2001: 183–98, Alexander and McLaughlin 2003).

There has been an awakening of interest in spiritual matters over the past several decades because modern civilization has failed to offer rich and compelling accounts of what it means to live a purposeful or good life (Alexander, 2001: 12–24). Avoiding the quagmires of extreme subjectivism and relativism requires that we seek life's purposes beyond self and society even if we can say little directly about that which is supposed to lie beyond everyday experience (55–108). Inquiries about the meaning of worthwhile living fall within the purview of classical ethics, which is concerned with envisaging conceptions of the good, not merely with the articulating, analyzing, or justifying codes of behavior. The spiritual quest, therefore, can be understood as a search for ethical vision to guide our lives.

Among educators and education scholars this spiritual interest has grown in the past few years because of the sense that schools and other contemporary educational institutions have lost their moral compass. The curriculum has become inarticulate about matters of life and death, good and evil, right and wrong, love and hate. It has focused almost exclusively on instrumental knowledge – on teaching what it takes to get ahead – often losing sight of the fact that we are no longer sure which way is forward and which way back (Purpel 1988). The children's spirituality movement is one of a number of efforts in educational thought to recapture some sense of transcendent purpose in schooling, including character education (Lickona 1991), values education (Lawton, Cairns, and Gardner 2000), the ethic of caring (Noddings 2002), and critical pedagogy (McLaren 2002) to name but a few.

Although often expressed in concrete religious or cultural symbols, the concern for spirituality in education, as elsewhere, should not be understood as the expression of a particular doctrine, ideology, or religion. There are many different accounts of spirituality, religious and secular, rational and mystical. Some focus inwardly on soul, or mind, or feeling, or inner-child. Others look to community or collective for a sense of belonging and solidarity. A third approach turns outward, toward public worship, or ritual, or God. Most combine aspects of each approach, and many different varieties both within and among faith traditions, as well those reflecting no particular tradition at all, are reflected in these pages.

Anthropologist Clifford Geertz commented not long ago that there is a blurring of disciplinary genres among the humanities and social sciences today (Geertz 1983). This can certainly be said for this volume. The treatments of children's spirituality and spiritual education which follow are influenced by a variety of intellectual disciplines, analytic philosophy, pragmatism, existentialism, neo-Marxist critical theory, Catholic and Protestant theology, Jewish thought, Bahá'í religion, psychoanalysis, experimental psychology, sociology, and anthropology. In many cases these traditions are integrated in a single chapter. Thus, philosophers Nicholas Burbules and Terence McLaughlin understand the pedagogy of Jesus of Nazareth in terms of the philosophical analysis of the concept of teaching, Pamela King uses a quantitative research design drawn from experimental psychology to depict communities of character among Korean and American youth, and Ilan Gur-Ze'ev argues for a new counterspirituality based on Frankfurt School critical theory. Any organization of these essays, therefore, will be somewhat arbitrary, for a paper that appears in one category might just as readily be found in another.

With this in mind, I have found it useful to present the essays in three categories. **Part I** contains philosophical perspectives that clarify key issues in relation to educating spirituality, such as what it might mean to teach ethics and spirituality; the role of the soul, the psyche, and the mind in spiritual development; and the relation of others, experience, and religious practice to children's spirituality. **Part II** discusses the theological positions that represent classical faith traditions – Christian, Jewish, Bahá'i – in relation to spirituality and children, or that address how these traditions can be interpreted or imparted, through empirical or rational discourse, or through narrative and literature. **Part III** contains cultural and critical points of view, which consider the relation between children's spirituality and a variety of overt and covert forms of power.

Although these essays address a wide array of concerns within children's spirituality, this volume pays special attention to the connection between ethics, spirituality, and education. Modern philosophers often distinguish between morals, which relate to the right and wrong things to do, and ethics, which deal with inquiry into the justification of moral judgments. Discussions of this kind tend to focus on what rational people ought to do or what rights should be afforded in reasonable, just, or fair societies (Pring 2000: 140). An alternative advocated by feminist and existentialist philosophers understands morality in affective rather than behavioral or cognitive terms, as a particular sort of feeling. Ethics, in this view, entails a subject–subject or caring relation in which the other "fills the firmament," to use a phrase Noddings borrows from Buber (Noddings 1984). I have used the term ethics in a third sense drawn from ancient and medieval philosophers, and popular today among so-called "virtues" ethicists and "character" educators, having to do with the search for a good life (Alexander 2001). A fourth approach to ethics, with roots in Marxist and social democratic thought, is concerned with social justice, the abuse of power, and alleviating oppression of the poor and the downtrodden (Apple 1982). In the essays that follow there are authors who argue for connections between one or another account of spirituality and each of these orientations to ethics.

An intellectually honest treatment of our subject, however, requires that we not presuppose that a connection indeed exists between spirituality, ethics, and education. Some would argue, for example, that the very idea of spirituality is inherently childish; so education for spirituality is either a stage leading to a more mature religious stance or "miseducative" in the Deweyan sense that it undermines the sort of growth education implies (Dewey 1938). Others hold that all normalizing education necessarily entails an act of violence against the child, and so education per se can never be ethical or spiritual in the strictest sense of these terms. This volume gives voice not only to those who embrace a relation between some account of ethics, spiritual education, and children's spirituality but also to those who are skeptical about the merit of the entire enterprise.

It is perhaps characteristic of the new interest in spirituality that contributors to this volume represent a variety of religious backgrounds and cultural orientations, and that some quite intentionally represent no faith or tradition whatsoever. An important aspect of the recent spiritual awakening especially as it relates to children is a desire to seek that which unites humankind in solidarity with one another. The desire to connect self and society with matters of ultimate significance is not the concern of organized religion alone. Nor can secular or political ideologies claim exclusive ownership of the spiritual quest. The passion to live meaningful and purposeful lives stands at the very core of human existence and presents itself naturally in the very earliest stages of childhood.

As editor, I have endeavored to leave the views of each author entirely as they are, standardizing and clarifying style where possible, but recognizing also that such a diversity of intellectual, religious, and spiritual traditions must necessarily entail differences in approaches to expression as well. This places a burden on readers to shift from one approach to comprehending a text to another as they move through the volume, which makes the task of reading a bit more difficult. But, at the end of the day, this approach treats each view with the respect it deserves. Genuine dialogue between traditions, faiths, and perspectives does not come in neatly digestible packages. It follows, of course, that I take responsibility for the choice of essays in this book, but not for the views or traditions of expression chosen by each of the individual authors.

It is not insignificant that the conference from which these papers were taken was held in Haifa, Israel during the early stages of the Palestinian uprising that began in October 2000. Several of the authors refer to this. The struggle that has ensued since, including the terror that engulfed the cities and streets of Israel, the Palestinian Authority, and in some sense much of the world, represents more than the next phase of a war between two peoples over who will control a land holy to three great religious faiths. It also stands at the core of a global battle over how arguments will be settled among peoples with vastly different interests and visions of how life should be lived and over how people all over the world will relate to others very different from themselves.

The contributors to this volume do not represent a single view on how Israelis and Palestinians should resolve their differences or how we should engage the "other" in a world in which we come into increasing contact with diverse cultures, religions, races, and attitudes. However, they do agree that these issues ought to be placed at the center of educational thought and practice today and that the exploration and development of connections and disconnections between self, society, and our highest ideals which is the heart of children's spirituality – constitutes a significant way to do so. These essays are offered as a contribution to the growth of this new academic field extending our understanding of the roles children's spirituality can play in educational renewal through reengaging and reassessing ethical visions. We can only pray that in some small way this will also contribute to reconciliation among peoples in a world all too dominated by conflict.

I would be remiss not to acknowledge the assistance of many individuals and institutions whose help made it possible to publish this volume. The conference and publication of this volume was made possible by a generous grant from the Zeigler Family Trust. I am especially grateful to Mrs. Ruth Ziegler for her support in this and many other activities of the Center for Jewish Education. The conference was also supported by grants from the Office of the President, the Office of the Rector, the Research Authority, and the Faculty of Education of the University of Haifa. Thanks to Professors Yehuda Hayuth, President, Aaron Ben Zeev, Rector, Moshe Zeidner, Dean for Research, and Rachel Seginer, then Education Dean, for their continuing support.

I was able to complete work on this book while on study leave at Cambridge University during the summer of 2003. I am grateful to the Master and Fellows of St. Edmund's College, for electing me to a Visiting Fellowship during that period, and especially to my host, Professor Terence McLaughlin, for arranging such a warm reception for me in Cambridge. I am also thankful to Dr. Rebecca Nye and Ms. Rosalind Paul of the Faculty of Divinity for arranging a Visiting Fellowship in the Center for Advanced Religious and Theological Studies and for their equally cordial welcome.

I am similarly grateful to Drs. Clive and Jane Erricker and to Dr. Cathy Ota of the Children's Worldview Project at University College, Chichester and of the *Journal for Children's Spirituality* for envisaging this challenging new trend in educational scholarship and for entrusting the Center for Jewish Education at the University of Haifa with convening the second conference in Israel. Special thanks go to Debora Gottlieb Fattel, our unflappable conference coordinator, for her extraordinary efficiency and indefatigable good cheer; to Baruch Zilberman, Administrative Director of Haifa's Center for Jewish Education for his unflinching support and spirit of volunteerism; to Vered Meir and Sharon Riesfield, the Center's Administrative Assistants; and Susan Tornheim and Liz Steinberg, the book's copy-editors, for their dedication and persistence in bringing this volume to press; and of course to Anthony Grahame, our editor at Sussex Academic Press, for his patience and gentle prodding.

Finally, my wife and soul mate Shelley has brought spiritual inspiration to children and parents for more than 20 years first in Los Angeles and now in Haifa. Much of what I know of children's spirituality I learned from her. So, to Shelley, for agreeing to manage both our household and your business while I was away finishing this book, for following me to the ends of the earth, and for all that you have taught me about spirituality, children, and much, much more, this book is dedicated to you.

References

Alexander, H. A. 2001: *Reclaiming Goodness: Education and the Spiritual Quest.* Notre Dame, IN: University of Notre Dame Press.

Alexander, H. A. and McLaughlin, T. H. 2003: Education in Religion and Spirituality. In N. Blake, P. Smeyers, R. Smith and P. Standish (eds.), *The Blackwell Guide to the Philosophy of Education.* Oxford: Blackwell.

Apple, M. 1982: *Education and Power.* Boston: Routledge and Kegan Paul.

Dewey, J. 1938: *Experience and Education.* New York: Macmillan.

Erricker, J., Ota, C. and Erricker, C. (eds.) 2001: *Spiritual Education: Cultural, Religious, and Social Differences – New Perspectives for the 21st Century.* Brighton & Portland: Sussex Academic Press.

Geertz, C. 1983: *Local Knowledge: Further Essays in Interpretive Anthropology.* New York: Basic Books, pp. 1–36.

Heubner, D. 1999: *The Lure of the Transcendent.* Mahwah, NJ: Lawrence Erlbaum.

Lawton, D., Cairns, J. and Gardner, R. (eds.) 2000: *Education for Values: Morals, Ethics, and Citizenship in Contemporary Teaching.* London: Kogan Page.

Lickona, T. 1991: *Educating for Character,* New York: Bantham.

McLaren, P. 2002: *Life in Schools: An Introduction to Critical Pedagogy in the Foundations of Education,* 4th edn. Englewood-Cliffs, NJ: Prentice-Hall.

Noddings, N. 1984: *Caring: A Feminine Approach to Ethics and Moral Education.* Berkeley: University of California Press.

—— 2002: *Educating Moral People: A Caring Alternative to Character Education.* New York: Teachers College Press.

Phenix, P. H. 1971/1974: Transcendence and the Curriculum, in E. Eisner and E. Valance (eds.), *Conflicting Conceptions of Curriculum.* Berkeley: McCutchan; reprinted from *Teachers College Record* 73(2).

Purpel, D. 1988: *The Moral and Spiritual Crisis in Education: A Curriculum for Justice and Compassion in Education.* Westport, CN: Greenwood.

Pring, R. 2000: *Philosophy of Educational Research*, London: Continuum.

Part I

Philosophical Perspectives

T HE ESSAYS in this volume address six interrelated questions. Every author does not attend to each question, but from the range of the views that follow we can map out a variety of responses to them all. (1) The ontological question: what is the "stuff" of spirituality; what does it consist of? (2) The ethical question: what is the relation between spirituality and ethics? (3) The naturalistic question: are children born as spiritual beings; is spirituality innate, or inherent in childhood? (4) The developmental question: how does spirituality develop? (5) The pedagogic question: what might it mean to teach spirituality to children? And related to the latter, (6) the hermeneutic question: how should we read documents that speak to spiritual issues such as sacred texts?

Part I opens with an exchange between Nicholas C. Burbules and Terence H. McLaughlin concerning the pedagogic and hermeneutic questions. What, they ask, can be learned from the depiction of the pedagogy of Jesus in Christian Scripture about teaching in general and about teaching spirituality and ethics in particular? They agree that Jesus should be considered among the foremost teachers in the Western tradition, on the importance of considering him among other nonconventional teachers such as Socrates in the agora or Rousseau's tutor in *Emile*, on the essential "moral" and "relational" nature of teaching exhibited by Jesus, and on the central features of his pedagogy, such as his use of parables and proverbs. However, Burbules appears to hold that one can separate the essential characteristics of Jesus' teaching method from his religious message and his role for Christians as Messiah or Christ. McLaughlin, on the other hand, questions whether Burbules's interpretation is closer to an appropriation than an exegesis of Scripture, and by extension whether in spiritual teaching, as in pedagogy more generally, the medium can be so readily disconnected from the message. I suspect as well that one underlying difference between Burbules and McLaughlin may lie not only in their distinct approaches to interpretation but also in their responses to what I have called the ontological question, on which the former may be more open to secularism and less enamored with organized religion and theological realism than the latter.

This is followed by Amihud Gilead's discussion of the ontological and developmental status of spirituality viewed through the prism of D. W. Winnicott's psychoanalytic theory and Gilead's own "panenmentalism." Winnicott, a mid-twentieth century British pediatrician and child psychiatrist, held that young children should be allowed the illusion that what they imagine really exists. However, as they mature they should be encouraged by means of "transitional objects" – such as teddy bears – to move from a stage in which there are no limits on creativity to one in which they learn to distinguish between fantasy and reality (Winnicott 1971/1991). This bears a striking resemblance, argues Gilead, to his conception of the relation between possible and actual existence. There are no limits to the purely possible. The actual is possible too, but limited by other actualities. Both are mental concepts, because actuality is subsumed under potentiality. Hence, like the notion of panentheism, which holds that all of existence is subsumed by the Divine, panenmentalism holds that existence comprises mental possibility. Gilead equates spirituality with this conception of mentality. All of existence is spiritual, according to this view, yet the mental life of children represents a purer form of spirituality than the more realistic worldview of adults because children are less constrained by the actual.

In the third chapter, Claudia Eppert locates the education of ethics and spirituality in the surprising convergence of ideas between Simone Weil's "gymnastics of attention" and Emmanuel Levinas's attentiveness to the "other." "It is not so much that students should be encouraged to pay attention in order that they may acquire subject knowledge," writes Eppert following Weil. "Rather they learn subject knowledge so that they can practice paying attention." Attention, for Weil, is the "orientation of all . . . which the soul is capable toward God" (Weil 1951/1973: 105). This entails waiting and receiving, not mastering or controlling. When we attend in this way we prepare to accept our basic ethical responsibility for what Levinas calls "alterity." "To be attentive," Eppert quotes Levinas, "is to recognize the mastery of the other, to receive his command, or, more exactly, to receive from him the command to command" (Levinas 1961: 178). This entails a radical openness, exposure, and vulnerability. Acquiring a spiritual education lies not in coming to recognize the possible within my own mind, as Gilead holds, but rather in learning to receive the needs of another who is beyond and, in important respects, radically different from me. In Eppert's view, spirituality is located in between at least two subjects, not within an individual mind. Learning this relational attitude is essential to becoming an ethical being.

If Gilead located spirituality in pure possibility and Eppert in attention to others, Inna Semetsky follows Dewey in locating the spiritual moment in experience. Unlike Gilead's possible and actual, which exist within consciousness, for Semetsky all experience, even concepts, inhabit an "empirical happening" (Deleuze and Guattari 1994: 160). In addition, rather than prioritizing potential experiences as does Gilead, she is interested in the learning that transforms the possible into the actual, into what Deleuze calls "becoming-world." More particularly, Semetsky describes that state of childlike innocence just prior to the possible becoming actualized, the meeting of old and new that sparks into reality that which was previously only imagined – only virtual, pure possibility. The vitality of that moment is genuinely religious in that it returns us to the origins of creativity and teaches us to transcend the perceived boundaries of current habit or circumstance to grasp or initiate something new through the miracle we call learning. Spiritual education – or more precisely the spiritual moment in education that is the engine of all genuine learning – entails inhabiting that instant of pure possibility in which we return to the innocence of childhood prior to "becoming-world," that flash in which we "become-child."

If Burbules and McLaughlin engage Christian scripture with philosophical analysis, and Gilead, Eppert, and Semetsky interpret authors in the traditions of psychoanalysis, continental philosophy, and pragmatism, Ari Bursztein draws on the influential Israeli philosopher Yeshayahu Leibowitz. A prominent interpreter of the medieval Jewish philosopher Moses Maimonides, Leibowitz is known as a religious behaviorist for whom the observance of Jewish law – halakhah – is the essence of Judaism. Bursztein's essay centers on Leibowitz's interpretation of a passage in Maimonides' *Guide for the Perplexed* in which it is stated that the aim of halakhah is the welfare of the body and the soul (Maimonides 1190/1963: 510).

The early Leibowitz (1976) appears to follow the more standard interpretation of Maimonides according to which the observance of God's commandments, an "objective" undertaking, is preparation for contemplation of God's essence, a "subjective" or "spiritual" task. In this view, the publicly observable ritual behaviors of Jewish law attend to the welfare of the body, both of the individual, through the dictates of proper ethical conduct, and of the society, through the proper organization of social relations. Only when the welfare of the body is achieved can one turn to contemplating the correct understanding of the Divine, which is what Maimonides means by the welfare of the soul. According to this interpretation, observance of halakhah is a form of spiritual education in that it prepares one for the spiritual task of perfecting the soul.

According to the mature Leibowitz (1982), however, the idea that we must learn faith in God from religious practice entails a certain amount of what he calls "existential childishness." Both practice and faith are to be pursued, he holds in this later view, for their own sake. This reading of Maimonides hews more closely to the behaviorism for which Leibowitz is famous. It holds that observance of Divine commandments entails not only attention to the welfare of the body but of the soul as well. There is no way to contemplate God, in this interpretation, other than through the medium of observance. Halakhah is not preparation for the pursuit of spiritual perfection. Rather, the spiritual life – contemplating the correct understanding of God – is found in the very ritual observance itself. Bursztein argues through an analysis of Leibowitz's stance toward biblical criticism that the latter is his preferred reading and perhaps that of Maimonides as well.

Based on these essays, what can be said about the questions outlined at the outset? Concerning the ontological question – what is the 'stuff' of spirituality, what does it consist in? – Gilead suggests that it entails pure-possibility, which is a mental state, while Semetsky holds that it resides in the empirical moment just prior to the possible becoming actualized. Eppert holds that spirituality consists in "attention to the other" through which we can come to know God while Bursztein suggests that it entails contemplation of the true God through observance of His commandments, through which we can come into proper contact with others.

Burbules and McLaughlin both understand the ethical dimension of the life of Jesus in terms of modern moral philosophy and existentialist or feminist relational ethics, although McLaughlin appears also willing to consider Jesus as the Divine role model embodying an image of goodness or virtue. For Eppert, the spirituality of "attending to the other" is just what it means to embrace Levinas's notion of ethical responsibility. And according to Bursztein, the religious practice required for the perfection of body and soul entails commandments about relations between people, as well as between humans and the Divine.

Concerning the question of whether spirituality is innate in childhood, two authors, Gilead and Semetsky view the quintessential spirituality of childhood in a positive light. Bursztein, on the other hand, suggests that depending on religious practice to achieve faith may entail a childishness or less mature form of spirituality. For the former, becoming more spiritual requires a return to the "purity" or "innocence" of childhood; for the latter it requires growth toward the capacity to practice God's commandments for their own sake.

How does spirituality develop? According to Gilead, it emerges by means of Winnicott's transitional objects in which the child learns to distinguish the possible from the actual. As children become increasingly aware of the difference between the two, they gain the capacity not only to realize the actual but to value the purely possible as well. Eppert suggests that spirituality and ethics are not natural developments within the growth of children. These qualities must be learned. In Semetsky's view, spirituality is neither developed nor learned. Rather it is inherent in the miracle of learning itself – of becoming-world, of moving from old to new.

How then might spirituality be taught? According to Burbules and McLaughlin the spiritual and moral life can be taught through written communications such as sacred scriptures through oral communications, such as stories, parables, proverbs and puzzles; and through interpersonal communications, such as the very person of the teacher and the relations he or she creates with students or disciples. Eppert suggests that spirituality and ethics are taught not through specific subject matter, but in the way we learn to attend to ideas, ideals, and one another in the process of engaging any and all subject matters. And Bursztein returns us to the practice of religion itself, not as a means to some spiritual end external to observance, but as the very way in which to engage faith for its own sake.

Finally, the hermeneutic question: how might these texts, stories, parables, subjects, and practices be interpreted? McLaughlin suggests that there is a distinction between exegesis, in which we uncover meanings present in the material itself, and appropriation, in which we apply these meanings to contexts for which they may not have otherwise been intended. He prefers the former and suggests that at least in this context Burbules has tended toward the latter. Interestingly, Bursztein follows Leibowitz in suggesting that the exegesis closely associated with historical criticism of the Bible may be of less concern to the religious practitioner than appropriation, such as that found in rabbinic sources. To fulfill God's commandments, one needs to know how they are to be applied today, not what they meant in the past.

These perspectives by no means offer a definitive philosophical account of children's spirituality or of spiritual education, but they go a long way toward laying out many of the issues and alternatives any such account must address.

References

Deleuze, G. and Guattari, F. 1994: *What Is Philosophy?* H. Tomlinson and G. Burchell (trans.). New York: Columbia University Press.

Leibowitz, I. 1976: Education Towards the Commandments, *Judaism, Jewish People, and the State of Israel*. Tel Aviv: Schocken (Hebrew).

—— 1982: *Reciting the Shema: Faith, History, and Values*. Jerusalem: Academon (Hebrew).

Levinas, E. 1961: *Totality and Infinity: An Essay on Exteriority*, A. Lingis (trans.). Pittsburgh: Duquesne University Press.

Maimonides, M. 1190/1963: *Guide for the Perplexed*. S. Pines (trans.). Chicago: University of Chicago Press.
Weil, S. 1951/1973: *Waiting for God*. New York: Harper and Row.
Winnicott, D. W. 1971/1991: *Playing and Reality*. New York: Routledge.

Chapter 1

Jesus as Teacher

Nicholas C. Burbules

I

IN THE TWENTY-FIRST CENTURY, the image of the teacher has become so thoroughly the product of a professionalized, institutionalized society that it is increasingly difficult to imagine radically different alternatives of what a teacher might be. A teacher has a classroom, a certain number of students, an advanced degree, a supervisor; across nations and cultures we can envision this archetype in our mind's eye. If a young person says he or she wants to become a teacher, everyone has a pretty similar idea of what that means. Of course, the word "teacher" is used more broadly, and people who do not fit all these characteristics are called teachers. Nevertheless, in general, most people (including those who work in university departments or colleges of education) proceed from day to day on the assumption that preparing teachers means preparing students for a very particular role and context.

Recent changes, especially changes in technology, are beginning to shake up these assumptions about where, when, and how teaching takes place. Yet even here there is often a tendency to assimilate those new possibilities into recalcitrant assumptions about the nature of teaching with which we are familiar and comfortable.

Philosophers and theorists of education have a special duty, I believe, to resist such tendencies, to keep multiple and even radically unconventional models of teaching clearly in front of the educational audience not necessarily to advocate for any one of them, but to keep our thinking fresh and dynamic about what constitutes good teaching. The search for one best way of teaching has preoccupied philosophers in the West since Socrates. Today this search is more typically couched in the language of scientific efficacy and efficiency. In the process, teaching in many schools is becoming less and less creative, personal, and rewarding. The scope of options for teachers is becoming more constrained, their subject matter and purposes more determined by the decisions of others, their outcomes measured more mechanically and impersonally.

For this reason, I believe it is important to recover images of teaching that do not fit into these conventional roles and contexts. Moreover, I believe it is important to resist demands to subject alternative models of teaching to common standardized procedures of comparison, not only because these procedures are suspect but because doing so would simply reinforce the idea that our goal is to winnow many possibilities down until we find the "best" one.

There are many such alternative models of teaching: Socrates in the agora, Rousseau's tutor in *Emile*, the mother teaching her child, the wise man or shaman, the Zen master. One of my students is completing a very interesting thesis on the character of the Fool in literature as a kind of teacher (McDonough 2002). Generally these unconventional models are ignored in the development of teachers. If they are discussed, it is as testing grounds for the exploration of methods that might be reinterpreted or adapted for use in the classroom and what cannot be adapted for classroom use is, *ipso facto*, taken as irrelevant. This misses the fundamental point of such examples, which is that *being* a teacher means something different in all of these cases. It is not simply a matter of different pedagogical methods but of different relations of teacher to student, different settings, different criteria of success. What these examples give us, more than anything else, is room to imagine a new scope of possibilities when the pressures of routine and conformity tend to draw us back into conventional business as usual.

These considerations are even more salient when we reflect on the intrinsically *moral* character of teaching – not simply as a matter of professional ethics, but as a deeper choice about a way of being in the world, a way of being with others. To be a teacher of one kind or another is also to inhabit a set of ethical relations to others.

And so we come to the topic of this essay. Theological considerations aside, one of the foremost exemplars of teaching, particularly moral teaching, within the Western tradition is the figure of Jesus. I say "theological considerations aside" because I am not concerned here with the status of Jesus as the Christ, or Messiah, for certain religious traditions; nor will I be saying much about his specifically religious teachings, or his preaching (Hinsdale 1985: 1–5). Even those who are not Christian are familiar with, and frequently invoke, the proverbs and the parables of Jesus. Certainly all the examples I use here will be familiar. It is as a cultural icon, a moral exemplar, that Jesus will figure in this account, and so I will hew closely to a secularized interpretation of his status and influence (Manson 1951: 285–6).[1] Nor is the actual historical accuracy of these stories and statements necessarily relevant. The Gospel texts are part of our literary heritage, and whether one reads them literally, as historical records, or as a set of legends, based on oral traditions, committed to writing years after the death of Jesus, their influence on our vocabulary of teaching, particularly moral teaching, remains unmatched.

II

The kind of teaching Jesus practiced poses a sharp contrast to the didactic styles of most instruction, including most moral instruction. His use of various rhetorical forms drew from the longstanding Jewish tradition of *meshalim*, which included proverbs, riddles, aphorisms, and allegories. I start with the assumption that Jesus was a Jew who always regarded himself as part of the Jewish tradition, though certainly as a critic, even a revolutionary, from within (Klausner 1925). However, Jesus' distinctive use of parables, short fictional narratives told in the third person, represented a type of *mashal* not evidenced in the Hebrew Bible, although they were part of the wider rabbinic tradition (Scott 1989; Crossan 1973). These figurative devices allowed Jesus to teach in a style that provided for both "popular intelligibility and impressive pregnancy," an unusual achievement that managed to draw from familiar, concrete, and accessible examples, while at the same time inviting rich, multiple interpretations that "avoided pedantic modes of teaching and the petty arts of the scholastic learning" (Wendt 1909: 109, 148). As I will argue later, this invitation to open-ended interpretation and avoidance of strict moral edicts reveals something basic about Jesus' conception of moral agency and motivation.

It is not my purpose here to generate a strict typology of the teaching styles of Jesus. The terms "proverb," "parable," "allegory," and so on, do not carve out distinct types; in the Gospels, for example, the term *parabole* is used to refer to both parables and proverbs (Hinsdale 1985: 159; Scott 1989: 19–30; Stevens 1907: 41–2).[2] Nevertheless, within this constellation of figurative forms there are some interesting differences in how they subject themselves to interpretation, and in these variations of interpretation we see important differences in moral teaching sometimes tuned, for example, to different audiences (Perkins 1990: 41–6).

There is no evidence in the Gospels that Jesus taught children directly. Presumably there were children in some of the large crowds who heard him. He did, however, use children as an object lesson for others (Matt. 8:2–4; 9:36–37; 19:13–14; Mark 10:14–16; Luke 9:47–48; 18:15–17). Nevertheless, one can speculate about the relevance of Jesus' teaching style for teaching children, particularly in his use of figurative forms. Proverbs and parables can stay with children; good stories are memorable. But to understand the teaching of Jesus we need to get away from the notion that one simply starts children with simple proverbs, parables, and fables, then later gives them more mature moral instruction. For Jesus, these forms were as profound as moral teaching gets; they can be understood at different levels, revealing meanings over time.

Overall, two features of this teaching style stand out. The first, already mentioned, is that it is almost entirely devoid of explicit moral directives. In fact, Jesus had almost nothing to say about the varieties of conduct that constitute specific immoral acts (stealing, lying, and so on). His heavy reliance on figurative utterances suggests that moral guidance requires more general guideposts, and that moral sensitivity is not gained primarily through exhortation but through the thoughtful internalization of proverbs, examples, and cases, the analysis of which opens up a process of moral reflection that guides conduct in a less determined manner.

The other feature, linked to the first, is that the teaching of Jesus is entirely oral. Like Socrates, that other great exemplar of teaching in the Western tradition, Jesus did not produce any texts and appears to us exclusively as a character in narratives written by others after his death. There is only one instance in the Gospels where we see Jesus writing anything (I will discuss that event later). Otherwise his teaching was often opportunistic in the sense that he drew from circumstances at hand to make his points, and his folksy, aphoristic style was undoubtedly part of what has made his influence so enduring. One might even go beyond this to suggest that his refusal to write anything was itself a pointed comment on the uselessness of formal moral doctrines or codes; for him, moral agency operated within broader standards of conduct and character.

Jesus' rhetoric of moral teaching comprises four broad types, though these frequently overlap. The first is questioning or disputation, typically applied in cases where the interlocutor is either hostile or simply slow to make a connection (Hinsdale 1985: 140–4; Horne 1920: 45–62). These dialogues are not generally Socratic or open-ended; the questions tend to be strongly leading, and so (ironically) it is often in these questioning moments that we actually see Jesus the moral teacher as the *most* directive. As with Socrates, these disputatious dialogues often seem to be directed very little toward changing the mind of the interlocutor (which may not be possible anyway) and more toward influencing the audience to the dispute – including, of course, the readers of the text. Jesus certainly believed that some hearers would not be open to his moral instruction, and he did not waste much time with them.

A second type of moral teaching is more discursive and straightforward; we see a prime example of it in the "Sermon on the Mount" (Matt. 5:1–7:29; Luke 6:20–49).[2] Although these passages combine several forms of moral teaching, they begin with a kind of declaration, a summons, an invitation or a calling-forth that asks for a response (Hinsdale 1985: 137–8). One commentator suggests that this indicates the initial phase of a teacher/disciple relationship that Jesus sought to establish with the learner (and again there are interesting parallels with Socrates here) (Robbins 1984: 108–19). As elsewhere, Jesus seemed to assume that a necessary precondition must exist in order for teaching to go forward: without an active, interested response and an openness to moral reflection, teaching in one of his most-repeated parables is like casting seed upon barren soil (Matt. 13:4–9; Mark 4:3–9; Luke 8:4–8).

A third type of moral teaching is generally classified as proverbs: an aphoristic style that is strongly based in the Jewish wisdom tradition (Piper 1989: 11–13; Scott 1989: 7; Crossan 1983).[3] In the Gospels such proverbs are far more numerous than parables (Piper 1989: 11–13). They encapsulate in a memorable, pithy way some insight into human conduct or character, often framed in a provocative or paradoxical manner: "Many who are first will be last and the last first" (Mark 10:31); "If salt loses its saltiness, what will you season it with?" (Mark 9:50; Matt. 5:13); "Physician, heal yourself" (Luke 4:23; Stevens 1907: 37–8). Proverbs compose the bulk of the *moral* teaching in the Gospels; while there are a few moral parables in the Gospels, most of the parables serve to represent aspects of the religious doctine of Jesus, such as the Kingdom of Heaven.

Proverbs can have a special appeal for children; they are simple, easy to remember and provide something to ponder. They may not be enormously complex, but they can be profound. Moreover, proverbs and other figurations can come to be *shared* as part of a common cultural heritage; they provide a resource that can be referred to and discussed.

The use of parables constitutes a fourth, and very important, aspect of the teaching of Jesus: "In all this teaching to the crowds Jesus spoke in parables; in fact, he never spoke to them without a parable" (Matt. 13:34). In some respects, parables act as allegories, as objects of interpretation, in which circumstances of the world are taken as symbols for spiritual truths (Horne 1920: 90). However, this strictly allegorical interpretation of parables, in which each element is presumed to represent some other thing, vastly underestimates the richness and complexity of the parable form (Stevens 1907: 42–4). Parables are not simply illustrative, and taking them as purely representative betrays an overly literalistic reading of their figurative form. On one account, allegories are more like similes, parables like metaphors (Liebenberg 2001: 53). The meaning of parables (like metaphors) cannot be exhausted in a simple summation.

Nor are parables like fables, which tend to serve as straightforward lessons in "prudential morality" (Stevens 1907: 40). For Manson "The object of the parable is to work through the imagination and understanding of the hearers in order to arouse the conscience, and the real goal of parabolic teaching is not attained unless the conscience is aroused" (Manson 1951: 71; Liebenberg 2001: 157; Scott 1989: 29–30).[4]

For children, parables and fables can *entertain* and *delight*. They teach as narratives, not as arguments, and invite an active response from the hearer. Children can use their imaginations to visualize these stories, picturing the characters, and filling in or adding story elements, to make these stories their own.

The parables of Jesus generally draw either from common, natural events and human conduct or from a singular event or circumstance (Wendt 1909: 117–21; Winton 1990). Either way, they rely in large measure for their effectiveness on their modest and highly familiar subject matter: mustard seeds, fig trees, vineyards, wedding feasts. Yet at the same time, "it is as plain that Jesus used the parable to obscure truth, as that He used it to illuminate truth" (Hinsdale 1985: 167). This seems a strange kind of teaching indeed!

III

In order to understand why Jesus adopted the styles of moral teaching that he did, we need to speculate on his underlying moral psychology: why people act, or fail to act, morally (Hinsdale 1985: 230).[5] I think it is clear that Jesus believed that moral conduct depended on an internal commitment to, and an interest in, being good. This is not as tautological as it sounds. Many moral theories begin with the assumption that people would be good if they knew what the right thing was to do; moral theory is meant to help them by identifying what those right acts are. Other moral theories seem to assume that their role is to convince people *why* they should act morally; if their arguments are convincing, people (at least, rational people) will be persuaded by those arguments and act accordingly. Jesus seemed to begin from a different assumption, namely, that there are actual barriers to being good, and without addressing those barriers, the effect of moral exhortation, didactic instruction, or arguments will be nil.

One of the most difficult of these barriers, and a particular concern for Jesus, was the attitude of moralism and self-righteousness itself. Notice Luke 18:9: "Here is another parable that he told. It was aimed at those who were sure of their own goodness and looked down on everyone else." The story of the Samaritan woman accused of adultery, and Jesus' famous challenge "That one of you who is without sin shall cast the first stone" (John 7:53–8:11) clearly speaks to the same problem. For Jesus, smugness and moral superiority are moral barriers because they foster a sense of complacency and inhibit the ability to empathize with or forgive others, two crucial dimensions of morality. Similarly, arrogance and egoism tend to encourage selfishness or cruelty. Resentment and bitterness tend to justify blaming others for one's failings or making excuses for one's misconduct. Misery and hopelessness tend to produce moral passivity and fatalism.

Unless one speaks to the underlying traits and attitudes that lead to immorality, trying to change people's actions will be futile. Hence, for Jesus, moral teaching requires a *transformation* in these underlying traits and attitudes; self-righteousness, complacency, arrogance, egoism, resentment, and hopelessness must be *unlearned* before morality can take root. As Manson summarizes, "The moral demands of Jesus presuppose a changed nature and disposition" (Manson 1951: 299). This transformative model is utterly different from, for example, Kohlbergian or other developmental models because Jesus believed that there were actual impediments to being good.

The process of trying to transform moral character, in the way I have been describing it, has several elements. First, it involves identifying and confronting barriers like those mentioned above. While there is certainly no one-to-one correspondence between social groups and these personal traits and attitudes, it is not hard to see that people in certain situations, like poverty, tend to be more susceptible to hopelessness and resentment; those who are more privileged and affluent tend to be more susceptible to complacency and self-righteousness; and those in positions of unquestioned power tend to be more susceptible to arrogance and egoism. We see Jesus interacting with people in these sorts of groups in very different ways.

The types of traits and attitudes described here are also distinctive in that people have to *give them up* in order to change. While this is not simply a matter of choice, there is a willing component to that process, especially in view of the fact that these traits and attitudes can have a strong, if perverse, appeal for people – they can be pleasurable or gratifying in various ways, and so it is difficult to *want* to give them up. Jesus clearly believed that failing to do so (for example, failing to give up a grievance and forgive others) is a fundamental moral shortcoming and makes one incapable of moral recovery.

For children we might ask how and when these impediments are acquired. Jesus did not say. Clearly children are capable of selfish or mean acts, but perhaps they are not capable of forming the traits and attitudes described here – their misconduct is more "pure" in this sense. Perhaps such deeper faults of character can only be based upon a corpus of experience: how we act and respond, and how others interact with us. This would suggest that, in part, moral education for children might try to identify and defer these impediments *before* they settle in, in short, helping young people form the *desire to be good.*

Another part of this process is the *recognition* of one's self in a parable or example: "Why do you look at the speck of sawdust in your brother's eye, with never a thought for the great plank in your own?" (Matt. 7:3–5; Luke 6:41–42). Part of Jesus' talent for teaching was using teaching methods and examples that were intended to speak to *that* audience, in *that* place and time. But none of this can be more than an *invitation* to moral interpretation and reflection. The ambiguity and indirectness of figurative language was perfectly suited to Jesus' purpose; it attracts interest, it sparks an attitude of curiosity, but it also requires an effort for completion. Different hearers will take different messages away from common proverbs and parables, and this is what Jesus seems to have intended; while others will derive no meaning or benefit from them at all, which also seems to have been part of his purpose.

Without this type of transformation, moral teaching is pointless. Jesus reserved some of his most vivid images to make this point: "No one sews a patch of unshrunk cloth to an old coat; for then the patch tears away from the coat, and leaves a bigger hole. Neither do you put new wine into old wine-skins; if you do, the skins burst, and then the wine runs out and the skins are spoilt" (Matt. 9:16–17; Mark 2:21–22; Luke 5:36–38). Here Jesus seems to be saying that moral instruction without underlying moral transformation can actually make the character of people *worse* (for example, exaggerating their sense of self-righteousness, which impinges upon their actual moral conduct).

IV

In discussing the teaching episodes of Jesus, we start almost at the beginning of the first Gospel, the so-called Sermon on the Mount (Matt. 5:1–7:29; Luke 6:20–49). It begins with what I called above a declaration or summons, what is traditionally called the Beatitudes ("How blest are those . . . "), a discourse intended to attract, to reassure, and to invest his hearers with a sense of their importance ("You are light for all the world," Matt. 5:14). This is followed by a series of proverbs contrasting a morality of rules and a morality of compassion ("You have learned . . . eye for eye, tooth for tooth. But what I tell you is this . . . If someone slaps you on the right cheek, turn and offer him your left," Matt. 5:38; Luke 6:28–29). Jesus spoke repeatedly against self-righteousness ("When you do some act of charity, do not let your left hand know what your right hand is doing," Matt. 6:3; "Pass no judgment, and you will not be judged," Matt. 7:1; Luke 6:37).

The epitome of this sermon is the so-called Golden Rule: "Always treat others as you would like them to treat you" (Matt. 7:12; Luke 6:31). This proverb, perhaps the most famous of all of Jesus' moral teachings, exemplifies the special quality of a morality of spirit and attitude. This principle, if followed literally and with calculation (treating others well *in order* to be treated well), could be seen as the opposite of morality. Yet even the most simple, plain person can recognize in it a moral value – the value of empathy, of trying to imagine from one's own perspective the needs and interests of others. Certainly, taken as a rule, this proverb would have countless exceptions (what I want for myself others may not want for themselves, etc.). While seemingly simple, even childlike, this proverb has sufficient depth and complexity to inspire sophisticated and profound moral theories, including Kant's Categorical Imperative and John Rawls's "veil of ignorance" argument in *A Theory of Justice*.

Proverbs can be found on nearly every page of the Gospels. Crossan identifies 133 distinct proverbs, not counting repetition (Crossan 1983: 2). Many of them have the same character as the Golden Rule: "Love your neighbor as yourself" (Matt. 22:39; Mark 12:31; Luke 10:27) or "It is better to give than to receive" (Acts 20:35, reported by Paul as a quote from Jesus). Other proverbs contain paradoxical assertions ("Many who are first will be last and the last first," Mark 10:31) that belie clear, literal analysis. Does this mean that one should not try for moral improvement? (Stevens 1907: 31–2). Many of Jesus' proverbs and parables seem to be saying that consistently virtuous people will not be treated any better than those who arrive at goodness only at the last moment (as in the parable of the Prodigal Son). Taken literally this is a very strange message for moral teaching.

Moreover, the moral map of all the proverbs and parables of Jesus does not form a consistent whole. Contrast the famous proverb about turning the other cheek with the injunction to his disciples "Whoever has a purse should take it with him . . . and if he has no sword, let him sell his cloak and buy one" (Luke 22:36). How are we to view these apparent paradoxes within, and contradictions between, proverbs and other moral teachings? One explanation, of course, is that the Gospels were written by different people in different situations at different times and thus should not be expected to present an entirely consistent doctrine. Another explanation is that Jesus was strongly situationist in his morality and did not value moral consistency for its own sake. I prefer a different explanation, which is that the representation of paradox and inconsistency itself teaches something important about moral thought and action: that it is not perfectionist, but inevitably incomplete; that it is not a search for a system of rules but a cultivation of moral sensitivity and conscience. Proverbs can be counterproductive to moral teaching when they are taken as directives rather than as broadly directional guideposts. The best moral proverbs of Jesus make clear the inevitability of interpretation, misinterpretation and different interpretations in guiding conduct.

This acknowledgement of moral difficulty and perplexity makes one commentator compare Jesus' method of teaching with John Dewey's "problem method" (Horne 1920: 31–2). The shortcoming of this comparison, however, is apparent when we review Jesus' own account of why he taught through parables and other figurative forms: it is, he said, precisely in order that he *not* be understood. The famous parable of the seeds thrown by the sower, some on the footpath, some on the rocky ground, some among the thistles, concerns a planting that does not take root (Matt. 13:4–9; Mark 4:3–9; Luke 8:4–8). It is a parable about the inaccessibility of parables. When his disciples then asked him why he taught in parables, Jesus had to explain to them in other words what the parable was about: parables are not meant to be understood by everyone; for those not prepared to receive them, "they look without seeing, and listen without hearing or understanding" (Matt. 13:10–15; Mark 4:10–12; Luke 8:9–10). He then went on, just in case they missed the point, to give an exegesis of the parable he has just given them: "This is what the parable means . . . " (Luke 8:11–15; Matt. 13:16–23; Mark 4:13–20). In short, they were not allowed *not* to understand. What manner of moral teaching is this?

A parable about why he taught in parables: parables are meant to be misunderstood, "revealing truth to friends and concealing truth from enemies," says Horne (Horne 1920: 88). But why should moral (or spiritual) truth be concealed from anyone? Earlier I suggested that Jesus seemed to believe that without the precondition of an appropriate moral commitment or receptivity, moral teaching of the sort he offered would be ineffective and even counterproductive. Hence the point is not a matter of purposive concealment; it is adopting a figurative method *knowing* that those who are impatient, incurious, or of an insufficiently motivated spirit will derive little from it. Wanting something literal and unambiguous, they will lose interest or reinterpret the message to suit their preconceptions. The disciples, here and elsewhere in the Gospels, were given an explicit explanation of the parables because it was important that they truly understood this one root parable. Moreover, with texts like the Gospels, there is always the second perspective of the observers of the interchanges (including the reader of the text); *they* see the meaning of the parable, and *they* see who understands it and who fails to understand it. This communicated an important message to the observers not only about the meaning of the parable but about the characteristics and attitudes of those who understand it and those who do not and this conveys to the observers a crucial moral message as well.

As I have said, the Gospels contain a few primarily *moral* parables (and at least one narrative about Jesus that reads like a parable). The story of the Good Samaritan (Luke 10:29–37) is an elaboration of the proverb "Love your neighbor as yourself." The story is familiar: a man traveling from Jerusalem to Jericho is waylaid by robbers, who leave him for dead. The victim is presumably a Jew, and he is passed by a priest and a Levite who travel on the opposite side to avoid dealing with him. A third man, a Samaritan, stops and comes to his aid. In the context of Luke's Gospel, this was certainly meant as a snipe at the Jewish religious men, who would not care for their own. And the irony intended by the story is that there was no love lost between Jews and Samaritans at that time but *this* Samaritan proved to be a good neighbor. So there are many levels of moral meaning here: the virtue of compassion for strangers or of caring for those in need generally; avoiding stereotypes about which nations or cultures are morally superior; marking the difference between official piety and personal decency; and so on. This is not simply a moral fable with a pat conclusion; it can be variously interpreted and in these different readings reveals something about the moral sensibilities of the reader.

The parable of the Unforgiving Servant (Matt. 18:23–35) deals with another recurring theme in Jesus' moral sphere, forgiveness. Here a servant owes his master a large sum of money; the man throws himself on the mercy of his master and pleads, "Be patient with me . . . and I will pay in full." The master, moved to pity by these entreaties, releases the man and even agrees to cancel his debt. Yet the man no sooner leaves than he encounters a fellow servant who owes *him* money. Grabbing him by the throat, he orders, "Pay me what you owe." When the master learns of this, he summons the man he had forgiven, punishes him severely, and reinstitutes his debt.

Forgiveness is an unusual sort of moral response; it involves giving up something: a sense of entitlement to be angry or resentful, or a desire for revenge or restitution. You cannot compel forgiveness. This parable explores one of Jesus' primary themes: that in order to be forgiven we need to be prepared to forgive others (Manson 1951: 311). In Jesus' moral universe, how we treat others is intimately tied up with how others treat us, and vice versa: "Pass no judgment, and you will not be judged"; "Always treat others as you would like them to treat you"; and so on. Forgiveness plays a central part in this moral universe because others sometimes treat us badly, but this does not entitle us to treat them, or others, badly as a consequence. Yet the parable does not say, "You must always forgive others." There is clearly a limit to the master's ability or willingness to forgive. The parable's main moral point is that forgiveness should be contagious. The web of moral contingency means that we will always need forgiveness from someone, and that others will always need it from us; actions have too many unforeseeable consequences to avoid ever doing harm. But many complications are not addressed here. Should we forgive unintended wrongs more readily than intentional ones? Do we have less of an obligation to forgive repeated instances of the same harmful act by the same person? Are some things unforgivable? A parable is not designed to answer these sorts of questions definitively; its efficacy lies elsewhere.

The theme of forgiveness also arises in my last example, a parable about a Samaritan representing Jesus, a woman accused of adultery and sentenced to punishment by stoning. This parable culminates in the famous proverb "That one of you who is without sin shall cast the first stone" (John 8:7). I am treating it here as a parable because by most scholarly editions this passage was not part of the original Gospel of John but survived through separate oral traditions and was added to the text later (Buttrick 1952: 591–2). There is something else unique about this passage: it is the only instance in which we see Jesus writing anything; he wrote with his finger on the ground both before and after his proverbial statement. What was he writing, and why? We are not told. One interpretation might be that writing in the dirt and sand was his way of indicating the transience of written moral pronouncements. Here, as elsewhere in the Gospels, he refused to address a moral problem through formal rules that subject particular cases to universal laws. In the words of Manson, Jesus' morality was based on "a standard of example rather than precept" (Manson 1951: 302). He was, as noted earlier, trying to undermine the confidence of the righteous that they know whose sins to judge and what punishment they deserve.

V

I have made four general points here about the moral teaching of Jesus. The first is that it is aimed at achieving a transformation of moral character; without changing certain traits and attitudes that impede moral responsiveness, moral teaching remains merely exhortative. Second, moral teaching cannot be moralizing; it must begin with an understanding of moral agency and motivation, and sometimes the way to influence these is *not* through direct moral instruction, but through other kinds of teaching. Third, many deep moral insights are gained only indirectly, through reflection on complex and puzzling cases that do not yield simple truths or directives. Hence, fourth, Jesus' use of proverbs, allegories, paradoxes, parables, and other figurative forms reflects, on the positive side, a desire to cultivate in listeners a breadth and flexibility of moral imagination and, on the negative side, a willingness to see many listeners misunderstand or not understand at all.

Toward the end of the Gospel of John, Jesus said, "Till now I have been using figures of speech; a time is coming when I shall no longer use figures, but tell you of the Father in plain words" (John 16:25). In keeping with the more eschatological character of that Gospel, this promise anticipated the end of days. But if Jesus had done this, he would no longer have been *teaching*. Certainly it would not have been in keeping with his views on moral teaching (although I suppose moral teaching will no longer be necessary should that day arrive).

The figure of Jesus presents us with an exemplar of teaching through non-literal forms; he used these not merely for embellishment, or as a way to entertain his audience, or to hold and sustain their interest. He taught morality this way, I believe, because he could not conceive of any other way to teach it. His relation to his subject matter and his relation to his audience demanded that he cede to his listeners the discretion to hear him in different ways and to some the choice not to hear him at all. This may not be a very conventional way of thinking about Jesus or about teaching but I hope that even through disagreements with this view our capacities to imagine different kinds of teaching, and different roles for the teacher, can be enlarged. The aspiration to be a teacher, particularly a moral teacher, need not be bounded by the constraints of a specific professional role; indeed, it may be that for moral teaching an institutionalized context is among the least suitable.

Notes

1   I should say here that the possibility of splitting off Jesus' moral from his religious teachings is explicitly denied by many Christian writers, for example, Manson.
2   All Gospel passages quoted are from the New English Bible.
3   Crossan disputes whether Jesus' aphorisms should be thought of simply as proverbs.
4   Scott distinguishes two types of parable: the metaphoric and the metonymic.
5   "A theory and method are . . . implicitly contained in all his teaching."

References

Buttrick, G. (ed.) 1952: *The Interpreter's Bible,* Vol. 8. New York: Abbingdon Press.
Crossan, J. D. 1973: *In Parables: The Challenge of the Historical Jesus.* San Francisco: Harper and Row.
—— 1983: *In Fragments: The Aphorisms of Jesus.* San Francisco: Harper and Row.
Hinsdale, B. A. 1985: *Jesus as a Teacher.* St. Louis, Missouri: Christian Publishing Company.
Horne, H. H. 1920: *Jesus the Master Teacher.* New York: Association Press.
Klausner, J. 1925: *Jesus of Nazareth.* New York: Macmillan.
Liebenberg, J. 2001: *The Language of the Kingdom and Jesus.* New York: Walter de Gruyter.

Manson, T. W. 1951: *The Teaching of Jesus*. Cambridge: Cambridge University Press.

McDonough, T. 2002: The Rhetoric of the Fool's Pedagogy. Master's thesis, Department of Educational Policy Studies, University of Illinois, Urbana/Champaign.

New English Bible 1970: Oxford University Press and Cambridge University Press.

Perkins, P. 1990: *Jesus as Teacher*. Cambridge: Cambridge University Press.

Piper, R. 1989: *Wisdom in the Q-Tradition*. New York: Cambridge University Press.

Robbins, V. K. 1984: *Jesus the Teacher*. Philadelphia: Fortress Press.

Scott, B. B. 1989: *Hear Then the Parable*. Minneapolis: Fortress Press.

Stevens, G. B. 1907: *The Teaching of Jesus*. New York: Macmillan.

Wendt, H. H. 1909: *The Teaching of Jesus*. Edinburgh: T. & T. Clark.

Winton, A. P. 1990: *The Proverbs of Jesus*. Sheffield: JSOT Press.

Chapter 2

Nicholas Burbules on Jesus as Teacher

Terence H. McLaughlin

N ICHOLAS BURBULES has written a very interesting and thought-provoking essay on a topic of perennial importance and interest. I find myself in agreement with a number of claims that Burbules makes in his essay about Jesus as a teacher. I do, however, have some queries, criticisms, and further issues to raise in this reply. In the spirit of Burbules' essay, my reply is intended to contribute in a tentative way to ongoing exploratory discussion of a topic that is elusive and complex.

The reply has five sections. In the first section, I outline a number of points of agreement between Burbules and myself. The second section offers a sketch of the central features of Jesus as a teacher that emerge in Burbules' account. In the third section, I draw a distinction between two differing kinds of activity in which one might be engaged in considering Jesus as a teacher. I describe these activities as involving "exegesis" and "appropriation" respectively, and I briefly outline the requirements and scope of each kind of activity before viewing Burbules' argument in light of the distinction drawn between these two kinds of engagement. The fourth section offers an outline of Jesus as a teacher that emerges from the activity of "exegesis" and that, through the fuller and more complex picture that it paints, places Burbules' account in critical perspective. In the fifth section, I explore the general implications of the discussion as a whole for the activity of teaching.

Points of Agreement

Three points of agreement between Burbules and myself can be highlighted. First, I agree with Burbules that it is a good thing, for the reasons he gives, to be alert in an open-minded way to alternative and unconventional models of teaching. Burbules insists that philosophers and theorists of education have a special duty to resist tendencies to think of teaching solely in terms of familiar, professionalized contexts and to help keep "multiple and even radically unconventional models." It is also important, as Burbules urges, that we do not lose sight of the essentially moral character of teaching as a "way of being" both in the world and in relation to others.

Second, Burbules is surely justified in his general view that Jesus was one of the foremost exemplars of teaching, particularly moral teaching, in the Western tradition, and in his implicit claim that an appreciation of this example is not wholly dependent upon the possession of Christian faith. Writing as a Jew and a former Christian, Geza Vermes refers to the "incomparable superiority" of Jesus, which he considers to consist in part in the sublimity, distinctiveness, and originality of his ethical code and the "remarkable art" of his parables (Vermes 2001a: 195–6).[1] Burbules' broad assessment of the nature and impact of the teaching of Jesus is echoed in the judgments of most scholars. Bredin, for example, represents a common view in his observation that Jesus was a teacher "who taught in a remarkable and memorable way . . . who captivated his audience, who impressed them with his authority and who had the knack of enshrining his insights in unforgettable language and discourse" (Bredin 1986: 23).

Third, much of what Burbules says in detailed terms about Jesus as a teacher compels acceptance. For example, Jesus was not for the most part didactic (at least in any straightforward way); his teaching contained an unusual combination of linguistic elements (proverbs, riddles, aphorisms, allegories, analogies, parables, and the like), some of them striking. The "constellation of figurative forms" deployed by Jesus has the broad character that Burbules describes: for example, the aptness of the proverbs for progressive understanding at different levels over time, the centrality to the forms of teaching of an invitation to a certain kind of response on the part of the hearers, the presence of a puzzling element of opacity, and so forth. Burbules is also correct in indicating that the language used by Jesus *constitutes* his teaching and does not stand in a contingent relationship to it.[2]

However, not all the claims that Burbules makes about Jesus as a teacher are unproblematic, and a number of points of query and disagreement emerge as Burbules' general portrait of Jesus as a teacher is brought into more precise focus.

Central Features of Burbules' Account
of Jesus as a Teacher

It is important to note that Burbules does not set out to provide a complete picture of Jesus as a teacher. Crucially, he restricts his attention to what he takes to be the specifically *moral* teaching of Jesus and deliberately sets aside the *religious* teaching of Jesus and questions about the status of Jesus as a religious figure. Burbules writes, "I am not concerned here with the status of Jesus as the Christ, or Messiah, for certain religious traditions; nor will I be saying much about his specifically religious teachings, or his *preaching*" (my emphasis). Burbules therefore offers a self-consciously restricted and specific perspective on Jesus as a teacher, presenting him in "secularised" terms as a moral teacher.

The picture of Jesus as a teacher that emerges from this perspective is one that is very attractive to contemporary educators in a broadly liberal tradition. Burbules sees the teaching of Jesus as not only devoid of "moralizing" but also (almost) devoid of "explicit moral directives." Jesus, he argues, "had almost nothing to say" about the immorality of specific acts but emphasized the need for "general guideposts" in a process of moral guidance involving the cultivation of moral sensibility (including a broad and flexible moral imagination) through internalizing the proverbs and other linguistic elements that constituted his teaching. Jesus, Burbules claims, saw moral sensibility, reflection, and agency as best situated within "broad" standards of conduct and character rather than as determined by "formal moral doctrines or codes." Indeed, Jesus can, he suggests, be seen as pointing to the "uselessness" of such doctrines and codes. The proverbs of Jesus are "broadly directional guideposts" making clear the inevitability of "interpretation, misinterpretation, and different interpretations" in relation to moral conduct. According to Burbules, therefore, Jesus favored a morality of "spirit and attitude" and of "moral sensitivity and conscience" rather than a morality of rules, and was also alert to the incompleteness, imperfection, difficulty, and complexity of moral thought and action.

Burbules also sees Jesus as identifying attitudes and traits such as "moralism," "self-righteousness," "smugness," and "moral superiority" as obstacles to the achievement of moral sensibility, reflection, and agency, and as inviting and bringing about a certain kind of personal transformation in his hearers, involving processes such as the identification and confrontation of personal "barriers," the achievement of "self-recognition," and the development of appropriate desires for change and for the pursuit of the good.

The picture of Jesus as a teacher that emerges in this interpretation is indeed harmonious with, and attractive to, contemporary perspectives. But how adequate is it?

The way in which adequacy should be understood here requires attention to contrasting activities that I shall describe as "exegesis" and "appropriation."

Exegesis and Appropriation

In distinguishing the activities of "exegesis" and "appropriation" my aim is to bring Burbules' depiction of Jesus as a teacher, and the issues it raises, into clearer focus. The distinction is therefore drawn for a specific purpose and requires considerable further sophistication in a fuller discussion. Some of the complexities to which the distinction gives rise will be acknowledged.

In my account of these notions, the activities of both exegesis and appropriation involve forms of interpretation, but they are governed by somewhat different ends. I describe the activity of exegesis in the context of the present discussion as involving an attempt to offer an account of Jesus as a teacher based on an interpretation of texts and other data where the primary end is to offer an account that, as far as possible, provides a full and accurate depiction of (to put matters roughly) the original "realities" involved. In this activity the meanings (motives, concepts, understandings, responses, and so on) and the context (historical, theological, political, and so on) relevant to Jesus' life and work receive sustained attention and elucidation. The criteria for the adequacy of any account offered are not primarily related to the present significance, meaning, importance, or usefulness of Jesus as a teacher for particular persons or situations, but to the extent to which a faithful depiction of the original "realities" has been offered. An indication of the range of questions that arise in a complex activity such as this is given by Michael McCrum:

> How far is Jesus' original message faithfully conveyed by the evangelists? How unique is it? How far do rabbinic parallels shed light on the parables? How subversive and unconventional are they? How limited to particular contexts? What . . . theology, or Christology, can we legitimately derive from them? (McCrum 1999: 75–6)

The difficulties inherent in such an activity cannot be underestimated and are now widely acknowledged. A central difficulty is captured in Stefan Reif's observation that exploration of the figure of Jesus reveals "a rich kaleidoscope of differing images" (Vermes 2001a: viii).[3]

I describe the contrasting activity of "appropriation" as involving an attempt to offer an account of Jesus as a teacher in which the criteria for the adequacy of the account are not primarily related to the extent to which the original "realities" have been faithfully depicted, but to the extent to which Jesus as a teacher has been "brought alive for" and applied fruitfully to, particular persons or situations. The activity of appropriation is not intended to have negative connotations. The notion of "making one's own" (Latin: "proprius") does not in itself imply that the activity involves motives and judgments of the kind captured in the word "proprietorial" or that it involves inauthentic or implausible inter-pretations. The recent illuminating meditative exploration of the Gospels by the Dalai Lama can be regarded as a kind of appropriation (Kiely 2002).

Is Burbules seeking to engage in exegesis or appropriation? It is tempting to see him as engaged solely in the activity of appropriation. After all, in explicitly pursuing a secularized interpretation of Jesus, Burbules sets aside elements of the life and teaching of Jesus that many will see as central to an account that aspires to accuracy and complete-ness. Furthermore, Burbules says clearly that he is not concerned with the historical accuracy of the Gospel texts but with their literary signif-icance. One should not conclude too quickly, however, that Burbules is uninterested in exegesis. Burbules is attentive to, and locates his inter-pretive efforts within, the scriptural material relating to the teaching of Jesus, and he seeks to some extent to offer an account of how (at least part of) this teaching should be properly understood. Burbules is there-fore in part engaged in the activity of exegesis. This fact invites recognition of the point that the distinction between exegesis and appro-priation should not be drawn too sharply. Any convincing attempt at appropriation involves a degree of exegesis of what is to be appropri-ated if it is to avoid accusations of distortive or even falsifying reinterpretation.[4] Deidun identifies a central danger here when he observes that "interpreters who turn to biblical texts in search of 'rele-vance' will surely find what they are looking for, but only after imposing on the texts their own notions of what counts as relevant" (Deidun 1998: 4). In a similar vein, Smith and Shortt alert us to the danger of projecting onto the example of Jesus what we already regard as good teaching (Smith and Shortt 2002: 141). Overall, however, notwithstanding the sensitivity of his account, it is fair to see Burbules as primarily engaged in a form of the activity of appropriation.

Jesus as a Teacher Revisited

I return here to the portrayal of Jesus as a teacher in light of the distinc-tion between exegesis and appropriation.

The activity of exegesis reveals a fuller and more complex picture of Jesus as a teacher than can be found in Burbules' account. Three important, and relatively uncontroversial, general features of this picture require emphasis. First, as Burbules acknowledges, much of the teaching is specifically religious. The full scope of this aspect of Jesus' teaching is wide-ranging. It includes the announcement that the reign of God had arrived in his own presence; that a period of impending catastrophe and judgment on Israel was imminent, which invited repentance and belief; that eschatological forgiveness and salvation were available through him; that the law and the prophets had been fulfilled; that a new covenant was being brought about through his death; that there was to be a final apocalyptic judgment including eschatological reversal; and so on. The "content" of this teaching is, of course, the subject of considerable debate and critical enquiry, and one of the central issues that arises is the relationship between the teaching of the historical Jesus and the teaching superimposed on this in the light of the subsequent development of the Christ of Christian faith. A further issue is the extent to which there is a political dimension to Jesus' teaching about the "Kingdom" of God (on this see, for example, Nolan 1992, ch. 6). For our purposes, however, it is sufficient to emphasize the general point that much of the teaching of Jesus was specifically religious.[5]

Second, it is not easy to separate the religious from the moral elements of Jesus' teaching. Some of the teaching involves the radicalization of common morality, as seen, for example, in the insistence upon unlimited forgiveness for injuries and of love of neighbor, challenging ethics that transcend the ethics of minimum reciprocity and strictly conceived rights and duties and that oppose self-conscious goodness (Preston 1991: 95–6).[6] Jesus was a Jewish teacher located in a specific religious and ethical tradition and context.[7] He offered a vision of a flourishing life that embodied inseparable religious elements.

Although there are complexities in working out just what Jesus' ethical teaching actually was (on this see, for example, Deidun 1998: 17–20, Hays 1996, ch. 7), it is widely recognized that the moral teaching of Jesus is inseparable from his religious teaching.[8] Richard Robinson, for example, argues that Jesus "is primarily not a teacher or moralist but a mysterious and miraculous divine leader" whose major precepts involved devotion to God or piety and belief in Jesus (Robinson 1964: 142–6).[9] Patrick Hannon puts a similar point in this way:

> It is . . . important to remember that Jesus was not primarily a moral teacher. True . . . what he taught had a bearing on morality. And he did sometimes teach morality directly: the primacy of the love-commandment, the scope and quality of the love which it enjoins, something of what it precludes as well as what it asks to be done. But as with the call to repentance his moral teaching is consequent upon his gospel. It opens up the

path of love for one in whom God's love has resonated. (Hannon 1992: 35)[10]

The basis of Jesus' teaching has been described as "a joyful response in life to the overflowing graciousness of God" (Preston 1991: 101).[11] McCrum claims that "Jesus was a great charismatic teacher . . . the substance and style of whose teaching was essentially similar to those of Jewish Rabbis but was more demanding, authoritative, and controversial" (McCrum 1999: 73). Bredin argues that the sayings of Jesus go far beyond common sense, balanced judgment, and "the accumulated wisdom of the ages" that are the usual stuff of proverbs; their radicalism, indication of final reversal and reference to conflict make them better seen as "counter-proverbs" (Bredin 1986: 26–8).

Bredin points out that Jesus is always concerned with God and His reign and that the parables, while secular in appearance, encourage their hearers to think about God in a new way: they are "threshold" stories that hint at what is involved in belonging to "the kingdom of God" (Bredin 1986: 35–46). He suggests that it is "precisely through the shattering effect of parables that the reign of God takes root in my life and begins to grow and to take over" (Bredin 1986: 44). Vermes argues that the synoptic sayings of Jesus "are centered on the heavenly Father, the imminent arrival of the Kingdom of God, and on the religious and moral requisites for people to enter the Kingdom through the gateway of repentance." Jesus was "wholly theocentric" (Vermes 2001b: 23, 257).[12] The extent to which Jesus' teaching was conflictual is significant.[13] Another important point to note is that the distinction between the "natural" and the "supernatural," for example, was not one recognized in the Bible (Nolan 1992: 41).

Third, it is important to acknowledge that the teaching of Jesus was accomplished not merely through what he said but through *actions* (for example, healing, miracles, exorcism, prayer, washing the feet of his disciples, reacting to events, enduring suffering, and so on). The *example* of Jesus is therefore an important part of his overall influence as a teacher: his way of life embodies his teaching (Bredin 1986, ch. 6). Jesus taught by means of what he said but also via a specific *praxis* (Nolan 1992, Part 2). Familiar elements in this way of life, or *praxis*, include Jesus' association and identification with the poor and oppressed and his unrestrained compassion for them (Nolan 1992, ch. 3).

According to Nolan, Jesus removed the shame, humiliation, and guilt of "the poor and sinners" by mixing with, extending friendship to, and accepting them, which amounted to a kind of implicit forgiveness and wide-ranging liberation (Nolan 1992, ch. 5). The fact that Jesus actually mixed with such people and did not merely speak out in an abstract way on their behalf has been widely recognized as distinctive and significant

(Vermes 2001a: 196). Gordon Graham argues that the significance of Jesus lies more in what he was and did as "an agent of cosmic history" than in what he taught (Graham 2001: 73). The significance of the *example* of Jesus is inseparable from his religious *status*. Bredin, for example, claims that "every iota" of the New Testament is Christological, implicitly if not explicitly so (Bredin 1986: 233).

This fuller and more complex picture of Jesus as a teacher is less harmonious with, and attractive to, contemporary perspectives than the picture painted by Burbules. Indeed, from contemporary perspectives, this picture invites the real possibility of puzzlement, disagreement, and rejection. For example, the degree and kind of authority exercised by Jesus led to the following well-known observation by C. S. Lewis:

> A man who was merely a man and said the sorts of things Jesus said would not be a great moral teacher: He would either be a lunatic [or] the devil . . . You must make your choice. Either this man was, and is, the son of God or else a madman . . . [L]et us not come up with any . . . nonsense about his being a great human teacher. He has not left that open to us. (Lewis 2002: 52)

Jesus' moral teaching has been described as unsystematic, vague, puzzling, and obscure; as containing a "prominent strand of harshness"; as neglecting knowledge, truth, and reason; as depending upon promises and threats; and silent about important values (Robinson 1964, sections 2.86 and 2.87). Another important aspect of concern about Jesus' moral teaching is that his eschatological beliefs led him to propose an "ethics of the interim" that was designed to serve merely until the envisaged imminent end of the world and was therefore both impractical and distorted (on this see, for example, Deidun 1998: 17–20).

How does Burbules' depiction of Jesus as a teacher look from the perspective of this fuller and more complex picture? As indicated earlier, it is important to remember and acknowledge that Burbules is not engaging primarily in the task of exegesis but of appropriation. Furthermore, Burbules is aware of many of the elements raised in this fuller and more complex account. For example, his setting aside of the religious aspects of the teaching and status of Jesus is done self-consciously, and Burbules does acknowledge in the course of his discussion that the separation of the religious and moral aspects of the teaching of Jesus is questionable, that Jesus always regarded himself as part of the Jewish tradition, that his teaching had eschatological dimensions, that it did not amount to a coherent whole, that Jesus' moral teaching was not wholly devoid of direction, and that he did teach through example. In these and other respects, Burbules is sensitive to the demands of exegesis. However, the fuller and more complex picture of Jesus as a teacher that has been outlined puts Burbules' picture under pressure at a number of points and raises questions about the extent to which his appropriation is devoid of distortion.

For example, Burbules argues that in his moral teaching, Jesus extended invitations to "open-ended interpretation" and avoided issuing "strict moral edicts" as part of a morality of compassion rather than of rules. Given the fuller perspective indicated earlier, however, these claims require some qualification. The claims are rather inconsistent with some general features of the tone and "content" of the message of Jesus, especially his call for radical, single-minded (and often counterintuitive) commitment on the part of his disciples, which was perceived as taking priority over all natural relationships (as in "let the dead bury the dead") and as enjoining or prohibiting specific concrete actions (such as the abandonment of material possessions). In addition, the claims do not take account of Jesus' unequivocal statements on particular morally sensitive matters, especially his condemnation of divorce (on this see, for example, Hays 1996, ch. 15).

On the question of "rules" and the Law, Hays claims that it is unlikely that Jesus proclaimed an abrogation or even a critique of the Law as distinct from mounting a critique of those who professed allegiance to the Law but whose commitment to it was flawed in various ways (Hays 1996: 164). The Law, therefore, is the backdrop to much of Jesus' teaching, and much of the compassion of Jesus needs to be seen not as indifference to or rejection of specific norms, but as understanding and forgiveness extended to those who infringed them; here the classic distinction between "the sin" and "the sinner" is pertinent. Similarly, injunctions such as, "Do not judge, so that you may not be judged" are not seen as denying the relevance and importance of relevant norms. As Hays points out, the original context of the saying warns those who judge others that they are liable to the judgment of God (Hays 1996: 348). Neither, for the reasons indicated earlier, are proverbs as "open-ended" as Burbules implies.[14]

Furthermore, although Burbules acknowledges that the sorts of "transformation" in people brought about by Jesus are associated with "theological notions" like "original sin" and "spiritual conversion," his account of them in terms of processes such as "self-recognition" is partial. Also, Burbules' account of the opacity of the parables neglects the specifically religious elements and motives in play. In sum, therefore, the picture of Jesus presented by Burbules is limited when viewed from an exegesis-based perspective (see, for example, Vermes 2001b: 249–58).

Burbules is, however, not concerned to deny this. The potential limitations of his appropriation do, however, become apparent when we consider the implications of the discussion so far for the activity of teaching.

Implications of Jesus as a Teacher

Burbules is careful to resist the temptation to draw crude implications for teaching from his account of Jesus as a teacher. He does not, for example, attempt to identify "methods" that might be "reinterpreted" or "adapted" for use in the classroom.[15] Instead Burbules seeks to uncover an "image" of teaching that illuminates in general terms a particular way of "being in the world" and "being with others" and, more specifically, a series of insights into what might be roughly described as the "moral" aspects of teaching. Burbules sees this image not as a model to be emulated, even in general terms, but as inviting consideration and discussion in order to enhance our imaginative capacities about different kinds of teaching and teaching roles. As seen earlier, the insights about teaching that emerge from Burbules' account of Jesus as a teacher include an emphasis upon avoiding explicit moral directives in favor of providing "general guideposts" for moral conduct and the development of moral understanding, an indication of the distinctive role of proverbs and parables in promoting moral sensitivity via thoughtful internalization, and a recognition of the importance of transforming traits and attitudes that underlie moral failure, such as arrogance and egoism.

Each of these kinds of insights that Burbules draws from his account of Jesus as a teacher is eminently suitable for consideration and discussion by those concerned with teaching. The sorts of questions that are likely to arise in this process of consideration and discussion, which Burbules envisages as involving criticism and disagreement, can be readily anticipated. In relation to the "avoidance of moral directives" insight, for example, familiar queries and objections can be expected arising from claims about the need for a judicious balance between direction and openness in teaching and moral formation. These factors are likely in turn to give rise to reflection upon more general issues about, for example, the aims, principles, and constraints relating to these activities in a liberal democratic society. In light of this reflection, moral direction might be seen as appropriate and necessary in relation to certain matters (for example, where the moral issues at stake are fundamental and the subject of wide-ranging consensus), but not in relation to others (those, for example, that may be seen under the banner of legitimate diversity).

Furthermore, while indirect, opaque, and variably interpretable moral influence of the sort exemplified by Jesus might be seen as apt in relation to some moral issues (for example, where differential responses are seen as legitimate) this may not be so in relation to other moral issues. With regard to the "role of proverbs and parables" insight, questions are likely to arise about the effect of parables in contemporary contexts of teaching, where their impact might, for various reasons, be seen as superficial and eclectic.[16] Burbules notes that parables are part of our "shared common cultural heritage," but to what extent is this true in contemporary contexts? How can the effect of the parables that Burbules describes be achieved in these contexts? In relation to the "transformation of negative traits and attitudes" insight, questions are likely to arise about the nature of the mandate that a teacher might enjoy for engaging in "transformative" activities that are potentially intimately related to the personhood of individuals. What is the nature and justification of "charismatic authority" in the case of teachers? Consideration of the rights and duties that parents may be said to enjoy in relation to influence over their children is clearly significant here.

Many further examples of the sorts of questions that may arise in the kind of process of reflection upon Jesus as a teacher that Burbules envisages can be readily imagined. However, Burbules does not seem to see his portrayal of Jesus as a teacher as serving as a mere "trigger" for such questions. After all, questions of these kinds could be raised directly or in other ways. Burbules seems rather to invite us to be open to, and to appreciate, the imaginative *impact* that a ruminative reflection on Jesus as a teacher might have. An invitation to engage in ruminative reflection on Burbules' portrayal of Jesus as a teacher gives rise to the following phenomenological speculation: Any process of reflection on Jesus as a teacher is likely to explore the complexities and subtleties inherent in the "content" and "method" of his teaching. It is also likely to explore the distinctive "way of being" that was characteristic of Jesus. Both of these explorations involve engagement with questions relating to Jesus' motivation, self-understanding, and beliefs, as well as to the context of his life and work.

Yet Burbules' portrayal of Jesus is self-consciously restricted and selective. The kind of ruminative reflection that Burbules invites may therefore find itself naturally drawn, in its search for sensitive understanding of Jesus as a teacher, to the fuller resources of the wider imaginative canvas provided by a portrayal of Jesus from the perspective of exegesis. This is not to suggest that such a reflection, properly conducted, must terminate in Christian faith but that ruminative reflection is likely to be unsatisfied by the circumscribed portrayal of Jesus as a teacher offered by Burbules. Be this as it may, the salience of Jesus as a religious and not merely a cultural figure is also likely to drive ruminative reflection in the direction of a portrayal of Jesus from the perspective of exegesis.

A further reason why such reflection *should* extend to a portrayal of Jesus from the perspective of exegesis is that many of the questions about teaching alluded to above have an important religious, and not merely moral, dimension to them.[17] Again, the suggestion here is not that the questions at stake can only be properly understood from the perspective of Christian faith, but that such a perspective should not be ignored or excluded.

The tone of Burbules' chapter suggests that he would not object if the reflection he invites on Jesus as a teacher extended to reflection on a portrayal of Jesus offered from the perspective of exegesis. If this is so, it is consistent with his concern that philosophers and theorists of education should be alert in an open-minded way to a range of alternative and unconventional models of teaching; after all, the exclusion of a religious dimension from reflection upon teaching is one of the most prominent expressions of conventionality.

Notes

1   On Vermes' personal journey of faith see Vermes 1998.

2   Bredin argues that parables are not merely "teaching aids" used to illustrate the message of Jesus; they *are* in an important sense his teaching (Bredin 1986: 46). On the language used by Jesus, see for example, Bredin 1986, ch. 2.

3   For a review of the difficulties involved as revealed in contemporary scholarship about Jesus see Powell 2000.

4   Similarly, the exercise of the imagination involved in "exegesis" cannot be devoid of elements of "appropriation."

5   On the overall picture of Jesus that emerges from his teaching in the synoptic Gospels see, for example, Vermes 2001b: 193–209.

6   "It is certainly the case that Jesus challenged society's standards by the standards of the Kingdom of God in his attitude not only to the poor, but to heretics and schismatics (Samaritans), the immoral (prostitutes and adulterers), the politically compromised (tax collectors), society's rejects (lepers), those whom society neglected; and to women as a sex" (Preston 1991: 97).

7   On these matters see, for example, Vermes 2001a, 2001b, esp. ch. 7, Meeks 1986, Hays 1996, Sanders 1985.

8   "The moral teaching of Jesus is part and parcel of his religion and is not separable from it except by violence" (Manson quoted in Robinson 1964: 142).

9   According to Vermes, the whole synoptic tradition presents the essential ministry of Jesus in terms of exorcism and healing (Vermes 2001a: 40), and it is necessary to consider the teaching of Jesus alongside his work as an exorcist and healer (Vermes 2001b: 158).

10 In more technical language, moral *didache* (teaching) is subordinate to the affirmations of the *kerygma* – the message of the good news (Hannon 1992: 36). On the Christian faith and morality see, for example, Hannon 1992, ch. 3; Preston 1991; Deidun 1998; Graham 2001, esp. chs. 1–2; Hays 1996.

11 On Jesus as a teacher see also, for example, Vermes 2001a, esp. pp. 10–13; 2001b, esp. pp. 25–6, 154–8, 193–206; Smith and Shortt 2002, esp. chs. 12–13.

12 Vermes argues that if Jesus was primarily a teacher of morals he might have

shown a preference for "short, pithy, colourful utterances" (Vermes 2001a: 1). Similarly Gordon Graham has argued that Jesus cannot properly be seen as a distinctive and innovative moral teacher (Graham 2001: 29–31).

13 On this matter see, for example, McCrum 1999, ch. 15, 16; Hays 1996: 164–5.
14 Bredin argues: "We will never really know a parable until we cross the threshold into the world opened up for us *by* parable, a world of paradox and mystery, the antithesis of our everyday world" (Bredin 1986: 45).
15 On limitations inherent in overly crude attempts to draw "implications" for teaching from the Bible see Smith and Shortt 2002. On similar difficulties arising in relation to see Jesus as a "model" teacher see *ibid.*, chs. 12 and 13.
16 For an approach open to this kind of criticism see Templeton 1994 where two hundred "laws of life" drawn from the scriptures of the great spiritual traditions of the world are identified.
17 For a discussion of some of these dimensions see Alexander and McLaughlin 2003.

References

Alexander, H. A. and McLaughlin, T. H. 2003: Education in Religion and Spirituality. In N. Blake, P. Smeyers, R. Smith and P. Standish (eds.), *The Blackwell Guide to the Philosophy of Education*, Oxford: Blackwell.
Bredin, E. 1986: *Disturbing the Peace: The Way of Disciples*, 2nd ed. Dublin: Columbia Press.
Deidun, T. 1998: The Bible and Christian Ethics. In B. Hoose (ed.), *Christian Ethics: An Introduction*, London: Cassell.
Graham, G. 2001: *Evil and Christian Ethics*. Cambridge: Cambridge University Press.
Hannon, P. 1992: *Church, State, Morality and Law*. Dublin: Gill and Macmillan.
Hays, R. B. 1996: *The Moral Vision of the New Testament*. Edinburgh: T. and T. Clark.
Kiely, R. 2002: *The Good Heart: His Holiness The Dalai Lama Explores the Heart of Christianity and of Humanity*. London: Rider.
Lewis, C. S. 2002: *Mere Christianity*. London: HarperCollins.
McCrum, M. 1999: *The Man Jesus: Fact and Legend*. London: Janus.
Meeks, W. 1986: *The Moral World of the First Christians*. London: SPCK.
Nolan, A. 1992: *Jesus Before Christianity*, revised edn. London: Darton, Longman and Todd.
Powell, M. A. 2000: *The Jesus Debate: Modern Historians Investigate the Life of Christ*. Oxford: Lion.
Preston, R. 1991: Christian Ethics. In P. Singer (ed.), *A Companion to Ethics*, Oxford: Basil Blackwell.
Robinson, R. 1964: *An Atheist's Values*. Oxford: Basil Blackwell.
Sanders, E. P. 1985: *Jesus and Judaism*. London: SCM Press.
Smith, D. I. and Shortt, J. 2002: *The Bible and the Task of Teaching*. Nottingham: Stapleford Centre.
Templeton, J. M. 1994: *Discovering the Laws of Life*. New York: Continuum.
Vermes, G. 1998: *Providential Accidents: An Autobiography*. London: SCM Press.
—— 2001a: *Jesus the Jew*. London: SCM Press.
—— 2001b: *The Changing Faces of Jesus*. London: Penguin Books.

Chapter 3

Children's Spirituality: Between Winnicott and Panenmentalism

AMIHUD GILEAD

W INNICOTT'S *Playing and Reality* (1991) has left a great impression on numerous readers. For many the book has changed their view of life and their understanding of psychic life as a whole. Winnicott's thought has made a great contribution to our understanding of art, creativity, and their relation to the child in each of us. As I see it, Winnicott's contribution to our understanding of children's spirituality is immense.

In *Playing and Reality* Winnicott wrote:

> Should an adult make claims on us for our acceptance of the objectivity of his subjective phenomena we discern or diagnose madness. If, however, the adult can manage to enjoy the personal intermediate area without making claims, then we can acknowledge our own corresponding areas and are pleased to find a degree of overlapping, that is to say, common experience between members of a group in art or religion or philosophy . . .

> Transitional objects and transitional phenomena belong to the realm of illusion which is at the basis of initiation of experience. This early stage in development is made possible by the mother's special capacity for making adaptation to the needs of her infant, thus allowing the infant the illusion that what the infant creates really exists.

> This intermediate area of experience, unchallenged in respect of its belonging to inner or external (shared) reality, constitutes the greater part of the infant's experience, and throughout life is retained in the intense experiencing that belongs to the arts and to religion and to imaginative living, and to creative scientific work. (1991: 14)

Winnicott's own creativity has much to do with his special way of writing; his language is very precise, yet it never loses its artistic, poetic flavor. This special language enables him to keep in close contact with his readers. He deeply understands the somewhat mysterious area between inner psychic reality and external shared reality, the area that belongs to both kinds of reality and yet belongs to neither of them, a third kind of reality that necessarily leads to a paradox. Believing that this paradox should not be resolved, he writes, "My contribution is to ask for a paradox to be accepted and tolerated and respected, and for it not to be resolved. By flight to split off intellectual functioning it is possible to resolve the paradox, but the price of this is the loss of the value of the paradox itself" (1991: xii).

This loss may in turn entail the loss of creativity and even that of sanity and the flexibility essential to healthy psychic life. While creating, playing, enjoying life and creativity, utilizing language inventively, developing new theories, scientific and others, we are staying in that intermediate zone, suspending the test of reality. Without the great support that our mother gave us, we would be unable to do so, to create, to enjoy life, to know the secret of symbols, and to follow meanings and significance. At first, according to Winnicott, we use our imagination to create illusions – about our omnipotence to create the entire world, especially the heart of it, i.e., our mother, and to create ourselves as part and parcel of her. Thanks to the gradual, adaptive weaning of us from those illusions, our mother helped us cope with external reality, to make use of it as well as of her. And yet, from time to time, to come back to this playground of our creativity and imagination – while watching films and theater performances, reading books, enjoying pieces of art or creating them as well as forming new ideas, philosophizing, coining new words and expressions, believing in God, and much more.

Such, as a matter of truth, is our inter-subjective world of spirituality. The potential intermediate space for our spirituality must be in permanent and intimate contact with the child in each of us; the child that always keeps something of the primordial mother's encouragement as well as the capability of weaning and adaptation, with regard to our inner and external reality. Moreover, playing in the intermediate zone and utilizing the potential space and its objects enables children to face external, objective or inter-subjective, reality. For what has impinged on the spirituality of the children teaches and instructs them well where the inner reality of each of them ends and external reality begins. Impinging on fantasies and, mostly, weaning them from illusions are indispensable for becoming acquainted with external, inter-subjective or objective, reality. While under the influence of fantasies and illusions, children believe themselves omnipotent, ignoring their own limitations and boundaries. It is only by being weaned from illusions and recognizing the limitations of fantasies that human beings can face external reality

and make use of it within its borders. Note that at this point, my interpretation somewhat deviates from the above passage by Winnicott. In
it he does not make a distinction between illusion and fantasy. As I see
it, such a distinction is indispensable. I will turn to this distinction
below.

Although Winnicottian ideas of potential space, intermediate zones,
and transitional objects or phenomena are indispensable to our understanding of spirituality, they are still not enough. Metaphysically
speaking, we need much more. This was one of the reasons why I introduced my metaphysical view, panenmentalism, to say much more
about spirituality, mentality, and pure possibilities without which no
identification, meanings, significance, and values are possible at all
(Gilead 1999). Winnicott was not a philosopher, and yet his psychoanalytic thinking carries some metaphysical significance with which my
panenmentalism maintains an intimate dialogue. One of the ways in
which panenmentalism challenges Winnicott's psychoanalysis is in
replacing creation with discovery. Adults, like children, cannot create
anything out of nothing, but they can discover new possibilities for
identifying, recognizing, understanding, valuing, and imagining.
Panenmentalism adheres to the view that creativity is indeed a
discovery of pure possibilities, discovering new areas or dimensions of
spirituality. Pure possibilities are independent of actualization.
Regardless of actualization, all possibilities are pure.

What is panenmentalism? You cannot yet find this word in any dictionary. What can be found in dictionaries and lexicons is a related word,
panentheism, which means that God encompasses within Himself (or
Herself, if you like) the whole of reality, yet God is greater than the
whole, i.e., the world. Cordovero's mysticism, for instance, is a kind of
panentheism. Panenmentalism is a term that I have coined to mean that
everything is the mental, and the mental comprises all that is, including
the actual-physical (Gilead 1999). Now, the mental is the purely
possible, namely, the possible that is independent of the actual. The
actual is possible too, but the purely possible need not be actual at all.
Thus, the possible-mental is wider than the actual-physical, and the
former comprises the latter, as restricted, conditioned, and limited. It is
only the actual-physical that is spatiotemporal and causally conditioned, whereas the purely possible-mental is exempt from
spatiotemporal and causal conditions.

Let me explain how I realized that the psychic or the mental has to do
with pure possibilities and, moreover, that our mind as such is a pure
possibility partly actualized in our body, which is a physical–actual
entity. What really distinguishes mind from body is that the mind is
determined by means of pure possibilities that as such are not actualities at all. Although pure possibilities are neither spatiotemporal nor

causally determining or determined, they undoubtedly make an enormous essential difference to the mind.

By contrast, no pure possibility affects anything actual. Only actualities can determine, cause, or change other actualities. When the mind affects or causes something, it is only due to the actualization of it. The mind as such does not cause anything. All psychic activities and faculties have to do with pure possibilities. Such obviously is the case with psychic states, such as imagining, longing, aspiring, doubting, willing, believing, and thinking; all the cases in which no actual object is present. Any direct object of our thought must be first and foremost a pure possibility, a mental entity, regardless or independent of any actualization. The actualization of such pure possibility is secondary. We can, and indeed do, think of things that are purely possible and have never have been actualized. The very same holds for our intentions and intentionality as a whole, which many philosophers believe to be the distinguishing mark of the psychic. In any case, we are able to think about, believe in, aspire toward, or value because of pure possibilities.

Under panenmentalism, what distinguishes the mind is, therefore, the relation to the purely mental, consisting solely of pure possibilities. On the basis of all the differences between the body, as an actual-physical being, and the mind, as a possible-psychical entity, panenmentalism attempts to cope with the psychophysical question in an entirely new way or to meet it in such a way that is no longer unsolvable. The panenmentalist psychophysical approach is not reductive or dualistic. Rather it maintains that mind and body are not identical, but are necessarily united just as any pure possibility and its actuality are united. The purely possible is the main characteristic of spirituality.

The mental consists of pure possibilities, such as concepts, ideas, identities, symbols, meanings, significance, and values. As I have shown elsewhere (Gilead 1999 and 2003), the psychic, which is a special part of the mental, consists of pure possibilities that are singular. In other words, no two pure mental possibilities can be identical, whereas two psychic possibilities belonging to two persons cannot be even similar. Each of them is unique. Since no two possibilities can be identical, being different from each other, they all relate one to the other. Any psychical possibility, being singular, necessarily relates to all the others. Hence, the entire realm of the mental is open to any of us *in principle*, and solipsism has no place in it.

This comprehensive relationality is independent of experience or of empirical nature. Thus, this relationality must be innate, accessible for each of us. In principle, every child has the capability of relating to the entire world of imagination, to which any pure possibility is communicable, at least under relationality. Children's imagination can be open to any pure possibility by way of discovery and thus can be open to the entire realm of pure possibilities. In their future experience, children, becoming adults, will realize which of the possibilities–identities have been actualized and which have not. But first and foremost, they can recognize each thing because the accessibility of the possibility–identity of each thing has been available to them from the very beginning of their mental journey toward mature knowledge and judgment.

In this way, my panenmentalism is joined with Winnicott's concept of playing. Instead of his potential space, I refer to the entire realm of pure possibilities. Instead of his concept of creativity, I refer to our creative discovery of pure possibilities. And instead of Winnicott's sense of reality, I refer to "sense of actuality," for pure possibilities and our acquaintance with them are no less real than actualities and our acquaintance with them. Our sense of actuality rests on detecting the indications of space, time, causality, and contingency. Note that although the relations between pure possibilities are necessary, the existence of any actuality is just a matter of sheer contingency (consider Gilead 1999: 5–39).

Since the mental is the spiritual, children's spirituality gains an eminent status in panenmentalism. In principle, the mental-spiritual is the richest realm accessible to any child as well as to any adult. According to Winnicott, children have access to the potential space, and the child in each of us must be alive and well in order to create and play. However, according to panenmentalism, children have complete access to the realm of the purely possible, the realm of the mental-spiritual; adults are able to tour the land of pure possibilities-identities through their imagination, which is also the only source of values, meanings, and significance. The realm of pure possibilities, of spirituality, shows us not only what the identities of actual things are, but also what they ought to be – the values according to which we value and judge these actual things.

The universal meaning of the concept of God, not only among adults but no less among children, may serve as an adequate illustration of the spiritual accessibility of children's imagination to the realm of the purely possible. As I elaborate elsewhere (Gilead 2003: 213–24), God is first and foremost a pure possibility, which carries a universal meaning, not only for believers in God but even for agnostics and atheists, whether they are willing to admit it or not. No agnostic or atheist is entitled to claim, that the concept of God is meaningless, for this concept bears meanings, however negative, cynical, or critical, for these disbelievers. What they mainly question or repudiate is the actual existence of God. All the more, the concept of God bears meanings as well as significance for any child. In other words, for children the concept of God appears to be universally meaningful and significant. That children ask a lot of questions about God is acknowledged to be a worldwide phenomenon. For this reason, Kant thought that such questions, common to all human beings, bear an anthropological-metaphysical distinguishing mark. Although it is beyond our capability to answer or to meet such questions, they are inescapable. According to Kant, it is an inescapable part of our nature to ask unanswerable metaphysical questions, such as: Does God exist? And what is the meaning of God for us? (Kant 1787: xxix–xxi, 6–7; *cf.* xxi–xxii, and 1781a: vii–viii).

I must add that whether God exists is not a question of God's possibility, but of God's actual existence, which is quite a different question. According to Kant, other metaphysical questions, inherent in human nature, are about the soul and the world. Indeed children frequently ask the following metaphysical questions: Is the soul immortal (living forever) or does it die with the body? Is the world finite or infinite? Was it created (made) or not? Does it exist in time, or is it eternal? If not discouraged, children will ask such questions quite naturally. Even in an entirely atheistic atmosphere or upbringing, children naturally ask questions about their birth, future death, creation, the creator, or the supreme "Governor" of everything. If not unnaturally restricted, children's imagination is by nature open to the pure possibilities on which such questions are grounded.

Winnicott's view of education is quite sophisticated and realistic as well as insightful. Mentioning "the task of weaning," Winnicott refers to "the tasks of parents and educators" and adds:

> If things go well, in this gradual disillusionment process, the stage is set for the frustrations that we gather together under the word weaning; but it should be remembered that when we talk about the phenomena . . . that cluster round weaning we are assuming the underlying process, the process by which opportunity for illusion and gradual disillusionment is provided . . .

> It is assumed here that the task of reality-acceptance is never completed, that no human being is free from the strain of relating inner and outer reality, and that relief from this strain is provided by an intermediate area of experience . . . which is not challenged (arts, religion, etc.). This intermediate area is in direct continuity with the play area of the small child who is "lost" in play. (1991: 13)

Spiritual or cognitive weaning or disillusionment provides an essential stage in educating, but no less vital is the spiritual relief or liberty, both for children and adults, from the reality test, from deciding where inner reality ends and external, objective, public, or inter-subjective reality begins. In this intermediate area of freedom and liberty, which is possibly not challenged by the reality test, the arts, religion, philosophy, and value inquiry flourish. Education should give rise to these essential themes of spirituality, granting them the freedom they need. As sane human beings, we know quite well where no room exists for illusions and what actually delineates the clear borderline between internal and external reality.

Knowing this, we are able and free to entertain new ideas, to believe in God, to have values, to play, to imagine, to fantasize, to make love. Like making love, education is an erotic matter. All erotic activities indispensably need fantasy, an intermediate zone for our free imagination or creativity. Yet we need actuality's acceptance as well, even though actual reality may impinge on our imagination and creativity. The sane meeting or fruitful dialogue between our fantasy and actual reality is the most important aim of education. Playing has a decisive role in good education. When teachers lose their intimate contact with the child in each of them, they cannot function as good educators. Panenmentalism is entitled to adopt such a view, yet instead of a reality test, we use an actuality test, for under panenmentalism pure possibilities are no less real than actualities.

There is another essential point to be made. Since Winnicott emphasized the indispensable distinction between an inner-subjective reality and an outer reality, a distinction without which sanity would lose its footing, his views continue to contribute much to oppose postmodernism nowadays. Panenmentalism opposes postmodernism even more (Gilead 2003). Postmodernism is most perilous in my eyes, especially for education. Indeed, pluralism, openness, freedom, and liberty by no means oppose what is called modernism, whereas they are genuinely not compatible with postmodernism.

Sharply distinguishing between internal and external reality, between pure possibility and actuality, panenmentalism supports the sort of education that is widely open to the realm of pure possibilities and to attempts to save as many possibilities as possible, and it shows us time and again numerous ways in which actualities are distinct from their own possibilities–identities. Thus, panenmentalism supports both sides: spirituality on the one hand, and realism or empiricism on the other.

As for illusion, I certainly disagree with Winnicott. In panenmentalism, illusion consists of confusing the purely possible with the actual and thus ignoring or mistaking the spatiotemporal and causal conditions of the actual as well as of its contingency. There is a great difference between fantasies or imagination and illusion. We may fantasize or imagine our love, desiring to fulfill this fantasy, without which erotic experience seems to be meaningless or lacking identity; illusion, on the other hand, is susceptible to disillusionment, which may nullify the erotic experience. Erotic experience and pleasure consist of rendering one's fantasies fulfilled, met, actual (or real in *un*-panenmentalist terms). Knowing precisely where our fantasies end and actual reality begins leads us to realize whether our erotic desire or craving can be fulfilled or not. Without knowing that, the clear-cut distinction between, for instance, rape and making love is blurred. Without knowing that, the distinction between madness and sanity is blurred. At this point, I entirely agree with Winnicott, although I do not consider our fantasies to be illusions. Unlike Winnicott, I attempt to save many more possibilities for our fantasy and imagination. Such possibilities should *not* be thrown away due to disillusionment.

Panenmentalism is a novel modal metaphysics that I proposed in 1999. I hope that its future is still ahead and that it will contribute to our insight and understanding of children's spirituality and creativity as well as to ways to educate children much better and more humanely. These ways should lead to saving more and more possibilities for children's spirituality, as well as for that of adults. Under panenmentalism, education or learning may become an unforgettable, fascinating experience, making one's life deeper, richer, and fuller.

References

Gilead, A. 1999: *Saving Possibilities: A Study in Philosophical Psychology.* Amsterdam and Atlanta: Rodopi – VIBS, Vol. 80.

—— 2003: *Singularity and Other Possibilities: Panenmentalist Novelties.* Amsterdam and New York: Rodopi – VIBS (forthcoming).

Kant, I. 1781a and 1787b: *Kritik der reinen Vernunft.* Riga: Johann Friedrich Hartknoch.

Winnicott, D. W. 1991 (1971): *Playing and Reality.* London and New York: Routledge.

Chapter 4

Altering Habits of Attention in Education: Simone Weil and Emmanuel Levinas

CLAUDIA EPPERT

"The only serious aim of schoolwork is to train the attention."
Simone Weil (1986: 273)

ADDRESSING THE NEED for children's spiritual and ethical development in schools is of the utmost importance. Recent years have witnessed a burgeoning of literature intent upon establishing an emphasis on the contemplative in educational theory and practice (Glazer 1999). This literature draws upon an extensive body of writing to explore the possibilities of meaningfully transforming the contemporary state of education and the prevalence of violence and violation in our society. In this chapter I seek to contribute to this literature by investigating how "attention" as a mode of relation is and might be presented in current educational practice. The call for children to learn to "pay attention" is heard daily, if not hourly, in schools in North America. Yet how is this imperative predominantly articulated and received, if at all? And how else might we conceptualize and subsequently promote it? In posing these two questions, my intent is to challenge what I perceive as a widespread usage of a limited meaning of this term. I propose a deepening of the meaning of attention by drawing upon the philosophical and religious writings of Simone Weil and Emmanuel Levinas. Although Weil and Levinas have disagreed profoundly on biblical matters (Levinas 1990; Rose 1993), both provide a compelling redefinition that emphasizes a meaningful attentiveness at the heart of real learning.

The Pedagogical Imperative: "Pay Attention!"

We might begin by looking at what is involved in North American school life when teachers ask students to "pay attention." Most commonly, it seems, this phrase is an imperative understood as a stern plea for learners to return, to refocus and accomplish the task at hand. More often than not, this task encompasses accumulating the necessary content knowledge required to pass local and state tests and exams. Indeed, with educational initiatives increasingly centered on implementing standardized testing nationwide, the pressures to pay attention to these terms are increasing proportionately. Educators and parents are invested in having their students pass class and grade levels successfully. Teachers fear losing their jobs because of students' poor test scores, and parents worry about their children being left behind in what has become a highly competitive global market. Paying attention, consequently, has become a commodity, a good purchasable by students by enrollment in high-scoring schools – one that is rewarded with state funding and credibility.

As anyone with first-hand classroom experience attests, the frequency of the stated imperative to pay attention measures the absence of attentiveness. Each time students are asked to pay attention, it is because that is precisely what they're not doing. It is a call invariably voiced in the face of disruption, restlessness, and distraction. Habits of inattention are manifest in many of the public schools I have visited in the American South in these last couple of years. Students commonly arrive late to class, have difficulty settling down, can't find pencils or pens, investigate their backpacks, pass notes, and so on. "Pay attention!" insists one seventh-grade English teacher that I am observing one afternoon to a crowd that is doing anything but. She is preparing her students for the LEAP test by giving them a grammar lesson on direct and indirect objects. Her command is warranted. Sitting at the back of the classroom, I watch two girls exchanging notes, and one girl next to me playing with her glittering nail-polish collection. I'm wondering why the young woman beside me is practicing holding her breath. Two or three rows away, a boy is standing up to change his shirt and shoes for basketball practice, another is reading the comic book strategically located within his spiral notebook, and yet another is busily completing his homework for another class. At the other side of the room, a boy is teasing the child in front of him. Habits of inattention are also revealed in manifest inertia and absence: truancy, daydreaming, sleeping, and staring. In the same seventh-grade class, a small handful are missing, a young girl is sucking her thumb and staring into space, one girl is close to falling asleep, and three boys are staring vacantly at the teacher with their grammar books closed. In this class of about 24, it is apparent that even the teacher is having difficulty paying attention. It seems as if she is speaking without thinking, hearing without listening. Her expression betrays a shadow of the extent of her despair and resignation with the preoccupations of her students, and her frustration with the incessant intercom announcements and the choppy piano recital sounds pouring in from the music classroom next door. "Pay attention!" she insists again, adding, "Remember, this will be on the test!" All indications, however, are that her commands are falling on many deaf ears.

The scene I have just described is not one for which this specific teacher (quite competent in her instructional capacities) can be assigned fault. Indeed, teacher after teacher I encounter testifies to the large-scale familiarity of this pedagogical drama. Why the inability to pay attention has become such a widespread "problem" in North American schools is a question not easily answered. Certainly socio-historical, economic, and cultural factors regulating the functioning of and attitudes toward our educational institutions bear a significant portion of the responsibility. For how is it possible to pay attention when music from the next room invades the ears, or when intercom announcements and requirements to attend basketball practice interrupt classroom activities? Moreover, the current preoccupation with test preparation represents a significant departure from progressive initiatives centered on generating student interest and involvement. These issues require fuller examination. However, I emphasize another potential source: our common North American conceptualization of the nature of attention and its role in schooling. The problem of the pervasiveness of habitual inattention needs to be addressed, not through the band-aid measures of increasing pressures on children or placing greater emphasis on exams, but rather through a revitalization of our understanding of attention itself. Insofar as this revitalization is recognized as necessary and meaningful, it may contribute to the beginnings of structural reform, or at least constitute a productive intervention in the current mechanization of education. To consider its possible terms, I now briefly turn to the writings of Weil and Levinas.

Simone Weil's "Gymnastics of Attention"

Born in 1909, Simone Weil became a passionate philosopher, teacher, mystic, and activist. While raised in a middle-class agnostic Jewish family, she developed an abiding interest in Roman Catholicism. Although this interest did not lead to her conversion, it significantly informed her intellectual, emotional, and spiritual directions throughout her young life. Weil perceived spirituality as deeply inter-twined with political and educational endeavors. Part of her emphasis on the importance of this intertwining might also be attributed to the social and political climate in which she found herself. As Sylvie Courtine-Denamy points out, Weil was a witness to dark times (Courtine-Denamy 2000: 3). A "committed observer," she was acutely conscious (indeed, self-destructively so) of her responsibilities to others, and recognized that the perpetuation of evil needs to be combated through social work. Her activities involved forming a social-action group in the late 1920s, holding a series of factory jobs, and participating in the events of the Spanish Civil War. Weil held that public education represented a prime occasion for prompting awareness of the necessity of social action and change (Rose 1993: 217); this awareness, she main-tained, could be actively fostered only if education embodied a spiritual orientation.

The considerable emphasis Weil placed on the value of attention in schooling clarifies the interconnections among educational activities, sociopolitical involvement, and spiritual development that she invited us to consider. While "attention" appears as an integral concept throughout her work, its link to education is centrally elaborated in her essay "Reflections on the Right Use of School Studies With a View to the Love of God." In this essay she asserted that the "development of the faculty of attention forms the real object and almost the sole interest of studies" (Weil 1951/1973: 105). All school subjects, she maintained, should be equally and singularly directed to this development. Whether an algebraic problem has been solved or not is less important than the fact that, in the attempt, one has paid attention. Weil's view, therefore, might be regarded as the inverse of current educational practice. It is not so much that students are encouraged to pay attention in order that they might acquire subject knowledge. Rather, they learn subject knowledge so that they can practice paying attention. The reason Weil prioritized attention over subject matter is because the former leads beyond the limitations of the latter to spiritual dialogue and growth. For Weil, the school training of attention, applied to algebra or Latin, ultimately prepares the way for the ability to participate in the higher form of atten-tion to prayer. For Weil, then, attention is not simply a discipline of concentration, of attending to the task at hand, but rather the "orienta-tion of all . . . which the soul is capable toward God" (Weil 1951/1973: 105).

If the orientation of attention differed in Weil's view from its norma-tive conceptualization and concrete expression in school life, so too did her understanding of the *process* of paying attention. Today, it seems, we mostly pay attention by willfully applying and mastering our powers of concentration and physical self-control. For instance, we make ourselves sit still and be quiet. And often when we ask students sitting in an overcrowded classroom to pay attention, it is enough that they accomplish simply that. Yet Weil, influenced by eastern religions, believed that expressions of our willful intentions are manifestations of ego rather than attention. The ego's dominant life project is to establish and secure the sovereignty of the "I." As Gillian Rose put it in her discussion of Weil's thought, will "means to seize and possess the world for oneself" (Rose 1993: 217). We want to possess the world in order to affirm our significance in it. We fear the horror of the void and yearn to have our investments confirmed through externally endowed acts of reward such as the acquisition of wealth and acknowledgement from others; hence, the long and deeply ingrained lineage of our willful habits, and their destructive consequences. In contrast to willful aspirations, acts of attention are invested in enacting the breakage and disappearance of the sovereign "I." These acts involve moving "out towards the world and to God without the recoil which is self and possession" (Rose 1993: 217).

Paying attention, thus, is not about searching, mastering, controlling, acquiring and possessing, about becoming "fixed on a problem" (Weil 1951/1973: 170). Rather, it has us emptying ourselves, waiting, and receiving what comes to us from without, openly and with no attachment. Attention is a passive mode of relation to the world, though not passive understood as idle or indifferent. Weil maintained that the practice of attention "[c]onsists of suspending our thought, leaving it detached, empty, and ready to be penetrated by the object" (Weil 1951/1973: 111). It begins with simple detached looking: observance such that the "real becomes evident." Through extreme attention we become able to embrace contradictions. The mind cannot tolerate contradictions readily and struggles to dispel them. Yet contradiction is the very substance of creation, and its envelopment signifies spiritual understanding and development. When we perceive contradictions, a loosening occurs, and a path of creativity and insight opens for us (Weil 1951/1973: 151). Practicing attention in this manner and to this end is inherently transforming. Weil wrote, "we do not obtain the most precious gifts by going in search of them but by waiting for them" (Weil 1951/1973: 111).

More precious than possessions and outward rewards are the gifts of learning how to love and how to be humble, compassionate, and understanding. The importance of these treasures can only be realized in devotion to a spiritual path, because learning how to give and receive them beyond the limitations of the ego is so enormously difficult. This is fundamentally why Weil stressed that teaching should have no other aim than to be directed toward the (re)training of habits of attention – to be devoted to the exercising of what she calls a "gymnastics of attention" (1952/1973: 173). Ultimately the goal of learning is not the acquisition of subject matter but rather a lifelong struggle with the question of how to live in the world – how to live with ourselves, with each other, with our environment, and with what is greater than what we are. Acquiring productive habits of attention prepares the way for this profound struggle, opening us up to the transformational possibility of overcoming our faults and prejudices. Weil asserted, "Every time that we really concentrate our attention, we destroy the evil in ourselves" (Weil 1951/1973: 111). And as we increase our powers of vigilance, we become more cognizant of and able to respond to the plights of others. In both its orientation and process, learning to pay attention thus encompasses and reflects a disciplined spiritual and sociopolitical relationship to the world. Paying attention is an individual as well as a collective social action. Weil wrote that "real progress will be precisely proportional to the total amount of genuine attention which is brought to bear upon it amongst the bulk of individuals concerned (nowadays, this means the whole world)" (Weil 1952–5/1956: 287). Yet it is also an inherently joyful undertaking. Here too we see how Weil characterized attention in a way that differs radically from its current usage. Remembering the call to "pay attention" in my own school life invokes thoughts of pain and humiliation more than pleasure, dutiful and reluctant obedience more than inspired motivation. Yet for Weil a "gymnastics of attention is by necessity a joyful undertaking." Pleasure and desire are "as indispensable in study as breathing is in running" (Weil 1951/1973: 110), because it is these emotions that invite in, and enable us to receive, what is outside of us.

Levinas on Attentiveness to Another

Emmanuel Levinas was born three years before Simone Weil. A native of Lithuania, he too became a philosopher. Unlike Weil, however, he identified strongly with his Jewish upbringing, and learned Hebrew as his first language. Studying in France at the University of Strasbourg, he became influenced by the ideas of Heidegger and Husserl. Profoundly affected by the events of his time, in the 1920s he joined the Alliance Israelite Universelle, a group that sought "to promote the integration of Jews as full citizens within their states, with equal rights and freedom from persecution" (Aronowicz 1990: xi).

Levinas's philosophical and religious preoccupations centered upon working through the concepts of responsibility, conscience, trauma, remembrance, time, and language. He predominantly sought to articulate a theory of ethical relations that countered the ontological imperialism he perceived manifest in Western philosophy and life. He believed that Western traditions of ethics and epistemology have supported the ego's drive to consolidate the "I" in ways that prove fundamentally violent to what it does not recognize as a reflection or assertion of itself. In its aspirations for self-validation, the autonomous "I" aspires to possess or annihilate all that it encounters, and theories of being and learning have justified these goals implicitly, if not explicitly. His notion of ethical responsibility thus opposes these ambitions by positing an asymmetrical structure at the heart of one person's relationship with another. The "I" has an infinite, absolute, and unquestionable responsibility for another being, and this responsibility precedes and fuels the founding of self, exceeding the self's acceptance or refusal of its exigencies (Levinas 1985/1995: 96–7). When Levinas's subject encounters another, in particular, the alterity of another that cannot be thematized, it is traumatized, its egoistic foundations irreparably shaken. As with Weil, then, Levinas perceived the dismantling of the sovereign "I" as central to the responsible and responsive relation with another.

For both of these philosophers, one is called to be answerable to suffering. Weil maintained that attention to the passerby in the street makes his or her sacredness immediately manifest and demands a response to the "silent cry" located in the passerby's question "Why am I being hurt?" (Weil 1986: 72). Weil argued that this cry that seeks to be released from evil is constant, and that humans are eternally obliged in the name of justice and preservation to prevent violence and violation. Our obligations precede our rights, and, unlike rights, exist independently of conditions. She contended, "There exists an obligation towards every human being for the sole reason that he or she *is* a human being, without any other condition requiring to be fulfilled, and even without any recognition on the part of the individual concerned" (Weil 1986: 107). For Weil, this obligation is not based upon conventions, customs, social structures, historical heritage or orientation, but upon a spiritual "something" that does not constitute part of this world (Weil 1986: 108).

Levinas similarly asserts that in the address of alterity, the self hears the commandment "[T]hou shalt not kill" (Levinas 1985/1995: 87, see also Rose 1993: 215). He similarly perceived a radical attention as a defining characteristic of ethical aspirations. For him, the encounter with another commands an unparalleled attentiveness embedded in the awareness of the inherent authority of the other person's alterity. What fundamentally encapsulates ethics is its responsiveness to and reflection of illimitable alterity – a radical difference, unthinkable, unquantifiable, insatiable, otherwise than being, holy, manifest in the specificity and irreducibility of another. Levinas wrote that "being attentive signifies a surplus of consciousness, and presupposes the call of the other. To be attentive is to recognize the mastery of the other, to receive his command, or, more exactly, to receive from him the command to command" (Levinas 1961: 178). In this sense, he also described attention as not being about mastery, domination, and willful intent, but about receptivity. This receptivity entails a radical passive opening, self-exposure, and vulnerability (Levinas 1991: 141). Moreover, our passive attention is turned toward two directions, entailing a carefully negotiated sensitivity to the discursive (the "said") and to the illimitable (the "saying") (Simon and Eppert 1997: 179).

Susan Handelman points out that because Levinas prioritized ethics over epistemology, he accomplished an important pedagogical reversal (Handelman 1996: 222). An ethical learning is open to what exceeds the resources of the already known. Levinas, like Weil, linked paying attention with the learning of something more profound than mere fact and information. It does not involve acquiring "an abstract and general content already common to me and the Other" (Levinas 1961: 98). Rather, because learning is contact with something radically foreign, exceeding the resources of consciousness, it is subject to the experience of surprise and trauma. The experience is transformational. Levinas's subject learns that the "I" is nothing but that which is established in relation to his or her obligation to the alterity of another (Eppert 2000). Learning to attend to another signals the beginning not only of responsibility but also of response. As Robert Gibbs observes, "attentiveness makes me utterly vulnerable and places me into question. I become changed in this encounter – I learn to respond. I receive the authority to speak and to reveal myself to others" (Gibbs 2000: 32). While this authority is not equal to that of another, it supports a responsive voice and agency learned from the teacher. Ethical learning thus involves a singular attentiveness that brings the subject into contact with infinity, traumatically initiates self-questioning and self-justification, and calls for responsible and responsive relations with another and with the world. Like with Weil, then, Levinas considers learning to have value profoundly beyond the instrumental acquisition of information. It is directed to ethical, social, and spiritual development that pierces the pretensions of the ego and is accomplished through the pedagogical vehicle of a not-indifferent, passive, and open practice of attention.

Implications for Education

Although Levinas and Weil differ particularly with regard to certain of their religious convictions, I have sought to emphasize points of similarity centered upon their understanding of the nature and purpose of attention in relationship to education. My aim is not only to make evident the surprising overlap of these two thinkers but also, and more predominantly, to highlight a more profound and productive way of practicing attention than is currently being embraced in North America. What implications do their insights hold for addressing the pervasive problem of children's inattention in our schools?

Both these philosophers support the recent return to the contemplative by emphasizing that learning must extend beyond the parsing of sentences or the solving of mathematical problems. Learning must relate to the pursuit of life's deeper questions and the effort to expand the horizons of one's ethical awareness in ways that require the difficult, interminable work of deconstructing the ego and of meeting one's obligations to others. Indeed, against the background of the disturbing realities of 9/11; the current events in Afghanistan, in India and Pakistan, and in Israel and Palestine; global exploitation; sexual abuse; and mass shootings in American schools – it is worth debating what the current national emphasis on testing is suited to accomplish. My intent here is not to devalue initiatives for setting standards but to focus on what threatens to become excluded when these initiatives take an obsessive turn, and when our educational concerns are limited to the processing of data more than to the cultivation of spirit.

Although both Levinas and Weil were deeply religious, and their respective writings are suffused with references to God, I feel that the practice of a higher form of learning need not be invested in particular religious affiliations and traditions. While debate (see Vokey 2000) rages around what constitutes the cultivation of spirit and its place in education, I invoke the spiritual here with regard to this higher form of attention as a way of emphasizing relations that open beyond the empirically known. I suggest that, at the very least, education must encompass the pursuit of ethical relations with the self, the other, and the world in ways cognizant of possibilities present beyond an autonomous, all-knowing, and self-interested subject. Steven Glazer comments that "in bringing the sacred into our experience of the world, the call to moral or ethical behavior becomes stronger and stronger. Merely by seeing the writing on the wall – the traces of our causes and effects – our path in life can be illuminated. What is required is not code, law, or force but instead a scale, intimacy, and ethic where call and response – cause and effect – can be witnessed, experienced, understood" (Glazer 1999: 11).

Our current emphasis in education simply cannot provide answers to the young girl I observed in the seventh-grade class who was practicing holding her breath. From her teacher I found out later that there had been recent violence in family. Clearly this girl's situation points to larger societal problems and serves to remind us of the complexities underscoring any attempts to examine and transform the causes for a particular effect. Yet in the face of these difficulties – and if we recognize contemporary education as impoverished in its inability to address body, emotion, mind, soul and spirit collectively – we might nevertheless begin to cultivate humane and relational qualities through initiatives centered upon the encouragement of the practice of alternate modes of attention.

This requires, first and foremost, a concentrated unlearning of our current habits of attention. We need to examine closely what we are asking students to do when we repeatedly announce the imperative to pay attention. We need to keep in mind that, in its current popular usage, the command recalls threat, fear, and obedience in the midst of dire boredom or restlessness. And we need to recognize how entrenched and unambiguous this imperative has become. I borrow the term "habits of (in)attention" from Megan Boler's insightful examination of our contemporary emotional grammars. Drawing upon John Dewey's writings, she observed how habits penetrate the core of the self and entail the establishment and solidification of particular desires, purposes, and dispositions (Boler 1999: 180). Consequently, they potentially signify the impairment of our ability to reflect (Boler 1999: 180). In other words, our habits not only of inattention but also of attention have become so fully ingrained that we have lost perspective about the possibilities and underlying significance of the phrase. The familiarity of our habits makes the struggle of unlearning all the more arduous. Boler introduces the need for an explicit "pedagogy of discomfort" that gives emotional room for us to recognize when habits "have become rigid and immune to flexibility; and to identify when and how our habits harm ourselves and others" (Boler 1999: 186).

The imperative to pay attention is the common response not just to an inability to concentrate on grammar lessons. It is also the answer to complaints about the seemingly widespread apathy of today's youth, as well as the apathy of adults whose involvement in politics and social change has been shown to be diminishing. (This answer incidentally reinforces the connection between habits of attention and social awareness and change). Yet repeated insistence is not the way to transform apathy into a responsible responsiveness. Practices of unlearning include not only the deconstruction of current habits of attention and inattention but also their replacement with a more productive practice – in and through considered reflection of what a philosophy of subjectivity and patterns of relation the imperative really speaks to and reinforces. Such habits of attention as sitting still extend beyond mere motor activity. They signify a particular worldview, a particular way of perceiving and actualizing the self, a certain habit of being. Weil and Levinas made evident that the enforcement of our will entails our exertion upon the world and reflects a relation of force and determined control more than one of detachment, receptivity, and openness.

Having identified alternatives to current practices of attention, however, we might do well to debate the practical expression of their philosophies in, say a Southern seventh-grade English classroom in which students are exchanging notes, talking, changing clothes, holding their breath, sharpening pencils, and generally being neither willfully obedient nor attentive. Weil and Levinas were clearly unfamiliar with contemporary realities of the classroom as they developed their theories. How can we respond to teachers who might roll their eyes at these ambitious ivory-tower ideas? What possibilities are there for introducing young learners to the joys and intrinsic rewards of attentiveness, especially when they are paying little attention in any form or manner to begin with?

Certainly part of the answer here involves making learning more accessible – more desirable and relevant – for children and enabling them to apply their insights. A curriculum attuned to the deeper of life's questions does not oppose but instead nicely corresponds to student interests. It is my belief that students of every age are naturally drawn to these questions although, as a society, we have largely either not encouraged their posing or have responded to them dryly, dispassionately, or dogmatically. However, sensitivity to student interests does not point in the direction of a curriculum exclusively focused on these interests. Such a curriculum diminishes the possibility that students might become, and practice becoming, absorbed in something beyond the immediate circle of their passions. The antidote for boredom and apathy does not emanate from outside engagements but rather from an inner perspective and approach to the world. If we turn inward and come to appreciate the intrinsic worth of each moment (whether dull or fascinating) and realize that with our powers of attention we can learn from whatever we participate in, it becomes apparent that boredom constitutes an expression of the ego. Yet powers of attention cannot simply become visible at the first call to pay attention in a meaningful way. Rather than being effortlessly acquired, these abilities demand extended cultivation. In this regard, the cultivation of spirit is incumbent upon a certain spirit of cultivation.

Incorporating material of interest and relevance into our curriculum can therefore help facilitate acts of attention and bring joy into our educational endeavors. Yet perhaps most fruitful and necessary to a relearning is to expose our students to the awareness of inattention as a problem of our contemporary times. We might consequently initiate change by posing attention as a question for classroom discussion and making it a subject of collective inquiry and study. Following such discussion, during the remainder of the year in the regular curriculum we might take a daily moment or two simply to pause. And in the small space of this pause, we might begin to learn not to master but to receive, begin to awaken and attune our hearts with one small step to all that we have yet to know, experience and give.

References

Aronowicz, A. (trans.) 1990: Translator's Introduction. In *Nine Talmudic Readings by Emmanuel Levinas*. Bloomington: Indiana University Press.

Boler, M. 1999: *Feeling Power: Emotions and Education*. New York: Routledge.

Courtine-Denamy, S. 2000: *Three Women in Dark Times: Edith Stein, Hannah Arendt, Simone Weil*. G. M. Goshgarian (trans.). Ithaca: Cornell University Press.

Eppert, C. 2000: Relearning Questions: Responding to the Ethical Address of Past and Present Others. In R. I. Simon, S. Rosenberg, and C. Eppert (eds.), *Between Hope and Despair: Pedagogy and the Remembrance of Historical Trauma*. Lanham, MD: Rowman and Littlefield.

Glazer, S. (ed.) 1999: *The Heart of Learning: Spirituality in Education*. New York: Penguin Putnam.

Gibbs, R. 2000: *Why Ethics? Signs of Responsibilities*. Princeton: Princeton University Press.

Handelman, S. 1996: The "Torah" of Criticism and the Criticism of Torah: Recuperating the Pedagogical Moment. In Steven Kepnes (ed.), *Interpreting Judaism in a Postmodern Age*, New York: New York University Press.

Levinas, E. 1961: *Totality and Infinity: An Essay on Exteriority*. Alphonso Lingis (trans.). Pittsburgh: Duquesne University Press.

—— 1991: *Otherwise Than Being or Beyond Essence*. Alphonso Lingus (trans.). Dordrecht: Kluwer.

—— 1985/1995: *Ethics and Infinity: Conversations With Philippe Nemo*. Richard Cohen (trans.). Pittsburgh: Duquesne University Press.

—— 1990: Simone Weil against the Bible. In *Difficult Freedom: Essays on Judaism*, Sean Hand (trans.). Baltimore: John Hopkins University Press.

Rose, G. 1993: Angry Angels: Simone Weil and Emmanuel Levinas. In *Judaism and Modernity: Philosophical Essays*. Oxford: Blackwell.

Simon, R. I. and Eppert, C. 1997: Remembering Obligation: Pedagogy and the Witnessing of Testimony of Historical Trauma. *Canadian Journal of Education* 22 (2): 175–91.

Vokey, D. 2000: Longing to Connect: Spirituality in Public Schools. *Paideusis* 13 (2): 23–41.

Weil, S. 1951/1973: *Waiting for God*. New York: Harper and Row.

—— 1952/1997: *Gravity and Grace*. Arthur Wills (trans.). Lincoln, NE: University of Nebraska Press.

—— 1952–5/1956: *The Notebooks of Simone Weil*. Arthur Wills (trans.). London: Routledge and Kegan Paul.

—— 1986: *Simone Weil: An Anthology*. Edited and introduced by Sian Miles. London: Virago Press.

Chapter 5

Learning from Experience: Dewey, Deleuze and "Becoming-Child"

INNA SEMETSKY

A S LONG AGO as 1925 John Dewey, in his *Experience and Nature*, noted that to call someone spiritual does not mean to invoke "a mysterious non-natural entity" (1925/1958: 293). A particular person who, according to Dewey, is endowed with a soul,

> has in marked degrees qualities of sensitive, rich and coordinated partic-
> ipation in all the situations of life. . . . When the organization called soul
> is free, moving and operative . . . it is spirit . . . Soul is form, spirit informs.
> . . . Perhaps the words soul and spirit are so heavily laden with . . .
> mythology . . . that they must be surrendered; it may be impossible to
> recover for them in science and philosophy the realities designated in
> idiomatic speech. But the realities are there, by whatever names they are
> called. (Dewey 1925/1958: 294)

How should we, as educators, understand Dewey's words in our current postmodern, "*inform*-ation" age? This paper addresses Dewey's notion of continuity in terms of its being "the intimate, delicate and subtle interdependence of all organic structures and processes with one another" (Dewey 1925/1958: 295). Rather than aiming toward building any unified theory, I intend to tell a story that describes "a procedure in actual practice which demonstrates this continuity" (Dewey 1925/1958: 295).

The structure of this chapter is twofold. The power of "stories lives tell" (Witherell and Noddings 1991) cannot be underestimated, and first I will present an excerpt from the semiautobiographical short story written by a Russian-Jewish émigré to Israel, Julia Schmookler. In 1975 the Russian-language edition appeared in print in Israel, and I took the liberty of translating a part of it into English for the purpose of inclusion in this chapter.

Second, I will focus on the notion of *percept* as described by Gilles Deleuze and will connect it with Dewey's account of a qualitative whole. Percept, which has been related by Deleuze to Spinoza-type singularity, allows a lesson in becoming, specifically, as Deleuze called it, *becoming-child*. I will conclude by suggesting that if, as Dewey said, spirit informs, then a little girl – the story's protagonist – has received, without any direct or explicit instruction, a lesson of vital education that is, according to Deleuze, an immanent mode of existence, and one "created vitally . . . through the forces it is able to harness" (Deleuze 1997: 135).

Below is the abbreviated excerpt in my translation from the story by Schmookler entitled "The Miracle."[1] Its narrator is a four-year-old girl in Russia, whose father has been taken to the Gulag by authorities and whose mother struggles to support the family. The girl, surrounded by politically correct (meaning cold and uncaring) teachers in her preschool, feels estranged and lonely. But one day a miracle happens:

> *They didn't like me in that preschool.*
> *Somehow I was different and seemed strange; the kids teased me and did not let me play with them; all games were taking place without me. And I lost all my vigor and forgot all the lovely songs and all the poems and lovely tales that I used to know by heart. And all day long I would sit by myself on a stool, making up an imaginary dialogue, and the never-ending story was always full of really good events. . . .*
>
> *Once when I was sitting on my stool, the teacher came in. She was holding a book, and I recognized the cover of the book in her hands. It was one of those books that mama and papa used to read to me in that previous life and I knew all of those books by heart. And in a sudden inspiration I knew what I was supposed to do. My head started spinning; my heart started pumping – and then stopped – and at that very moment I got up from my seat of shame. "I can READ this book," I said very firmly, and I felt complete freedom and total weightlessness during this grandiose lie.*
>
> *Everyone looked at me – nobody among us four-year-olds could read, or even dream of reading, of performing this magical act – and here I am, the last becoming the first! Even the teacher looked sort of kind and amazed – and then it happened: all the children sat around me on their little white chairs, and I was put in the center, and I read those poems one after another, turning pages where necessary, because I knew all the pictures and knew what was written under each one of them, and everything turned out just right; one would not wish for more.*
>
> *Teachers praised me and set me up as an example, and all day long I played with many popular children, and they chose me in some games. . . . The next day the*

same scene took place; the teacher brought another book, and again I knew it, and I read it by heart . . . My future seemed settled . . .

That's why on the third day when I once more was called up to read, and everyone was taking a seat, and I, like some very important person, went calmly and with dignity to the teacher to pick up the book, the world suddenly collapsed! I had never seen THIS book. All the chairs were already in a circle, and mine was specifically in the center, as usual, and I knew that THAT WAS IT, fate just decided to kill me in one swift stroke, and I would be better off if I were really dead or simply if I had never been born. The walls were rotating in a milky fog, my head was spinning, my throat became dry, my soul, hit by the thunder, became silent.

My body, meanwhile, was holding on to the book and continued moving toward the central chair. "What for?" I thought, "I'd better tell the truth and do it right now before everything becomes even worse." But my body, separated from my mind, was still moving. Then it sat down. "What for?" I thought, or did I think this thought before? . . .

Time was shifting and very rapidly indeed – my hands were already opening the front page. "God," I remembered, "God . . . ." Certainly I knew very well that God did not exist, but there was no time left to make the right choice.

I opened my mouth to confess everything and repent and end the terrible torture at once, but my eyes fell on the page, and suddenly I heard my voice, which was quietly and rhythmically saying those words that were printed on the page. One half of me was reading, and the other was listening in sublime horror, and white trembling light was slowly spreading around. I was reading page after page as if in a dream, and no one knew that it was a miracle, and simultaneously I was seeing the text all at once and the very black letters and the very bright pictures and myself as well, surrounded by all the kids. I was saved, it was a miracle, and it was terrifying, too, to speak as if someone were putting words in my mouth.

At last the book ended. The light disappeared, the kids left, and I sat by myself, my feet cotton-like. I sat alone and totally empty like an abandoned dwelling, and as for the new knowledge, it was too much. I felt its weight as if it were putting itself on shelves in my head . . .

At home, in bed, all of a sudden I got scared that I'd forgotten how to read, and I jumped out of bed and ran to the bookshelf to pick up one of mama's books. I opened it in the middle and clearly saw the phrase "her right breast was naked." I read it but did not understand. What does it mean, "right breast" or "left breast"? A person has one breast, and I looked at mine, which was represented by a piece of veneer unevenly covered with goose bumps.

In amazement, and happy that the ability to read had not left me, I fell asleep quietly knowing that I was protected and would be saved if there was a need.

Let us pause. The purpose of philosophy, for Deleuze, is, apart from creating novel concepts, radically ethical in a manner of being worthy of what is to come into existence, to *become*. In fact, novel concepts are created so as to make sense of experiential events and, ultimately, to affirm this sense. For Deleuze and Felix Guattari, the major message of their philosophy is "to become worthy of the event" (Deleuze and Guattari 1994: 160).

The desire propelling an event into becoming is not some magical thinking or one's strong will. A concept inhabits the *empirical* happening; it is, as Deleuze and Guattari say, a *living* concept, but the *ethical* work consists in the will itself being transformed into affirmation so as "to set up, . . . to extract" (Deleuze and Guattari 1994: 160) an event in this living concept. Desire constructs a plane – immanence, for Deleuze, is constructivism – and because desire is impersonal, therefore subjectless, it is attained, indeed affirmed, at the very instant of desperation in which "someone is deprived of the power of saying 'I'"(Deleuze 1987: 89), like the little girl in the story.

Such desire would perhaps be called the will to power by Nietzsche. According to Deleuze, however, "there are other names for it. For example, 'grace'" (Deleuze 1987: 91). For Deleuze, "all desires come from . . . the Outside . . . [and] we can always call it [the] plane of Nature, in order to underline its immanence" (Deleuze 1987: 97–8). Noticing that Spinoza was the one who conceived of the plane in this manner, Deleuze is adamant that it is the immanent process of desire that fills itself up, thus constituting a process called *joy*.

On the other hand, and as applied to social psychology, self-fulfillment has traditionally been identified not with personal physical demands like, for example, one's biological or physiological needs, nor even with social and communitarian values, but with values identified as spiritual and considered ideal. But Deleuze's philosophy does not set apart the ideal from the real. In his radically empirical philosophy everything is real, including the virtual, which, however, is not actual.

As for Dewey, when he assigns an *ideal* status to the state of being beyond good and evil, he implies that this state "is an impossibility for man." Yet as long as "the good signifies only that which is . . . rewarded, and the evil that which is . . . condemned . . ., the ideal factors of morality are always and everywhere beyond good and evil" (Dewey 1934/1980: 349).

According to Dewey, going beyond good and evil, especially under certain oppressive circumstances, is equivalent to "going beyond the actual to the possible" (Garrison 1997: 136–7). It seems, however, that to Deleuze, the state of being beyond good and evil and the one of going beyond the actual to the possible, albeit denoting the same, would appear to have slightly different connotations. Let us try to elucidate this very subtle and seemingly almost indiscernible difference.

Only creative art, for Dewey, is capable of possessing such a moral potency as going beyond good and evil, and one of the reasons for this is that art is "wholly innocent of ideas derived from praise and blame"

(Dewey 1934/1980: 349). Innocence seems to be the key word here. Deleuze's so-called ontology of the virtual frees thinking from common sense. Life itself, for Deleuze, is what *activates* thought, and thought *affirms* life. If, as Deleuze asserted, *immanence* is *a* life, then miracles may happen.

In the world described by Deleuze and Guattari as *becoming-world*, however, the latter may not be called miracles after all; they belong to pure events constituting virtual reality. Accordingly, *becoming-child* – a child by definition embodying the concept of innocence – is the factor that, as it seems, Dewey would have described as *ideal*, beyond good and evil. Yet Deleuze would not equate the latter with going beyond the actual to the possible.

The possible can be realized, and the real *thing* is to exist in the image and likeness, as the saying goes, of the possible *thing*. But the virtual is real even without being actual and only actualizes itself via multiple different/ciations (see Deleuze 1994), so the actual does not resemble the virtual; it is different from it, and it cannot be otherwise because the virtual is just a tendency, therefore *no-thing*. Virtual tendencies, *no-things*, become actualized, that is, embodied in the actual *things*, objects, experiences, states of affairs.

Deleuze's ontology becomes reinforced by Dewey's naturalistic logic in which "there is no breach of continuity between operations of inquiry and biological . . . and physical operations. 'Continuity' . . . means that rational operations *grow* out of organic activities, without being identical with that from which they emerge" (Dewey 1938: 166).

Becoming-actual means manifesting the actual existence and Deleuze's concept of different/ciation describing the method for actualization is *intuition* – or the pragmatic way of knowing described by Deleuze (1994) as transcendental empiricism. What is striving to become actual is that which is *in virtu* and is only waiting for conditions in the *real*, not merely possible, experience to come forward.

This *real* becoming-life, as any becoming, takes place within what Deleuze called a zone of indiscernibility as the instance of connection or, in Dewey's world, the "meeting of the old and new" (Dewey 1934/1980: 266). At such a meeting the connection is properly assigned the name *intuition* not only by Deleuze, but by Dewey too, even if Dewey puts the word *per se* in quotation marks to emphasize its nontraditional sense:

> "Intuition" is that meeting of the old and new in which the readjustment involved in every form of consciousness is effected suddenly by means of a quick and unexpected harmony which in its bright abruptness is like a flash of revelation; although in fact it is prepared for by long and slow incubation. Oftentimes the union of old and new, of foreground and background, is accomplished only by effort, prolonged perhaps to the point of

pain. . . . [T]he background of organized meanings can alone convert the new situation from the obscure into the clear and luminous. (Dewey 1934/1980: 266)

The meeting of the old and the new, of repetition and difference, is possible through their "jump together," that is, by means of a transversal link crossing levels and thresholds. The image of spark used by both Deleuze and Dewey – "old and new jump together like sparks when poles are adjusted" (Dewey 1934/1980: 266) – implies a sense of connection that is established via *relation* rather than by an immediate contact.

The dynamic forces affecting selection and assemblages do bring the "mind . . . in contact with the world" (Dewey 1934/1980: 267), yet such a contact is what in contemporary physics would be called a non-local connection. The contact in question would be described by means of "non-localizable connections, actions at a distance, systems of replay, resonance and echoes, objective chances, signs, signals and roles which transcend spatial locations and temporal successions" (Deleuze 1994: 83).

The contact manifests by its material embodiment in the form of the artifact or the new knowledge which, sure enough, seems to the little girl as being too much: "As for the new knowledge, it was too much, I felt its weight." Something that was virtual and as yet disembodied – like spirit that, as Dewey says, *informs* but by itself is not a form – became actualized in the uniqueness of experience and, as a consequence of the latter, was "marked by individuality" (Dewey 1934/1980: 266).

Therefore, this real becoming-life, the meeting of the old and the new, can be described as

an impersonal and yet singular life that disengages a pure event freed from the accidents of the inner and outer life, that is, from the subjectivity and objectivity of what happens . . . . This is a haecceity, which is no longer an individuation, but a singularization: *a life of pure immanence*, neutral, beyond good and evil. (Deleuze 1997: xiv)

And, for that matter, beyond truth and lie, or right and wrong, that is, beyond the dual opposites that, incidentally, came into existence in the first place as a result of the symbolic loss of innocence. Again innocence seems to be a key word, a situational variable of sorts, which by virtue of itself being embedded in the dynamic process creates the conditions in real experience for the production of meanings.

As becoming, it is imperceptible, unless perception vitally increases in power, which is the characteristic of Deleuze's method of transcendental empiricism. What Deleuze calls *percept* is the future-oriented perception in becoming. Through organic resonances enacted by transversal communication, the continuity is carried further toward the ultimate "unity of sense and impulse, of brain and eye and ear" (Dewey 1934/1980: 22–3), overcoming the otherwise ineliminable dualisms. That unity may become manifest, by means of actualization of potentialities, through breaks in *continuity*, the latter therefore appearing to be, at the level of concrete experiences, *discontinuous* and abrupt.

The little girl's seemingly miraculous experience is Deleuze's atemporal pure *event* which nevertheless is, from the point of view of experience itself, "the focal culmination of the continuity of an ordered temporal experience in a sudden discrete instant of climax" (Dewey 1934/1980: 23–4). The increase in power is taken almost literally; there is an exponential growth there, but the transversal communication carries an exponent towards its limit as if crossing the otherwise asymptotic line, thus becoming a threshold provided the situation meets the conditions for actualization.

Deleuze notices that such an element of vitality is manifest in newborn infants who embody the very passage of life. The actualization of the set of virtualities refers to attaining a consistency. It seems that what Deleuze implies here is that a baby would still have the virtual presence of the umbilical cord as a sign of symbiosis with his or her mother. Such is a *"zone of proximity or copresence"* (Deleuze and Guattari 1987: 273) that constitutes an imperceptible becoming. Hence for Deleuze and Guattari, "the child [does] not become; it is becoming itself that is a child" (Deleuze and Guattari 1987: 277).

When the little girl was reading the new text, she could not possibly speak from the viewpoint of concepts but rather had to "speak directly and intuitively in pure percepts" (Deleuze 1995: 165). Such is, as Deleuze notices, the paradoxical style of Spinoza, who – while remaining, for Deleuze, the most philosophical of philosophers whose *Ethics* presents axioms and propositions in abundance – nevertheless brings forward an intense non-philosophical understanding. For the little girl, the concept of reading is yet unknown, and her perception undergoes transformation or increase in power into becoming-*percept*, which is necessary for the creation of novel *concepts*.

The very passage between the two is what Deleuze calls *affect*, inseparable from percept and concept alike. An affect is *what a body can do* or, in Dewey's words, this body's "enhancement of the qualities . . . [and] intensified . . . appreciation"(Dewey 1916/1924: 278–9) of an experience. The body's newly acquired power to read "must liberate joys, vectorial signs of the augmentation of power, and ward off sadness, signs of diminution" (Deleuze 1997: 144), thus bringing healing to the situation that would otherwise remain traumatic.

Although such an experience indeed may seem to be too much, and the little girl feels overwhelmed, her situation has been changed. It has been transformed *"into one so determinate in its constituent distinctions and relations as to convert the elements of the original situation into a unified whole"* (Dewey 1938: 171). Speaking in percepts as a form of intuition is therefore, as we said earlier citing Dewey, the meeting of the old and the new. Perception would not *become* a percept without the two-way communication, or Dewey's *transaction.*

In this respect *in-tuition* always contains a numinous, religious element, especially if we read *re-ligio* etymologically as the linking backward to the origin, that is, literally self-referentiality: learning from within. Learning implies an increase in complexity via an asymmetrical, connection, yet the role of *re-ligio* is to restore the broken symmetry and unity. *A unified whole* is, however, never the same because of its (self)-organizing principle expressed in what Deleuze called the repetition of the different, embedded in his philosophical method of transcendental empiricism.

Not least important is this new *different part* that entered the integral *whole,* this little girl. As Dewey emphasized,

> the unification of the self through the ceaseless flux of what it does, suffers and achieves cannot be attained in terms of itself. The self is always directed toward something beyond itself and so its own unification depends upon the idea of the integration of the shifting scenes of the world into that imaginative totality we call the Universe. (Dewey 1934: 407)

The newly acquired skill of reading, by means of breaking out of the old habit, means that the little girl is undergoing "a modification through an experience . . . to easier and more effective action in a like direction in the future" (Dewey 1916/1924: 395). The ability to read becomes a new habit for the little girl in her *becoming-other. Acquiring* is always preceded by "the act of *in*quiring. It is seeking . . . for something that is not at hand" (Dewey 1916/1924: 173).

That which is not actually at hand must, as Deleuze would have said, *subsist* in its virtual state, thereby affording empiricism its transcendental quality. Learning, for Deleuze, always takes place "in and through the unconscious, thereby establishing the bond of a profound complicity between nature and mind" (Deleuze 1994: 165), leading to the conjugation that determines, as Deleuze says, the threshold of consciousness: unconscious-*becoming*-conscious.

This is the aforementioned unity of sense and impulse, posited by Dewey, or "the readjustment . . . in every form of consciousness" (Dewey 1934/1980: 266), when that which is still obscure or unconscious becomes transformed into the clear and luminous. *Trans-formation* presupposes *in-formation,* and if, as Dewey says, spirit informs, then the little girl has indeed *learned* without any direct or explicit instruction but by means of the natural interaction between herself and the whole of the environment that has generated an "intelligence in operation" (Dewey 1934: 410). She became an apprentice, capable of raising "each faculty to the level of its transcendent exercise, . . . [in her] attempts to give birth to that second power which grasps that which can only be sensed" (Deleuze 1994: 165).

Dewey insisted that the role of the teacher should not consist solely in what customarily is called instruction, with its emphasis on what has been specified by Nel Noddings as the "forced feedings of theories" (Noddings 1993: 15). Dewey identified an impulse as "the large and generous blending of interests . . . in the meeting of mind and universe" (Dewey 1934/1980: 267). Such is the learning space created by the little girl; she has literally *undergone* learning from experience when trying to give birth to something new. Indeed, no instruction appears to be necessary because,

> to "learn from experience" is to make a backward and forward connection between what we do to things and what we enjoy and suffer from things in consequence. Under such conditions, doing becomes a trying; an experiment with the world . . . ; the undergoing becomes instruction – discovery of the connection of things. (Dewey 1916/1924: 164)

Dewey describes such a learning remaining at the existential level of actual experience. Deleuze takes it to the level of the virtual, which is no less real than any actual existence. Different/ciation, for Deleuze, presupposes an intense *field* of individuation, the Dewey qualitative whole of sorts. It is because of "the action of the field of individuation that such and such differential relations and such and such distinctive points . . . are actualized – in other words are organized within intuition along lines differentiated in relation to other lines" (Deleuze 1994: 247).

Jim Garrison (2000), addressing the possibilities of spiritual education, reminds us that for Dewey the idea of God is the active relation between ideal and actual. The active *striving*, what Spinoza called *conatus*, to unite the two belongs, according to Garrison, to "potentially spiritual acts" (Garrison 2000: 114). The situation itself acquires a tone that can be "designated by an adjective" (Dewey 1934: 402), the religious. The reconstruction always occurs in the direction of "security and stability" (Dewey 1934: 405). Indeed, as the little girl said, "I fell asleep quietly knowing that I was protected . . ."

Is calling something into existence and creation, in accord with "Dewey's testimony, the supreme act of numinous spirit" (Garrison 2000: 116), or is it the prerogative of mundane matter – the latter, not passive and inert but radically active and capable of self organization? Or should we, rather than dwelling in metaphysical questions, just try to do our best to modify *conditions* so they are altered up to the point at which something new and good would be produced? Isn't this exactly what Dewey's laboratory method would call for?

For Dewey, the lesson of the latter is precisely the one of altering conditions, and such is also "the lesson which all education has to learn. The laboratory is a discovery of the conditions under which *labor* may become intellectually fruitful" (Dewey 1916/1924: 322). Deleuze too has identified teaching and learning with the "research laboratory" (Deleuze 1995: 139).

The thinking process that takes place in a laboratory is *in actu;* thought itself becomes an experiment, and "that's where you have to get to work . . . As though there are so many twists in the path of something moving through space like a whirlwind that can materialize at any point" (Deleuze 1995: 161). The novelty may be created precisely at such a critical point, "at the point where the mind comes in contact with the world . . . When the new is created, the far and strange become the most natural inevitable things in the world," even if clothed "by the inertia of habit" (Dewey 1934/1980: 267-8) so they are disguised under the name of *miracle.*

Note

1   All possible efforts have been made to locate Julia Schmookler with regard to copyright permission.

References

Deleuze, G. 1987: *Dialogues (with Claire Parnet)*. H. Tomlinson and G. Burchell (trans.). New York: Columbia University Press.

—— 1994: *Difference and Repetition*. P. Patton (trans.). New York: Columbia University Press.

—— 1995: *Negotiations 1972–1990*. M. Joughin (trans.). New York: Columbia University Press.

—— 1997: *Essays Critical and Clinical*. D. W. Smith and M. Greco (trans.). Minneapolis: University of Minnesota Press.

—— and Guattari, F. 1987: *A Thousand Plateaus: Capitalism and Schizophrenia*. B. Massumi (trans.). Minneapolis: University of Minnesota Press.

—— and Guattari, F. 1994: *What Is Philosophy?* H. Tomlinson and G. Burchell (trans.). New York: Columbia University Press.

Dewey, J. 1916/1924: *Democracy and Education*. New York: Macmillan Company.

—— 1925/1958: *Experience and Nature*. New York: Dover Publications.

—— 1934/1980: *Art as Experience*. New York: Perigree Books.

—— 1934: Religion versus the Religious. In *A Common Faith*. See Hickman and Alexander: 1998, vol. 1.

—— 1938: The Problem of Logical Subject-Matter (From *Logic: The Theory of Inquiry)*. In L. Hickman and T. Alexander (eds.), 1998: vol. 2.

—— 1938: The Pattern of Inquiry (From *Logic: The Theory of Inquiry*). In L.

Hickman and T. Alexander (eds.), *The Essential Dewey*, 1998, Vol. 2. Bloomington and Indianapolis: Indiana University Press.

Garrison, J. 1997: *Dewey and Eros: Wisdom and Desire in the Art of Teaching*. New York and London: Teachers College Press.

—— 2000: Assaying the Possibilities of Spiritual Education as Poetic Creation. In M. O'Loughlin (ed.), *Philosophy of Education in the New Millennium*. Proceedings of the 7th Biennial Conference of the International Network of Philosophers of Education. 18–21 August, 2000. The University of Sydney, Australia.

Hickman, L. and T. Alexander (eds.). 1998: *The Essential Dewey*, vols. 1 and 2. Bloomington and Indianapolis: Indiana University Press.

Noddings, N. 1993: Excellence as a Guide to Educational Conversation. In H. A. Alexander (ed.), *Proceedings of the Philosophy of Education Society*. Urbana, Illinois.

Schmookler, J. 1975: *Uhodim iz Rossii*. I. Semetsky (trans.). Biblioteka ALIA, Israel.

Witherell, C. and Noddings, N. (eds.) 1991: *Stories Lives Tell: Narrative and Dialogue in Education*. New York and London: Teachers College, Columbia University.

Chapter 6

Leibowitz on Spirituality as Existential Childishness

ARI BURSZTEIN

I

IN THIS CHAPTER I will consider whether the term "spirituality" has any meaning within the thought of Yeshayahu Leibowitz (1903–1994), probably the most outstanding Israeli philosopher of his day. At first glance this would appear to be a mere rhetorical question, for any definition of spirituality will be identified with inner needs, which conceptually are an expression of religiosity "not for its own sake" (Leibowitz 1976: 13–36), centered around human needs rather than around God. Although Leibowitz regards this sort of religiosity as inferior to religiosity "for its own sake," in which human interests play no part, it does have an essential place in human development.

There are many definitions of spirituality, especially at a time when movements and trends calling themselves spiritual keep cropping up. I will look at the spirituality that develops and accompanies institutionalized religion. For this purpose I shall define spirituality as "the experiential side of religion, as opposed to outward beliefs, practices and institutions, which deals with inner spiritual depths of a person" (Goring 1992: 499). This definition fits the religiosity that Leibowitz identifies with man's inner needs, as opposed to the religiosity expressed in Jewish religious institutions, and more precisely in the Jewish law, the Halakhah.

I propose analyzing the interrelationship between the religious and educational aspects of these two types of religiosity by discussing the development of Leibowitz's approach to them.[1] For this purpose I shall use his views on the Bible and Bible criticism to analyze the educational consequences of his thought. Finally, I shall try to determine whether according to that doctrine sprituality may be spoken of at all.

II

Leibowitz has written only two articles dealing directly with his educational doctrine (Leibowitz 1976: 37–50, 57–67). "Education towards the Commandments" (henceforth EC, Leibowitz 1976: 57–67), the more detailed of the two, starts off with a quotation from Maimonides (Maimonides 1963: III:510), the philosopher to whom Leibowitz turns for support for his doctrine:

> The Law as a whole aims at two things: the welfare of the soul and the welfare of the body. "Welfare of the soul" in the philosophy of Maimonides is faith, "the true views"; "welfare of the body" is the behavioral perfection of man in his personal as well as societal life – ethics and societal order. (Leibowitz 1976: 57)

According to Maimonides, welfare of the body, the personal and societal order, is an essential stage and prerequisite to the welfare of the soul, philosophical perfection. While the practical commandments aim at both goals, welfare of the soul is only alluded to in the Scriptures, best illustrated by the verse, "And thou shalt love the Lord thy God with all thy heart, and with all thy soul, and with all thy might" (Deut. 6:5; Maimonides 1963:III:512). Leibowitz claims that religious education should distinguish ends from means, in Maimonides' terminology "primary goal" (welfare of the soul) from "secondary goal" (welfare of the body). Education should concentrate upon the latter, which Leibowitz identifies with the practical commandments. Leibowitz thus appears to be deviating from the thesis of Maimonides, identifying, as he does, only the "welfare of the body" with the practical commandments and leaving the welfare of the soul to be identified with the belief in God, a goal toward which it is impossible to educate. Anyone who attempts to teach faith inevitably faces an intrinsic contradiction, for faith is attained by personal decision, independent of historical facts or external influences, even those of teachers and educators.[2]

We have seen that, according to Maimonides, "the Torah aims at two goals," that is, "the Law of Moses has indeed come to grant us two perfections simultaneously." The commandments as a whole mean to educate toward both goals: welfare of the soul (founded upon the means), and welfare of the body. However, Leibowitz's interpretation of the relationship between the two in EC sees religious education as concentrating exclusively upon welfare of the body. The welfare of the body serves to prepare for welfare of the soul, the latter realm not being included in the commandments. Then to what domain does religious faith belong? Is it a subjective spiritual phenomenon accompanying objective institutional religiosity? This point has, in my opinion, remained vague in EC.

In an article published nearly forty years later entitled "Reciting the Shema" (Leibowitz 1982, henceforth RS)," Leibowitz appears to have retracted his earlier views, resorting to the circular reasoning common in his mature thought:

> The Torah interprets the vague verse 'And thou shalt love the Lord thy God . . .' using its continuation 'And these words, which I command thee this day, shall be upon thy heart.' The acceptance of the yoke of the commandments is the love of the Lord, and that is what is called belief in God. (Leibowitz 1982: 17)

At this juncture, the love of the Lord is seen as identical with observing the commandments and not as a goal beyond that observance. The small opening for theoretical (perhaps even spiritual?) aspects of the Torah that Leibowitz had previously allowed has been shut out in his later article by the circular reasoning equating the love of the Lord with observing the commandments.

If we interpret the above quotation of Leibowitz narrowly, distinguishing between "observing the commandments" and "the acceptance of the yoke of the Torah and the commandments," on the face of it, the former formulation refers to the act itself, whereas the latter one refers to the conscious decision preceding the act; the decision which, according to Leibowitz, provides the contents and true foundation of religious activity. Assuming that we are reading Leibowitz correctly in separating the act of acceptance from the act of observance, it turns out that the volitional dimension of his thought is the end of the educational deed (which may be reached solely through the means of the "practical commandments"). Although this end does not reach any other goal, being an end in itself, the conscious decision would be the most spiritual act in Leibowitz's philosophy, it being the love of the Lord.[3] In my opinion, however, Leibowitz has never distinguished between the two formulations. Elsewhere, in fact, he has interpreted the same verse as follows:

> In terms of perfect faith the true explanation is that observing the commandments is nothing but the expression and the realization of the love of the Lord, for the act of observing the commandments is not an inevitable consequence of something in nature or history, nor is it a means to achieve something in man's existence or destiny. (Leibowitz 2000: 783)

At a later stage Leibowitz attempts to harmonize his position in EC in which the practical commandments appear to have an end beyond their fulfillment within the Halakhic system, with that of RS in which they

have no such end. In his commentary on the *Guide* (III:51) Leibowitz
claims:

> Twenty long chapters in Book Three of the *Guide* offer us a rational inter-
> pretation of the reasons for the various mitzvot, presented in a utilitarian
> spirit, as if their purpose was to educate man towards true opinions and
> to repudiation of wrong opinions (the eradication of idolatry!), to the
> virtues, to controlling his impulses, toward an excellent organization of
> society and the state and toward decent human relations that are designed
> for a man and a good of man. Suddenly the whole spirit of the interpre-
> tation is altered, and we read: Know that all such religious acts as reading
> the Law, praying, and the performance of all other precepts serve exclu-
> sively as the means of causing us to occupy and fill our mind with the
> precepts of God, and free it from worldly business; for we are thus, as it
> were, occupied with God, and not with that which is other than He
> (Leibowitz 1987: 23–35, *Guide* III:51; Friedlander's translation, p. 386,
> amended in accordance with the Pines translation).

In the beginning of this section, the mitzvot (precepts, commandments) are means directed toward some "purpose." At the end of it, they
are the purpose itself. Herein lies our problematic: The practical
precepts or commandments, the mitzvot which are the embodiment of
Jewish religion in the Halakhah, are in the first place an instrument for
education in religious faith: but once genuine "philosophical" faith or
knowledge of God is reached it has no other practical expression except
the worship of God through the fulfillment of these commandments
themselves.[4]

The relationship between commandments and faith now becomes
mutually reinforcing. The process of education toward the commandments seems at first sight to have an ulterior goal: attaining faith, but
the successful process would lead the person thus educated to the
conclusion that faith, or "recognizing God," is but another of the 613
commandments. In this way the earlier view, which saw the welfare of
the soul as a goal beyond the welfare of the body, and the later circular
view, which saw the welfare of the soul as just another commandment,
merge.[5]

I shall accept this mutual view of education in observance as
Leibowitz's ultimate position in order to analyze the educational consequences of his thought, using the issue of the status of the Scripture and
Bible criticism. In addition, I shall return to the question of spirituality
and how it may be referred to within a system that rejects it outright.

III

In his article "The Sanctity of the Scripture" (Leibowitz 1976: 346–50), Leibowitz expounded his views on the connection between the Written and Oral Law; their relation is not of coordination but rather of subordination. Moreover, we would naturally assume that the Oral Law, being an interpretation of the Written Law, would be subordinate to it, but Leibowitz claims that just the opposite is true: the Bible as a whole is just one of the religious institutions of the Oral Law, represented by the Halakhah. Talmudic sages, following numerous debates, selected the various books of the Bible.[6] The Jewish people have never lived according to the Written Law but rather according to the Halakhah. In his opinion, we would be surprised, upon comparing the Bible to other types of literature, to discover that:

> as poetry and literature, there certainly are creations in world literature that surpass the scripture; as philosophy – Plato and Kant are more significant; as history – Thucydides is more interesting and profound. . . . (Leibowitz: 1976: 349)

The sanctity of the 24 books of the Bible derives from their selection by the Halakhah to be the Holy Scripture of the Jewish people. Leibowitz resolutely opposed setting up the Bible as "the Book of Books" that gives meaning to Jewish history or as the ethical program for educating the people, as David Ben-Gurion did. This, in essence, is Leibowitz's view of the status of the Scripture.

If the Halakhah determines the meaning of the Scripture, and if its primary task is to imbue people with reverence and love of God, what benefit may be derived from a critical study of the Bible? Biblical criticism becomes utterly irrelevant as far as observing the commandments is concerned. As we have seen, what makes Judaism meaningful according to Leibowitz is not belief in the revelation at Mount Sinai, but rather the personal decision of the Jew to accept the Halakhah as the only practical way to worship God. If that is true, such a decision turns the Halakhah into divine revelation. In other words, Leibowitz turns the idea of "Torah from heaven" into "Torah for the sake of heaven" (Rosenberg 1979: 113).[7] In his view, the sages involved in halakhic codification do not speak in the name of God, but the believing Jew, out of autonomous choice and faith, accepts their edicts as issued under the authority bestowed upon them by God.

In an educational model such as Yehudah Halevi's in *The Kuzari*, a reasonable pedagogical process would require basing theological choices upon empirical facts; the king of Khazar would have to be convinced by the eminent historical testimony that the Jewish people bear regarding the revelation at Mount Sinai (Halevi 1978: I:25). In this pedagogic system the role of a person's active choice is minimal. He is required only to be astounded by miraculous "seeing of sounds," which limit his judgment. What has a mere grain of sand to say to Him who occupies the whole cosmos? The pedagogical thinking leading to these conclusions is that the proof leads to the choice.[8]

In Leibowitz's thought we encounter an opposite pedagogical theory. One of Leibowitz's major epistemological principles is the separation of the realm of values from the realm of facts. Human knowledge belongs to the secular world. In the world of values there is one cardinal choice that one may make in life: the decision to worship God. Such a decision should not be affected by historical facts, such as the revelation at Mount Sinai, or by any sort of signs or miracles. A decision that is affected by factors of this kind has, according to Leibowitz, been made to satisfy human needs – out of secular, not religious, motives.

At this point we should ask why the revelation at Mount Sinai belongs to the secular rather than to the sacred realm. The answer seems to be that, following Kant, Leibowitz believes that human consciousness is unable to exceed its innate boundaries, otherwise it would reach antinomies (Sagi 1995b). Theoretically, whether there was a revelation at Mount Sinai is a historical fact that can neither be proved nor disproved. How then may we base faith upon it? The answer lies in the fact that the Bible belongs to the sacred domain, having been sanctified by the oral law. It contains no scientific, historical or other secular information.

May any religious benefit be derived from studying the Scripture per se? Leibowitz would answer affirmatively. The educational-exegetical process required of the reader is one of demythologizing (Sagi 1995a: 56–7). A glance in the very first verse of the Torah makes it clear that it states nothing as to how the universe was created. Proper reading of the Scripture involves "scraping off" the anthropomorphic layer to uncover the true philosophical content so as to put the genuine worship of God into practice. Thus we discover in the very first verse of the Torah that "the universe is not god." This important piece of knowledge is not, however, obtained from the Torah itself. Rather, the believer finds it in the Torah as part of his or her subjectivity.[9] Indeed, Leibowitz defines faith as "a way of life that constructs and shapes one's view of the world." It may be said that the believer knows in advance what he or she is looking for and finds in the biblical text what the "spectacles" provided by faith enable him or her to find. To Leibowitz, in philosophical terminology, the revelation at Mount Sinai is "recognition of the imperative imposed upon us" (Leibowitz 1982: 154). This recognition results from a subjective, meta-historical decision that turns the

"Torah from heaven" (Written Law) into "Torah for the Sake of Heaven" (Oral Law), at once turning the Halakhah into a human creation for the sake of heaven.

IV

We see then that in Leibowitz's view there exists a "childish pedagogy," such as Yehudah Halevi's, according to which faith is imparted through external signs and miracles to which any reasonable person would inevitably succumb.[10] Leibowitz turns such childish pedagogy upside down. He proscribes any external fact from affecting the internal value judgment. Let us consider some of the educational consequences of this view. This issue may best be viewed in two dimensions: the diachronic and the synchronic. The former dimension is associated with developmental psychology. Maimonides offers a good example. He describes the start of the process of indoctrination as "Read, and I will give you some nuts or figs, I will give you a bit of honey" (Twersky 1972: 404). In other words, to achieve perfection of the child it is permissible for the teacher to resort to various stratagies. The teacher is well aware that the stratagies have no value in themselves, but only as stratagies. To him or her the child still has "deficient understanding," and if the indoctrination is successful, the child will, at the appropriate developmental stage, understand the "truth of things" and realize that "the truth has no other purpose than knowing that it is true."

We have seen that, according to Leibowitz's thought, a commandment not done for its own sake is not valueless. He finds an expression for this idea in the first two segments of the *Shema* prayer, which he sees as representing two distinct levels of observation of the commandments. He sees the first segment (Deut. 8:4–9) as representing a loftier level of observance than the second one (Deut. 11:13–22), which speaks of earthly rewards for observing the commandments and punishment for transgression. The educational path of the believer must be one of constant movement from the second segment (not for its own sake) towards the first (for its own sake). As far as Leibowitz is concerned, the mythological view of the revelation at Mount Sinai as a historical fact, from which value conclusions are to be derived, is "childish pedagogy" akin to Maimonides' "nuts, figs, and honey." This sort of revelation at Mount Sinai is in the same league as the redemption and coming of the Messiah (in their non-Leibowitzian interpretation); able to lead to not-for-its-own-sake worship. How then does one progress from "not for its own sake" to "for its own sake" within the boundaries of the revelation, that is, the acceptance of the Torah as divine in a "non-childish" manner? How can we teach that authority of the revelation has turned from external to internal, and that the revelation at Mount Sinai has become a voluntary choice?

We are facing the educational and societal implications of Leibowitz's thought. That thought is intended primarily for an elite, that consists largely of skeptical intellectuals who usually do not participate fully in community life or, alternatively, whose skepticism is not sufficiently consistent with the life of the community as a whole.[11] Let us allow ourselves for a moment to psychologize Leibowitz and to ask: what came first, the subjective view of the revelation or the inability to believe in historical revelation? If the second possibility is the answer, it may be said that Leibowitz's view on this issue suits skeptics. Thus the child who had started to practice religion "not for its own sake" and over the years has sincerely "perfected his mind" would also find himself unable to believe in the revelation at Mount Sinai.

Leibowitz's skepticism originates in his personality but is also derived from the views of one of the most influential philosophers of the twentieth century, Wittgenstein, who taught "whereof one cannot speak, thereof one must be silent" (Wittgenstein 1949: 189).[12] Leibowitz applied this to the revelation at Mount Sinai. How then may one remain a faithful Jew? Leibowitz's thought is to a certain extent Wittgenstein's principle translated into Jewish tradition.[13] Had the Jewish child been educated during the Middle Ages according to Maimonides, his "perfection of the mind" would have been achieved by Aristotelian methods. A child brought up according to Leibowitz, on the other hand, lives in a world of doubts and uncertainty. Not only is there no longer any reconciliation between religion and science, in Leibowitz's approach there is no contact between them. Perfection is reached only if it includes a skeptical stage, in which one learns not to make fallacious claims regarding matters about which "one must be silent." In short, to a certain extent Leibowitz would become an "observant Jewish Wittgenstein." I do not consider skepticism a defect, just an intellectual state quite prevalent in this postmodernist era. A paradoxical conse-quence of Leibowitz's thought is the absorption of those whose skepticism makes them unable to believe in the revelation at Mount Sinai, turning them at the end of a process of "perfecting the mind" into worshipers of God "for His own sake."

There is another point to be made regarding the diachronic dimen-sion of education. If we were to ask Leibowitz when will the educational process be considered to have reached its goal?, we would get the answer "Never." Attaining such a goal is impossible, and human strife is endless. Observing the commandments is to some extent a deviation from reality, although that observance by no means entails detachment from reality:[14]

The task it casts upon man is permanent and endless, and no religious achievement may be considered a reaching of a goal which, once attained, would make it possible to see the task as completed. (Leibowitz 1976: 23–4)[15]

Sagi claims that the endless strife in Leibowitz's thought is an inevitable result of two factors: (1) the dichotomy between the spiritual world and freedom, on the one hand, and reality on the other; (2) the infinite distance between God and humankind. It turns out that one of the educational implications of Leibowitz's thought stems from the aim of education – training for incessant, endless effort, rather than toward reaching a certain goal. Paradoxically, the religious value of education toward effort without reaching goals is greater than that of education toward a faith that reaches its goals, because a person trained for endless effort keeps on clinging to faith even knowing in advance that the tenets of his or her faith are utopian, not amenable to realization or modification through any state of redemption.[16] I believe that the status of the revelation at Mount Sinai may be seen to parallel the attainment of the goal of the faith (impossible, as stated above), and the lack of certainty regarding the occurrence of the revelation to parallel the education toward effort without expectation of reaching a goal. Thus, according to Leibowitz, the believer has to live in the world of religious effort without being rewarded with "historical facts" such as the revelation at Mount Sinai.

In the synchronic dimension we are not dealing with a developmental educational process. Let us try to imagine how it is possible to educate toward practice "for its own sake" without undergoing an extended process of "not for its own sake," for which Leibowitz's model is appropriate. Maimonides' *Code* describes the kinds of behavior of a leader resulting in the "sanctification of the Lord's Name" (meaning raising the esteem, as it were, of the Lord and His Torah), so that "everyone praises and loves him and longs for his deeds" ("Laws Concerning the Foundations of Torah," 5:11). In this context, the leader is God's representative on earth, and his deeds have an overwhelming influence upon the masses. Although Leibowitz was by no means a leader of masses, for a significant number of people he has been a model to emulate, especially against a background of increasing "profanation of the Lord's name," as defined by the obverse of Maimonides' *Code* description within Israel's religious establishment. Leibowitz had combined extreme leftist political views, a pathos for social reform, the orientation of an outstanding scientist, unyielding practical religious orthodoxy, and skeptical philosophic theory. It seems that everyone may find in him one or more qualities worth emulating. A person considering Leibowitz's philosophy would think, "This outstanding man has succeeded in combining what seemed almost impossible to combine. Why should I not try to follow him in combining the same qualities?" Leibowitz as a person teaches himself.

These ideas may be applied to the question about the relation of the Written to the Oral Law, as well as to disabling the effect of biblical criticism. According to Leibowitz, the Written Law is a document concerned with reverence towards God. One brought up according to Leibowitz would not need signs or external historical events, since the revelation at Mount Sinai would mean "recognizing the imperative imposed upon us." In other words, Leibowitz himself functions as "a document concerning reverence towards God," leading the one thus brought up to recognize that imperative. The revelation takes place in the choice of the Written Law by the Oral Law or, alternatively, the Oral Law chooses Leibowitz to realize itself ideally. The educated Jew decides to submit to the Oral Law and does so by emulating the man who teaches himself or by being inspired by he who symbolizes the document concerning reverence towards God which the Oral Law chose to educate those who wish to worship God. From a certain aspect this educational act is paradoxical: that person teaches himself and his emulation may constitute a choice "not for its own sake." The educated Jew may erroneously decide to become a Leibowitzian not from a desire to worship God, but from a wish to emulate Leibowitz. This is a real danger, which, in my opinion, is inherent in the educational process described above. If we become convinced that it is both certain and inevitable, we would have to conclude that the only one able to educate himself by that process towards the worship of God "for its own sake" would be Leibowitz himself.

V

At this point I wish to use "meta-Leibowitzian" terminology.[17] I believe that a parallel may be drawn, using Leibowitz's terminology, between the relation of "practice for its own sake" (objective religion) and "practice not for its own sake" (subjective religion), and the relation of commandments to faith. As we have seen, Leibowitz describes the relationship between commandments and faith as one of constant feedback.[18] I believe that, on a meta-Leibowitzian plane, the existential state of one brought up on practical commandments is one of constant passage between "not for its own sake" and "for its own sake," between the second and the first segment of the *Shema* prayer; and this is a description of the endless effort and the permanent task one has to carry out.

According to Leibowitz, central figures in Jewish history such as

Abraham, Job, or Maimonides, indicate that the religious goal of the observer of the commandments is ultimately unattainable, remaining as a destination toward which we must forever strive.[19] The ceaseless existential status of passage between subjective and objective religiosity makes, according to Leibowitz, spirituality an essential and unavoidable stage in human development. This is the childish part, but since the direction of that development is in the form of a rising spiral, that person returns to the subjective religiosity of "not for its own sake" in all stages of life in an effort to be free of it, but with a complete awareness that the results of that liberation are not final, and his struggle will be endless.

We thus find Leibowitz again situated by himself against the current; contrary to most descriptions of the evolution of the religious phenomenon in which spirituality is the climax, Leibowitz sees spirituality as its first, primitive level. Spirituality, religiosity "not for its own sake," is the childishness that accompanies us at all times in our constant attempt to mature and be free of it, without final outcome. I believe that only in these terms may we speak of spirituality, which to Leibowitz is actually "childish spirituality." That stage is unavoidable and indispensable to one's development; no one is born a Maimonidean or a Leibowitzian. We recite the first segment of the *Shema* prayer as a declaration of intentions and as the aim of our religious life, but the second segment reminds us again that achieving that aim does not promise us everlasting rest but only the knowledge that achieving that aim is a task that never ends.

Notes

1   I do not wish to unpack Leibowitz's philosophical evolution for the sake of "philological–historical" research but rather to point to certain contradictions in his interpretation of the relationship between "for its own sake" and "not for its own sake" as a means to clarify the issue of spirituality. Quite a bit has been written about the relationship between the "early" and "late" Leibowitz. For example see Goldman 1995: 179–86.

2   From this follows, according to Leibowitz, that education toward the practical commandments is the preferred route to attaining faith, "preparation for the acquisition of values" as opposed to "imparting values," in his terminology, although the result is not automatic. Leibowitz quotes Maimonides' *Code*: "How shall a man train himself in these dispositions, so that they become ingrained? Let him practice again and again the actions prompted by those dispositions . . . and repeat them continually . . . and so the corresponding dispositions will become a fixed part of his character" (Laws relating to moral dispositions and to ethical conduct, Chap. I, law 7). For an in-depth analysis of that educational approach, see Rosenak 1987: 207–27. For a comprehensive analysis of Leibowitz's educational philosophy, see Ohana 2000.

3   The term "spiritual" may be used in reference to the conscious decision to

observe the commandments, in accordance with our definition of that term as the experiential contents associated with institutional religion.

4 In an English language interview Leibowitz interpreted "and free it from worldly business" in the above quotation as "welfare of the body." According to this interpretation Maimonides sees the ultimate goal in ending the occupation with "welfare of the body" as being occupied exclusively with "welfare of the soul." We have indeed understood the "welfare of the body" to be the basis for the "welfare of the soul," as did Leibowitz in "Education Towards the Commandments." See Haberman 1994: 144.

5 Shalom Rosenberg has written recently about the religious experience in Leibowitz's philosophy. In an article to be published in Hebrew titled "Paradoxes and faith in Y. Leibowitz's philosophy," Rosenberg claims to have discovered the religious experience that accompanies the observation of the Halakhah in "meta-Leibowitzian" terminology, as he calls it. To him, "Leibowitz has not given up on the experience of 'being commanded', i.e. on the psychological experience of the encounter with that 'something' that arrives from the outside." The way to the transcendental passes through the deed, which itself possesses a transcendental component – fulfilling the commandment for its own sake. According to Rosenberg, "The deed accompanies the theological silence, but that silence may express an internal existential experience which I am neither compelled, willing, nor able to express in words." It follows that, according to Rosenberg's interpretation, Leibowitz is an existentialist thinker in that the true religious experience is expressed solely through the proper observance of the commandments, which, paradoxically, means a complete dismissal of all personal interests and experiences. Toward the end of the present article I mean to avail myself of "meta-Leibowitzian" terminology the way Rosenberg has.

6 See, for example, *Babylonian Talmud*, Tract. *Meghilah*, 7a.

7 Regarding Leibowitz's views of the status of the Scripture, see also Sagi 1995a: 49–62, 2000: 4–7 and Granot 1991: 1–7.

8 In certain respects this pedagogy parallels modern testimonies to the revelation at Mount Sinai, claiming the discovery of hidden messages in the Torah. Many secular persons undergo under various auspices "learning experiences" involving the uncovering of mysteries of the Torah. It includes such things as computer programs that manipulate letters in the sacred text to reveal allusions to future events such as the Holocaust or the Gulf War. According to the pedagogy that guides those who use such "proofs," the "trainees" are left with no choice but to believe that the Torah is of divine origin.

9 The believer's subjectivity in this context has nothing to do with the definition of fulfilling a commandment "not for its own sake" as religious subjectivity.

10 Emil Fackenheim may be seen as carrying this sort of pedagogy into our era with his well-known concept of "Root Experiences." Regarding this see Fackenheim 1970.

11 This contradicts the communal dimension that Leibowitz the person needs to practice religion fully. I believe, however that, sociologically, the sort of

person who would adopt Leibowitz's views is one who does not need the community to express Leibowitzian philosophic principles. Michael Rosenak develops the importance of the communal dimension for Leibowitz in an article to be published entitled "Three Teachers and the Ways They Teach."

12   Of the relationship between Leibowitz and Wittgenstein see Sagi 1995b and Bareli 1993.

13   I am not speaking of direct influence. Leibowitz's early publications came out well before Wittgenstein's.

14   This is the reason why education towards the commandments entails some revolt and oppositionism. "A revolutionary education is easier, for it raises one's self-esteem by casting upon him the task of creating a new world, contrary to the present one" (Leibowitz 1976: 60).

15   For analysis of this issue, see also Sagi 1993.

16   Leibowitz has explained this view on a number of occasions. See, for instance Leibowitz 1995: 108–52.

17   See footnote 5.

18   See Leibowitz 1995: 18–19. This, it should be remembered, is a description combining the idea of education toward goals with the circular argument discussed at the beginning of the present article. This position may be assailed; it may be said that the relationship between commandments and faith described there is one of feedback, but not constant feedback. There exists a single passage from commandments to faith and subsequently from faith to commandments, but the feedback ends there. To me, however, this interpretation is inconsistent with the general picture emerging from Leibowitz's view of the observation of the commandments as an endless task one has to carry out. The dynamics of that process are defined not by linear evolvement but as a rising spiral that keeps on returning to a "childish" stage of "not for its own sake," but on a higher "childish" level reached as a desirable (though not automatic) result of the educational process. As far as I know, Leibowitz has not written explicitly about this, but I believe that my interpretation stems from his doctrine as an "existential implication."

19   This position is also based upon Leibowitz's view of messianism as an endless process, "a vision of redemption" according to his formulation, which is never realized. Accordingly, any self-proclaimed messiah or messianic phenomenon is termed by him "false messianism." Leibowitz has written about this quite considerably; see, for example Leibowitz 1976: 415–18.

References

Bareli, G. 1993: Faith and way of life – between Leibowitz and Wittgenstein. *Iyun*, 42: 493–507 (Hebrew).

Fackenheim, E. 1970: *God's Presence in History.* New York: New York University Press.

Goldman, E. 1995: Zionism as a Religious Challenge in Yeshayahu Leibowitz's

Thought, in A. Sagi (ed.), *Yeshayahu Leibowitz – His World and His Thought*. Jerusalem: Keter (Hebrew).

Goring, R. (ed.) 1992: *The Wordsworth Dictionary of Beliefs & Religions*. Edinburgh: Wordsworth Reference.

Granot, M. 1991: The Bible in Prof. Leibowitz's philosophy. *Ma'aloth*, Nisan 5741 (Hebrew).

Haberman, J. O. 1994: *The God I Believe in*. New York: The Free Press.

Halevi, Y. 1998: *The Kuzari*. New Jersey: J. Aronson Northvale.

Leibowitz, Y. 1976: *Judaism, Jewish People and the State of Israel*. Tel Aviv: Schocken (Hebrew).

—— 1982: *Faith, History, and Values*. Jerusalem: Academon (Hebrew).

—— 1987: *The Faith of Maimonides*. New York: Adama Books.

—— 1995: *Discourses on Rabbi H. M. Luzzato's Path of the Just*. Jerusalem: Informal Publication of Leibowitz's Students.

—— 2000: Discourses on Weekly Torah Portions. Jerusalem: Keter (Hebrew).

Maimonides, M. 1963: *Guide for the Perplexed*. S. Pines (trans.) Chicago: University of Chicago Press.

Ohana, M. 2000: *Yeshayahu Leibowitz – Educational Ramifications of His Thought*. Jerusalem: Ph.D. Dissertation, Hebrew University (Hebrew).

Rosenak, M. 1987: *Commandments and Concerns*. Philadelphia-New York-Jerusalem: Jewish Publication Society.

Rosenberg, S. 1979: Bible Research in Modern Jewish Thought. In U. Simon (ed.), *The Bible and Us*. Tel Aviv: Devir (Hebrew).

Sagi, A. 1993: Leibowitz and Camus: between faith and absurd. *Iyun*, 42: 460–92.

—— 1995a: The Scriptures and their significance in the thought of Leibowitz and Soloveitchik. *Badad*, 1: 49–63 (Hebrew).

—— 1995b: Religion without metaphysics – between Leibowitz and Wittgenstein. *Mahshavot 67*: 6–17 (Hebrew).

—— 2000: The revelation at Mount Sinai from fact to commitment. *Amudim*, 8: 642 (Hebrew).

Twersky, I. (ed.) 1972: *A Maimonides Reader*. New York: Berhman House.

Wittgenstein, L. 1949: *Tractatus Logico-Philosophicus*. London: Routledge & Kegan Paul.

Part II

Theological Perspectives

———

IN HER DELIGHTFUL essay on the use of children's literature in spiritual development, Ann Trousdale cites Jerome Bruner's (1986) distinction between paradigmatic and narrative thought. The former is concerned to explain reality in terms of the universal generalizations, causes, arguments, and verifications of logico-scientific reasoning. The latter hues closely to experience and seeks to illustrate and illuminate more than to prove essential or transcendent truths of the human condition through observations concerning concrete or particular cases expressed in symbols, metaphors, poems, and stories.

An intermingling of these two ways of conceiving the world can be found in both the philosophical and the theological sections of this volume. Yet the essays in this section tend to stand, or at least begin, more firmly within the confines of particular narrative or faith traditions than those in the previous section, even when they seek to demonstrate their point of view empirically or logically, whereas **Part I** selections tend to take as their starting point the universal claims of philosophy. Thus, although Burbules and McLaughlin reflect on Christian Scripture, they approach the text through the eyes of philosophical analysis; and while Eppert's account of Levinas and Bursztein's analysis of Leibowitz are both deeply grounded in the Jewish tradition, the former is so thoroughly steeped in Heidegger and Husserl and the latter in medieval Aristotelianism that it seemed appropriate to honor the philosophical emphasis of both essays by placing them in **Part I**.

Part II opens with a impassioned and poetic plea by Mary Elizabeth Moore, from within her own very open and liberal Protestantism – with sensitivity to the Jewish context in which her paper was delivered and directed to the violent struggle between Palestinian Arabs and Jewish Israelis – to travel the long road toward justice and reconciliation. Building on Alexander's (1999) account of education in the Hebrew Bible, she makes four important notes: first, that children are vulnerable and that adult society tends to be ambivalent toward them; second, that both Hebrew and Christian Scriptures value children highly; third, that children are to be blessed by us; and fourth, that they are to be received as a blessing from God. To walk with children toward hope, then, entails *lamenting* our ambivalence toward children; *celebrating* their special value; *blessing* them with care, guidance, inclusion, and empowerment; and *receiving* blessing from them as they help to return us to God.

It follows, responds Friedrich Schweitzer, that children have a fundamental right to religion, at least in the sense articulated by Schleiermacher (1799/1996) having to do with personal experience and feelings rather than institutions, traditions, or dogmas. He suggests that at least five sorts of religious questions arise in childhood having to do with death and dying, fairness, identity and self definition, religious diversity and multiculturalism, and God. These queries are basic to existence, so it is only proper to ensure that they be addressed in the course of a young person's education. This should be accomplished not by means of single-minded or simplistic answers, but rather through sophisticated, age-appropriate explorations that cannot help but turn the curriculum toward a variety of religious resources.

In the third chapter of **Part II** Iraj Ayman offers a Bahá'í perspective on children's spirituality. As a relatively young tradition, the principles of the Bahá'í faith are not well-known among Western scholars of religion, religious education, and children's spirituality. It is especially appropriate that a Bahá'í perspective be included in this volume since the conference was held in Haifa, the international center of the Bahá'í faith. Bahá'í religion is a global movement that seeks the unity of human kind by recognizing God as the "Supreme Source of Being" and the validity of Jewish (Hebrew), Christian, Moslem, and other prophets. Spirituality in this view is connected to the belief that humans were created lovingly by God with the capacity to reflect divine attributes, both individually and socially. The seeds of spirituality are inherent in each individual, as is free choice. The task of spiritual education is to empower the individual to make wholesome, wise, and ethical choices that reflect the attributes of the Creator through the development of intellectual discernment, moral judgment, and personal conduct.

In the next chapter Pamela Ebstyne King reports on her research concerning the relation between religious context and moral development among American and Korean youth. King draws on social capital theory, which discusses the benefits of social ties, to argue that the moral development of adolescents can be enhanced by religious contexts where social interaction, trust, and vision are shared among parents and children. One-way analysis of variance reveals that youth who attended religious congregations have greater access to social interaction, trust, and shared vision. These three factors of social capital explain a significant percentage of moral outcomes among American youngsters, but only a modest percentage among Korean youth, who appear more affected by trusting relationships, along with cultural values such as duty, loyalty, and authority, than by social interactions and shared vision. In societies such as the United States where religious institutions are often woven into the fabric of society, social capital can have a favorable impact on moral conduct. However, in cultures such as South Korea where this is not the case, religious participation only partially explains moral outcomes.

Ann Trousdale brings us back to Bruner's narrative perspective in her discussion of children's literature and spiritual development. Stories take children seriously, as Moore admonished; they propose answers to the queries outlined by Schweitzer; and they are storehouses of what King called social capital. What gives stories the power to affect us so profoundly, to take us to other worlds and return us to our own transformed? Too often we use stories to preach or sermonize. We ask children to recite the moral of the story, as if a good story can be summed up in a pithy phrase. The power of storytelling is not in the lesson, Trousdale argues, but in the images of real life that are created and the gaps that are left to be filled. Stories call us to respond, imagine, and interpret – to fill those gaps. In order to engage children on the road toward hope, empower them to explore existence, inspire them to walk with their Creator, and encourage them to enjoy the benefits of social interactions, we need to listen to how children respond. Stories can transform children's lives when we engage with them in interpretation.

Trousdale calls us to listen, and this is precisely what Howard Deitcher and Jen Glaser do in their discussion of theological reasoning. They suggest that a child's sense of the Divine may emerge not as a conclusion to carefully reasoned premises, as we find in the well-known five ways for proving God's existence, but in what Michael Polayni calls indwelling, the focal attention or tacit awareness present as we move from old to new truths, from the unknown to the known. Martin Buber, they remind us, referred to moments of this kind as "being in relation" as we attend to the world around us. Following Weil and Levinas, Eppert called this the "attention to the other," and in keeping with Deleuze, Semetsky called it "becoming-child" – that moment of innocence logically prior to creating or grasping something new. Gilead referred to this process as attention to pure possibility and Trousdale as "filling in" narrative gaps. Those integrative, synthetic, interpretive, originative, and relational moments that lie behind or beneath our knowledge, suggest Deitcher and Glaser, are where (or when) we discover Divinity. They learn this by listening to Maya, a 14-year-old Jewish Israeli girl of Sephardic origin, explain what she thinks and feels about God. Maya finds God not in rational proofs, but in biblical stories, such as Moses in the basket, or at the burning bush, or on Mt. Sinai; and in her contemporary Israeli narrative, despite those who challenge her faith by asking about God's absence during the Holocaust.

What do these theological perspectives add to the philosophical answers concerning the six questions outlined at opening of **Part I**? Spirituality, according to a number of authors, resides in a moment of indwelling, prior to creating or grasping something new, in which we attend or relate to – meet or care for – another. These moments are inherent in childhood. They lie within as potential waiting to emerge. But like muscles, although they develop naturally, they can be enhanced and strengthened with exercise. The exercise is often found in engagement with and interpretation of stories told across the generations that address questions of death, and fairness, and identity, and diversity, and God. Children want to address these queries, they have a right to do so, and we often enhance their social capital when we do.

But addressing them seriously may require that we move beyond what McLaughlin called "exegesis" or the narrow – simple, accurate, historic, critical – meaning of these stories to what he called application and what Trousdale dubbed "filling in the gaps," not only with what the story does not tell us about its own context but also what it may not say about our own. Some scholars call this eisegesis or reading into a text; the Talmudic sages called it *midrash*, from the Hebrew for explanation. Spiritual development and education in spirituality can be tied to *midrash*, which entails the application of family, communal, fictional, historic, or revealed narratives that address life's most basic questions to current circumstances. We would do well, nonetheless, to recall McLaughlin's admonition that "any convincing attempt at appropriation involves some degree of exegesis." To paraphrase theologian Abraham Joshua Heschel (1955), without exegesis stories are wild, but without appropriation – without eisegesis or *midrash* – they are dead.

When Moore calls us to walk with children toward hope and reconciliation and when Trousdale admonishes us to listen to their voices, perhaps they are saying that at the end of the day children may be among the best *midrash*ists of all. One path to spiritual development for them and spiritual renewal for us may be found in learning with and from their responses to the stories we and they tell.

References

Alexander, H. A. 1999: A Jewish View of Human Learning. *International Journal of Children's Spirituality* 4(2): 155–64.

Bruner, J. 1986: *Actual Minds, Possible Worlds*. Cambridge, MA: Harvard University Press.

Heschel, A. J. 1955: *God in Search of Man*. New York: Farrar, Straus, and Cudahy.

Schleiermacher, F. 1996: *On Religion: Speeches to Its Cultured Despisers*, R. Crouter (trans.). Cambridge: Cambridge University Press.

Chapter 7

Walking with Children toward Hope: The Long Road to Justice and Reconciliation

MARY ELIZABETH MULLINO MOORE

I COME TO THE PRESENT study as a mother who loves her children dearly – my two birth children and three stepchildren. I also come as a mother who cares about the children of others and realize that I have not succeeded well in inspiring *my* children to care, with their whole beings, for justice and reconciliation. My children and grandchildren are wonderful people, and my relations with them are strong. Yet I often blame myself for their uneven interest in the long road to justice. Furthermore, I have been surprised, saddened and finally gratified with the years of hard work and play required to build strong relations with my stepchildren. I make these comments to locate myself socially – as one who seeks to walk with children toward hope, yet finds herself on the road to justice and reconciliation without having arrived at the goal.

I also acknowledge that I come to this study with a sense of tragedy, grounded partly in the conference venue, where Palestinian and Israeli children die weekly from the ravages of war, where they listen to threatening bombs bursting in the night, where they are displaced and thrown into poverty by acts of war that rip apart the fragile social fabric, where they learn distrust and hate in societies that are struggling toward justice and reconciliation. The sense of tragedy is also fed by voices of children I know in the United States – children who live in poverty, children who live in abusive family situations, children who live in a culture of violence and strive to feel important by inflicting violence on others. The sense of tragedy is exacerbated by recent studies of children in poverty, from the United States, Germany, Brazil and other countries of the world (Couture 2000; Johnson 2001; Mette 2001).

These contextual reminders may awaken all of us to the vulnerability of childhood and the high stakes of this collection focused on children and spirituality. Why have the authors given the time and effort to reflect on children's spirituality if we do not hope that children's lives will be deepened, enriched, and strengthened through our work? If this volume is to make a difference, it will need to awaken people to children who live in our contemporary world and within various religious traditions. I will focus particularly on Jewish and Christian traditions, knowing that others will add different perspectives. The purpose of all these explorations is to *discern ways to walk with children toward hope, especially on the long road to justice and reconciliation.*

Children within the Jewish tradition are understood, first, as a blessing. They bless their family and the larger community, and they are to be blessed by those same families and communities. As Hanan Alexander explains, however, "The Bible . . . contains no clearly defined picture of the child" (Alexander 1999: 155). This is largely because the concept of childhood as a distinct time of life only emerged in the post-Enlightenment era; it is a construct of the past 200 years. On the other hand, the Bible does offer guidance for educating children; it simply says little about distinguishing children from adults. With this caution, I will expand on Alexander's work, sounding notes that stretch beyond his analysis.

The *first note* is children's vulnerability and society's ambivalence toward them, as revealed in Scripture and the contemporary world. *Second* is the high value that Hebrew and Christian Scriptures place on children. The *third* and *fourth* notes are the need for adults to bless children and the call to people of theistic religions to recognize God's revelation in children's lives. Attending to these four notes can potentially guide adult mentors to walk with children on the uncharted paths toward justice and reconciliation.

Note #1: Children's Vulnerability and Society's Ambivalence

Walking with children toward hope begins with recognizing their vulnerability and society's ambivalence toward them. Susanne Johnson describes the "strange self-contradiction" in the United States: "On the one hand, we idealize and romanticize children and childhood. Yet, at the same time, daily we allow children in America and all over the world to go to waste, physically, mentally, morally, emotionally" (Johnson 2001: 1). She argues that the church is guilty as well, often claiming to place high value on children, yet failing to protest and organize against "the scurrilous injustices that kill our children every day" (Johnson 2001: 1; Arnold 2000).

Scriptural descriptions of children are also ambivalent, as reflected in "Remember the Children" (Moore 2001b):[1]

> Remember the children –
>> Ishmael, Isaac, the children of Job –
>> Children silent,
>> Children vulnerable,
>> Children whose parents seem nothing but trouble.
> Remember the children –
>> Children of Zarephath and Syrophoenicia –
>> Children with illness,
>> Children who are poor,
>> Children whose lives have problems and more.
> Remember the children –
>> Ishmael, Isaac, the children of Job –
>> Children from Zarephath and Syrophoenicia –
>> Children whose parents do intercede,
>> Children of covenant, the community's seed;
>> Children with whom God enters a pact,
>> Children of covenant, by the grace of God's act.

The biblical views glimpsed in this poem are mirrored in twenty-first century life.

Case Study of Ambivalence and Vulnerability

Consider a case study of recent times, actually based on three cases merged for anonymity.

A young married couple was learning how to live well together. They had one recurring argument, however. He wanted a child; she did not. In particular, he wanted a son to follow him in the family business. The woman insisted that she did not have the patience or care-giving qualities to rear children. Finally, the husband said he would leave her if they did not have children. She consented. They had a son, but from the beginning, she was angry. She handled her son roughly, even injuring him at times. Her husband was eager for the son to grow up to be responsible, so from the time the boy was an infant, the father disciplined him hard, sometimes leading to cuts and bruises.

The child was told daily that he needed to be a good boy; he was told daily that he was rarely good. In every public setting or gathering with family and friends, the parents evaluated their son's behavior for others to hear, usually finding it sorely lacking. Now, as a teenager, this young man is walking with danger – acting out physical violence, giving verbal abuse to teachers and other youth, and experimenting with drugs. This boy lives in the middle of an adult power struggle, as does his sister who was born several years later.

This case reveals a family's life and much more. The patterns in the case are widespread: tensions between wanting and not wanting children, imposing adult needs and frustrations on children, using children for adults' ends. One could draw from many other cases, but a look at statistics in the United States (the country in which the three merged cases took place) will reveal some of the patterns in bold relief. In the United States, 13.5 million children live in poverty today. That means that one in six US children lives in poverty, one in five young children, and one in four children of color. Of these, 8 percent live in extreme poverty (Child Poverty Fact Sheet 2000). Many of these children have no health care, and many move from school to school three to four times a year. Many of their families are the working poor, suffering from the inequitable distribution of income in the US (Consumer Expenditure Survey 2000).

While many children strive for survival in the United States, children and their families also spend large sums of money for entertainment and material acquisition. In fact, people in the US spend three times more on entertainment than on education (Consumer Expenditure Survey 2000).[2] In Canada, 4 million children between ages 2 and 12 spend $1.5 billion of their own money per year and influence about $15 billion in home purchases by their families (Media Awareness Network 2002; Kline 1993). These figures reveal something of the corporate domination of families, whose children are captivated by the desire for acquisition. In fact, the family in the case study reveals how this pattern unfolds. In their home, the television is on 12 hours a day, and the two children receive every new toy on the market. Commercial advertising patterns have actually fed the ambivalent and vulnerable relationships of their family by promising happiness through possessions.

Vulnerability in Biblical Sources

One would hope that the descriptions above are a new and easily eradicated moment in human history, but this is not the case. Turning to biblical sources, even early narratives are ambivalent about children. God promised Abram and Sarai that they would be blessed with many heirs; yet their long wait for children, and the conception and early life of Abram's two sons, were fraught with ambiguity and vulnerability. After many years, when Sarai had born no children (Genesis 16:1–16), she took matters into her own hands. She said to Abram: "You see that the Lord has prevented me from bearing children; go in to my slave-girl; it may be that I shall obtain children by her" (Genesis 16:2).[3] Abram did go to Hagar and she conceived. Hagar then looked with contempt on Sarai, who complained to Abram. Abram responded, "Your slave girl is in your power; do to her as you please" (Genesis 16:6). Sarai dealt harshly with pregnant Hagar, who finally ran away. Hagar (a young girl herself) had been used by Sarai and Abram; she, and later her child Ishmael, were caught in an adult triangle.

Vulnerability Continues

Although the Bible uncovers a world very different from ours, it also illumines our world. The vulnerability of children continues today, as illustrated in the opening case study, the circumstances of which are repeated in many families. This vulnerability is repeated in social systems, as poverty levels in the United States reveal. We can also see evidence of children's vulnerability in the worldwide culture of war, where one-third of the people killed in armed conflicts in the 1990s were children; approximately 2 million children died in war. At the present time, 300,000–400,000 children (mostly under age 16) are fighting wars in more than thirty countries (Information Resource Centre 2001). Guns made of lightweight material are being manufactured so that children can hold them.

These patterns are also affected by racism, sometimes in dramatic forms. Aboriginal children of Australia were actually stolen from their families as late as the 1960s, partly in an intentional effort by government leaders to absorb their race into white Australia (Hollinsworth 1998). The same pattern was common across Canada and the United States (Tinker 1993).

In many countries of the world, such matters pass with little notice. In fact, the lack of notice can even compound the situation, as Norbert Mette describes in relation to his native Germany. In his country, a major academic and political discussion questions whether German children can be considered poor at all. Mette estimates, however, that more than 13 percent of children and youth under age 18 are considered poor by income standards. Children are now the highest population group in poverty; youth are second (Mette 2001: 8–9). Mette argues that highlighting the plight of impoverished children is part of forming an adequate political or religious response, which includes charity, structural change and reformed political awareness (16).

We are faced with the genuine vulnerability of children, but also with society's ambivalence. Children are people of worth. Furthermore, they abound with vision. Young people were major influences in igniting the Civil Rights movement in the United States (Halberstam 1998). For many decades, they have also been critics of war across the world, and of escalating weapons of mass destruction. This leads naturally to a second note.

Note #2: Children as God's Blessing to the Community

Even with diverse images of children in scripture, the theme that children are a blessing is continually reiterated. Consider a second poem based in scripture (Moore 2001a):[4]

> Blessing, blessing, and blessings more –
> Children are the blessings God has in store
> for a waiting creation,
> crying and torn.
> Children bless their families with a new generation,
> They carry God's promise for transformation,
> They are blessings who bring people great delight –
> blessings who herald God's reign into sight –
> beacons of hope in a barren land,
> the holy works of God's own hand. . . .

In light of these poetic references to scripture, we turn to the theme of blessing, recognizing that children are God's blessing to the community. Blessings are not just sentimental; they are fraught with difficulty in biblical writings. In Christian scriptures, Mary, the Mother of Jesus, is told that she will be blessed among women or, in some versions, that she has "found favor with God" (Luke 1:30). When the angel of the Lord comes to her, he tells her that she will bear a child and is to name him Jesus. This event and the words of the angel echo the story of Hagar and God's announcement of her child Ishmael (Genesis 16:11). Annunciations are not daily occurrences in the Bible, but here we find two – both to women, which is even more unusual, and to announce the birth of a blessed child. Yet the blessing of childbirth is a problem for both Mary and Hagar. Neither is properly married; one is betrothed and the other has been married as a slave and second wife to bear children for the first wife. Both will face much hardship, as will their children.

In light of this analysis, one has to ask whether children are really a blessing. According to the Hebrew tradition, they are. Consider Psalm 128:3: "Your wife will be a fruitful vine within your house; your children will be like olive shoots around your table. Thus shall the man be blessed who fears the Lord." In biblical worlds, children were a blessing in many practical ways – carrying on the legacy and livelihood of a family; they were also a spiritual blessing.

Children continue to be a blessing in both practical and spiritual ways, though the forms vary across the globe. They are also a blessing in small, undramatic ways. In the past three years, I led two events on children's ministry in British Columbia, Canada, one with children and one without. The one with children was more fun, and the children provided a wisdom that adults did not have; they even provided a barometer for me as the leader, indicating when to move to a new topic or activity. They were a blessing just by being themselves. Warning: appreciating children does have a drawback. When people recognize children as a blessing, their concern for children's vulnerability is heightened and their critique of ambivalent attitudes is sharpened. This leads naturally to a third note.

Note #3: Children as People to Be Blessed by Others

> And children are people who need to be blessed –
> to grow up with Yahweh
> to find God's good way.
> Children need to be taught the ways of the world
> the ways of good living,
> the paths of full giving . . . (Moore 2001a)

Children are not just a blessing; they are to be blessed by others – their parents and others in the community. Children are to be dedicated at an early age, and boys are to be circumcised (Exodus 12:48; Luke 2:21). Furthermore, parents are to teach their children the ways of God and God's covenant people (Deuteronomy 4:9–10; 6:7; 21; 11:19; 31:12–13; Joshua 4:6–7; Psalm 78:4) and children are expected to grow in God's favor (Luke 2:40).

Some people embody the blessing of children in inspiring ways. When my father-in-law died a few years ago, five of his nephews traveled across the country for his funeral. Each of these nephews had spent a teenage summer with PaPa and MaMa; each had worked with PaPa in his business and enjoyed MaMa's good cooking. PaPa and MaMa knew these boys were blessings; they knew their responsibility was to bless them.

Walking with children toward hope is giving children this kind of time, living and working with them. Spiritually, walking with children toward hope is more than introducing them to religion, even more than incorporating them into religious practices. According to Hanan Alexander, teaching within the Hebrew tradition is affirming "the moral potential of each person through the internalization of divine teachings" (Alexander 1999: 155). In short, one is walking with children respectfully and in awe of divine possibilities.

Of course, blessing children with such teaching is difficult. The act of blessing *all* children is particularly demanding. We are sometimes selective with groups of children. For example, we are sometimes able to take responsibility for blessing children close to us while ignoring those more distant, or blessing children in general rather than blessing particular children. We are sometimes able to take pity on children in poverty, but not on their parents, whose rise from poverty will be essential if the children are to emerge from poverty (Johnson 2001: 7–9). Here is where we are stirred to consider public policy, becoming critically aware of our own biases and failings, and also of biases and failings in the larger society.

This discussion suggests that people have a grave responsibility to care for their own children, to offer direct services to all children, and to develop a just public policy (Johnson 2001: 16–25; Mette 2001: 16–17; Anderson and Johnson 1994; Couture 1991, 2000). The urgent need is for families, congregations and schools to create places of sanctuary for children and to influence public policy so that it will offer hope to all children.

These various acts are not as separable as we often assume. One church agency initiated an anger-management program for parents, which was so successful that the local courts now refer juvenile offenders and their families to them for anger management workshops. Another church body – a local congregation – undertook a study of the schools of their city, discovering major inequities. They prepared a formal report, which they presented to the city council. The council has undertaken educational reforms as a result. These are examples of people merging acts of mercy with acts of justice, and merging individual, local acts with public acts in the larger sociopolitical arena. These are all ways that people collaborate to bless children on the road to hope.

Note #4: Children as Revelation of God's Blessing

> But our children are even more than this
> They are more than promise – more than bliss;
> They lead the way to the Kingdom of Heaven
> They represent promise and life-giving leaven!
> They light the path toward regeneration
> And point the way to God's new creation!
> (Moore 2001a)

The discussion to this point leads to a final theme – more blessing. Turning to the Gospel of Mark (Mark 10:13–16), consider the children who were brought to Jesus:

People were bringing little children to him in order that he might touch them; and the disciples spoke sternly to them. But when Jesus saw this, he was indignant and said to them, "Let the little children come to me; do not stop them; for it is to such as these that the kingdom of God belongs. Truly I tell you, whoever does not receive the kingdom of God as a little child will never enter it." And he took them up in his arms, laid his hands on them, and blessed them.

This story appears in Mark amid strong discipleship teachings. It follows soon after another story about taking up one's cross and following Jesus (Mark 8:31–38). Jesus had had an interchange with his disciples in which Peter had identified Jesus as the Messiah; Jesus then foretold his suffering and death. When Peter rebuked Jesus for such talk, Jesus responded: "If any want to become my followers, let them deny themselves and take up their cross and follow me" (Mark 8:34b).

In light of such strong talk, the disciples may have been confused by the response of Jesus to the children. Mark seems eager for his readers to see that confusion, placing the story in proximity to another story of children. In the earlier story, Jesus responded to the disciples' dispute about who was the greatest by placing a child among them. He said, "Whoever welcomes one such child in my name welcomes me, and whoever welcomes me welcomes not me but the one who sent me" (Mark 9:37). Perhaps the disciples did not understand such teaching; more likely, they simply did not like what they heard.

Jesus was placing children – the marginalized of the Greco-Roman society – in a place of honor. Recent biblical scholarship on Mark intensifies the sense of scandal in these two texts. Emphasis is placed not on the passivity of children (a common traditional interpretation), but on their representation as marginalized members of society. Thus, when Jesus asks his hearers to "receive the Kingdom of God as a little child," he is asking them to identify with the marginalized and, in fact, to be marginalized themselves (Bailey 1995: 58–67; Johnson 2001: 1–3).

Jesus said, "Truly I tell you, whoever does not receive the kingdom of God as a little child will never enter it" (Mark 10:15). Then he took the children in his arms and blessed them. He laid hands on them, conveying God's call. This was a severe breach of convention; yet the story embodies the Hebrew tradition of valuing children as a blessing and taking responsibility to bless children. Why, then, is the story controversial?

I suggest that the story introduces an incarnational element – the idea that the children actually *incarnate* God's Kingdom. This theme is particularly strong in Christian scriptures. The use of incarnational language might be unnecessarily provocative in an interreligious context, but I use it to preserve the radicality of the story. One might speak instead of the power of children to reveal God. This is more adequate in crossing theistic religious traditions, and it preserves much of what is meant here by incarnation. Focusing, then, on children as revealing God, we see that the marginalized of society are revealers of divinity. This is indeed compatible with many theistic traditions. Consider the baby Moses, for example, placed by his mother in a basket among reeds in the river, watched by his sister, and found by Pharaoh's daughter. Not only do we see three women walking with the baby Moses toward hope, but we also see the baby as a revealer of God. His presence in Pharaoh's house reveals that God is still present and active in Egypt during these hard times. Further, Moses is an Israelite – a child of migrant people, called by the name "Hebrew" (*habiru*) in Exodus 1:15–22. The very name *habiru* can be translated as refugee or fugitive; these were marginalized people. Moses is a mere baby among the marginalized; yet he is the primary sign of hope in these texts.

Children are revealed in these texts as not only vulnerable, but as *revelations* of God's being and *channels* of God's work. Thus, United Methodist Bishops have proclaimed that the church's mission is not only to mediate grace to the vulnerable, but also to welcome "God's transforming grace *through* the vulnerable" (Council of Bishops of The United Methodist Church 1996, 2001). Likewise, the Campaign of Brother- and Sisterhood 1987 by the Catholic Bishops Conference in Brazil carries this theme in declaring an "option for the children" (Mette 2001: 16–17).[5] They make explicit connections between the marginalization of children and their identification with the weak and excluded of society.

So what *is* revealed of God through the marginalized? Certain features of God's work can be discerned if we think of children as revelatory of God's intentions for the world. I will name three revelatory qualities of children, but others could be added.

Interruptive

Children reveal, first, that God acts through interruptions. In Mark's narrative, the children's arrival at Jesus' knee was clearly interruptive, and the incident still raises interruptive issues – issues of belonging (who is included) and faithfulness (what is the appropriate human response to God). Questions related to children have continued to be evocative for Christianity. For example, the words "as a little child" were likely invoked in discussions of infant baptism in the early church (Nineham 1978: 267–9; Bowman 1965: 211–12). Indeed, children still pose interruptive questions for faith communities.

Receptive

Children also reveal that God intends the world to be receptive (to "receive the kingdom of God as a little child"). While adults around Jesus were trying to earn the approval of Jesus, the children simply received. Children also lead contemporary communities to appreciate the power of receiving.

Wondering

Children further reveal that God intends for the world to wonder. Drawing this conclusion from Mark 10:10–13 is an act of imagination; however, the experience of being received and blessed by Jesus, especially amid controversy, surely stirred wonder in these children. Other texts reveal the theme of wonder more explicitly. In Luke's Gospel, we find Jesus lingering in the Temple asking questions (2:22–40), being true to his Jewish tradition. Consider also the writings of mystical religionists, such as Abraham Joshua Heschel (1951: 11–13, 40–1) and Howard Thurman (1961: 19–20), and religious educators, such as Karen-Marie Yust (in press) and Anabel Proffitt (1998: 102–13; 1994; cf: Hay, Nbye, Murphy 1996).

This discussion suggests that the marginalized – represented by children – dare to be interruptive, receptive, and wondering. In so doing, they uncover God's work and point the way for communities to follow.

Walking with Children toward Hope

We return now to the central question with which this study began: how do we walk with children toward hope? Certainly we cannot expect to find one simple road to justice and reconciliation. The personal and contextual comments with which I began suggest an almost overwhelming complexity. At the same time, the question is not without answers. Remarkable work has been done in South Africa and Australia during the past 20 years promoting justice and reconciliation. Archbishop Desmond Tutu marvels that South Africa has become a symbol of reconciliation for the world (1999). Australians – both aboriginal and white – marvel at the slow but sure movements of reconciliation in their country (Brennan 1992; Harris 1998; Reynolds 1981; Tickner 2001). Neither situation is simple; both countries face major challenges. Australians, for example, seek now to act justly toward new immigrants without slowing reconciliation between aboriginal people and the white descendents of earlier European arrivals. Despite problems, the movements in South Africa and Australia have been exemplary. They have involved initiatives from government and religious authorities, as well as many grassroots movements. These have not always been in sympathy with one another, but they have reinforced and challenged each other, contributing to the continuation of a movement.

Differences between the two countries are also in evidence. In the case of South Africa, an extensive, carefully developed plan was undertaken in setting up the Truth and Reconciliation Commission. In Australia, no effort has been so fully accepted and widely practiced, although major efforts were made to gain approval of the Australian Declaration Towards Reconciliation, 2000.

The people of these two countries are quick to point out their limitations, failures, and despair, so neither case is presented as an unconditional success story. On the other hand, interviews with people involved in both struggles have evoked a common refrain from those actively working for change in local, grassroots communities: "We are moving; we can see change; we will not give up." Interviews with people less involved are more discouraging. These people are more likely to take a pessimistic view, emphasizing the absence of action, the slowness of change. One might conclude from this brief commentary that movement toward justice and reconciliation is possible, that the people most injured need to be especially heeded, that successful movements will often involve initiatives from authorities *and* grassroots groups, and that hopefulness often emerges among people most involved in working for change.

With this background, we return to children – the people most marginalized in almost any conflict or oppressive situation. The analysis of this paper suggests four steps that we might take as we walk with children on the long road to justice and reconciliation. In fact, we might walk, roll, crawl, run, or dance these steps, but they can indeed guide our journey with children.

The first step is *lament*, in which we recognize and critically analyze the ambivalence and vulnerability that surround children and childhood. We protest the forces that tear at children and bring us to fiery anger or bitter tears. We grieve for the pains of children in the present, the pains of children far away, and the painful realities that have endured throughout recorded history. We not only grieve for the pain, but also for the social and religious structures that have perpetuated that pain.

The second step is *celebration*. We celebrate the blessings of children – the creative marvel of their births, the promise of the future that they hold, the delight of their presence, the stability and freshness they bring to human community, and the uniqueness of each child. This is the step that thrives on ritual acts and spontaneous acts of thanksgiving.

The third step is *blessing*. Here we bless children with care and guidance, ritual inclusion, and opportunity and empowerment. In biblical texts, we see such blessings enacted. Jesus took the children into his arms (a symbol of caring), laid hands on them (a symbol of commissioning), and blessed them (a symbol of abiding promise). In Exodus, the midwives, the mother and sister of Moses, and the daughter of

Pharaoh blessed Moses with protection, care and hope. Blessing children will take many forms, but it frequently involves responding to their vulnerability and marginality. It involves risk.

The fourth step is *receiving blessings from children*. This is the step in which we receive the delight of children, but also the marginality. It is the step in which we receive all that children have to give, which includes interruptions, receptivity, and wondering. While each of these has a romantic dimension, each also has a terrifying dimension. We will be faced with accepting the delightful and disturbing interruptions children bring to our lives; receiving the happy and challenging gifts they give us; and wondering at the agonizing questions, unresolved issues, and movements of God they uncover.

Looking back on the earlier case study, the family in this case had no place where they could lament, and they did not know how to receive the laments of one another. The only form of celebration they had learned was to purchase things or spend money on expensive meals; these were short-lived celebrations. The mother was never taught to bless her child, although she had sparks of desire at times. The father wanted to bless his son, but only knew how to do it through harsh discipline. Neither parent could receive blessings from either of their children; they rarely delighted in their lives. If this study is to have value, it must speak a word to this family.

What would be transformed in this family, and for their children, if a community were present for them, guiding and creating space for them to lament and celebrate, to bless and be blessed by their children? What would be transformed if public policies supported them and their children – in education, legal systems, and social support structures? I dare say that hope travels in these very footsteps – not an easy hope based on immediate rewards for good works, but an abiding hope that rises from the ground as people travel in the path of God's promises and blessings.

Notes

1   The poem is based on biblical texts alluding to children, especially: Genesis 16:1–18:15; 21:1–21; 22:1–19; I Kings 17:8–24; Job 1:13–22; 42:10, 13–17; Mark 7:24–30.
2   Percentages are based on 1999 figures.
3   All biblical quotes are taken from the New Revised Standard Version of the Bible.
4   The poem, in its entirety, is based on biblical texts of children, including those listed in Note 1 and those found in: Exodus 1:7; 20:10; Deuteronomy 4:9–10; 6:7, 21; 11:19; 31:12–13; Joshua 4:6–7; Psalms 78:1–8; 127:3–5; 128:3–6; Proverbs 17:6; Isaiah 29:22–23; 30:1–3; Hosea 4:6; Matthew 1:1–3:17; Mark 9:14–29, 33–37; 10:13–16; Luke 1:5–2:52; 3:8; John 6:1–14, esp. 9; 8:39; Acts 2:14–18. Succeeding verses of this poem introduce the next two sections.

5   Mette translates some of this text and also refers to a pastoral letter on chil-
     dren in Germany.

References

Alexander, H. A. 1999: A Jewish View of Human Learning. *International Journal of Children's Spirituality* 4(2): 155–64.

Anderson, H. and Johnson, S. B. W. 1994: *Regarding Children: A New Respect for Childhood and Families*. Louisville, KY: Westminster/John Knox.

Arnold, J. C. 2000: *Endangered: Your Child in a Hostile World*. Farmington, PA: Plough Publishing House of The Bruderhof Foundation.

Bailey, J. L. 1995: Experiencing the Kingdom as a Little Child: A Rereading of Mark 10:13–16. *Word and World* 15(1): 58–67.

Bowman, J. 1965: *The Gospel of Mark: The New Christian-Jewish Passover Haggadah*. Leiden: E. J. Brill.

Brennan, F. (ed.) 1992: *Reconciling Our Differences: A Christian Approach to Recognising Aboriginal Land Rights*. Victoria, Australia: Aurora Books.

Child Poverty Fact Sheet 2000: National Center for Children in Poverty, July 2002, www.childstats.gov.

Consumer Expenditure Survey 2000: US Bureau of Labor Statistics, 27 December 2001, http://stats.bls.gov/csxhome.htm.

Council of Bishops of The United Methodist Church 1996: Children and Poverty: An Episcopal Initiative, Biblical and Theological Foundations. Nashville: The United Methodist Publishing House.

—— 2001: Community with Children and the Poor: Renewing the Episcopal Initiative. Nashville: The United Methodist Publishing House.

Couture, P. D. 1991: *Blessed Are the Poor? Women's Poverty, Family Policy, and Practical Theology*. Nashville: Abingdon.

—— 2000: *Seeing Children, Seeing God: A Practical Theology of Children and Poverty*. Nashville: Abingdon.

Halberstam, D. 1998: *The Children*. New York: Random House.

Harris, J. 1998: *We Wish We'd Done More: Ninety Years of CMS and Aboriginal Issues in North Australia*. Adelaide, Australia: Openbook.

Hay, D., Nbye, R. and Murphy, R. 1996: Thinking About Childhood Spirituality: Review of Research and Current Directions. In Leslie J. Francis, William K. Kay, and William S. Campbell (eds.), *Research in Religious Education*. Macon, GA: Smyth & Helwys.

Heschel, A. J. 1951: *Man Is Not Alone: A Philosophy of Religion*. New York: Farrar, Straus and Giroux.

Hollinsworth, D. 1998: *Race and Racism in Australia*, 2nd ed. Australia: Social Science Press.

Information Resource Centre 2001: War, Peace and Security World Wide Web Server. Canada Minister of Public Works and Government Services, http://www.cfcsc.dnd.ca/links/wars/index.html.

Johnson, S. 2001: Women, Children, Poverty, and the Church: A Faith-Based Community Revitalization Approach to Addressing Poverty. Paper presented to the International Academy of Practical Theology, Stellenbosch, South Africa, April.

Kline, S. 1993: *Out of the Garden: Toys, TV, and Children's Culture in the Age of Marketing*. New York: Verso.

Media Awareness Network 2002: www.media-awareness.ca/eng/issues/stats/indad.htm.

Mette, N. 2001: Children's Poverty in the Midst of an Affluent Society: A Challenge to the Churches and Practical Theology in Germany. Paper presented to the International Academy of Practical Theology, Stellenbosch, South Africa, April.

Moore, M. E. M. 1998, revised 2001a: Blessing, Blessing and Blessings More. Unpublished poem.

—— 1998, revised 2001b: Remember the Children. Unpublished poem.

National Council of the Churches of Christ in the United States of America 1989: *The Holy Bible: New Revised Standard Version*. Nashville, Tenn.: Thomas Nelson.

Nineham, D. E. 1978, 1963: *St. Mark*. Philadelphia: Westminster.

Proffitt, A. C. 1994: Mystery, Metaphor and Religious Education: The Challenge of Teaching in a Postmodern World. Paper presented to the International Seminar on Religious Education and Values, Goslar, Germany.

—— 1998: The Importance of Wonder in Religious Education. *Religious Education*, 93(1):102–13.

Reynolds, H. 1981: *The Other Side of the Frontier: Aboriginal Resistance to the European Invasion of Australia*. Ringwood, Victoria; Harmondsworth: Penguin.

Thurman, H. 1961: *The Inward Journey*. Richmond, IN: Friends United Press.

Tickner, R. 2001: *Taking a Stand: Land Rights to Reconciliation*. Allen and Unwin.

Tinker, G. 1993: *Missionary Conquest*. Minneapolis: Fortress.

Tutu, Desmond M. 1999: *No Future Without Forgiveness*. New York: Doubleday.

Yust, K.-M. (in press): The Toddler and the Community (12 months–3 years). In F. Kelcourse (ed.), *Human Development and Faith*. St. Louis: Chalice.

Chapter 8

Children's Right to Religion: A Response to Mary Elizabeth Moore

FRIEDRICH SCHWEITZER

BEING A RESPONDENT can mean many different things. Sometimes it means that the respondent is to identify all the possible shortcomings of the first paper. This would be perfectly inadequate and even tactless in relationship to a paper that is as moving, spirited, and poetic as Mary Elizabeth Moore's.

Another possibility for a respondent is to point out what disagreements he or she has with the first paper. But this task also is not appropriate. I deeply agree with almost everything in Mary Elizabeth Moore's paper so it would be highly artificial to focus on the few little details on which we might disagree. Let me say it in my own words: With Mary Elizabeth Moore I am convinced that *hope* is something like the core and precondition of all education. Whoever has no hope cannot educate children but can only supervise them and train them. All true education presupposes hope in a future to which children can be introduced. Without hope there is no education.

For me this is actually one of the reasons why all education has to do with faith, spirituality, and religion. Hope in the future can never be reduced to science and technology. It is always related to our deepest feelings and convictions. Therefore education has an underlying religious structure.

It should be clear that my use of the term "religion" is quite close to the term "spirituality," at least in some sense. My use is informed by classic works like that of Friedrich Schleiermacher that speak of religion in a generic or human sense. For the early Schleiermacher, religion is first of all a matter of personal experience and feeling, not of institutions like the church or of tradition and dogma (Schleiermacher 1799/1967).

Institutions, traditions, and dogma may also belong to religion since individual religion tends to become institutionalized, but they are not the core of religion. So when I speak of education having an underlying religious structure, I am referring to this kind of generic understanding of religion.

Given my agreement with Mary Elizabeth's views in "Walking with Children toward Hope," I have chosen to focus on some additional aspects of an education for hope from my own perspective as a religious and moral educator. What does it take to sustain hope in children? And what are the consequences for an education that wants to do justice to this task?

There are of course many different answers to these questions, and I will not be able to discuss all of them. In my own work I have found it increasingly important to focus on the questions that children ask and that children are. It is important that we do not only think of those questions that children pose to us explicitly. We must also include questions that children *are* for us and with which they confront us through their being with us as educators. Only in this way will we get a full understanding of what education for hope entails for children and adults.

I am deeply convinced that in the life of all children there are questions of at least potentially religious or spiritual meaning. And this is true quite independently of their background, religious or not. I am also convinced that any education for true hope depends on not closing our ears to those questions that are related to children's spirituality and moral feelings.

Over the years I have identified five such questions of potential religious meaning; I believe that most of them are also present in Mary Elizabeth Moore's paper even if she considers them in a different way than I phrase them. I have to limit myself here to a shorthand description of these questions, which I have developed more fully in some of my earlier publications, especially in my recent book on children's right to religion (Schweitzer 2000, also see Schweitzer 2002).

The first question is the question of death and dying. All children encounter this question sooner or later, many of them all too soon in this world of violence and aggression. But even with the most protected childhood, children will eventually come across a dead bird on their way home from preschool or learn of the death of their friend's relative, or maybe even experience the death of a parent.

Do all people have to die? Do you have to die? And what will happen to me after you die? These are some of the most moving questions children can confront their parents with.

In her important book, *Do Children Need Religion?*, Martha Fay, a mother and journalist in the United States, relates how her three-year-old daughter Anna started asking questions about death and dying after her grandmother died. Anna wanted to know *why* her grandmother died, and no reference to old age or failing health seemed to be sufficient answer to her repeated questions. Moreover, Anna wanted to know what "dead" really means and where "people go when they die." It is fascinating to read how the mother slowly but surely came to understand that Anna's questions were not about rational explanations, not about "mechanistic explanations alone," as Martha Fay puts it. And Anna's questions remain a challenge for adults who, even as parents of a three-year-old, have to be prepared for what they do not want to hear:

> Nor, we soon realized, would her father and I long remain her exclusive informants. Within a few months, her friend Ian's grandmother had also died, but unlike Nanny [Anna's grandmother], this lucky woman, according to her grandson, had gone straight to heaven, which turned out to be right where I had left it as a child, and where Anna – hearing about it, as far as we knew, for the first time – seemed to think it properly belonged: directly overhead, out of sight behind the clouds. (Fay 1993: 6–7)

I like this story very much because it shows that we can indeed answer our children's questions about death and dying without any reference to religion, for example, by limiting our responses to the "mechanistic explanations" to which Martha Fay first resorted. But what are we really telling children in this case? That a mother of three young children "just had cancer" and that she "had to die" – because this is how the world happens to be? If the world just is "like that," there is no room for hope. There only is space for resignation. This is why listening to children's questions about death and dying is so important for any education toward hope, and this includes doing justice to the religious or spiritual meaning of such questions. For children, no rationalist or mechanistic explanations will do *vis-à-vis* their perceptions of death and dying. They need answers that are in line with the meaning of their questions – about the *why* and about the future of the dead (and of the living).

The second question is of a different kind. It may be a question that children ask less often but it certainly is a question with which they confront us many times: why be moral in a world that is not moral? Why be fair to others who are not fair to me?

Again there are nonreligious answers, and many of today's parents are actually trying them out. *You want to be fair because that's the way you want to be treated by others!* But what if the others still react unfairly? What if there really is no positive reciprocity but only the never-ending spiral of violence and aggression? And what adult would really be able to demonstrate that fairness necessarily leads to fairness in this world?

In my view the only way to give children a positive basis for their morality is to share a faith with them, to let them participate in our own nonviolent relationships with other people and with the world. In other words, the reason for being moral in a world that is not moral must come from a religious or spiritual attitude that the children can share.

To be sure, it is possible to have a nonreligious basis for ethics like, for example, the basis that discourse ethics has offered. But the abstract reasoning on which this model is based is not accessible to children. Children's moral thinking and acting is embedded in their social life and especially in their relationship to parents or other adults around them. Moral education must take account of this and must offer them an ethical basis that is in line with their ways of experiencing the world.

Death and dying and the motives for being moral in a world that is unjust are two topics that show the interconnection between education for hope on the one hand and spirituality or religion on the other. The same is true for my third question, which concerns the self or identity of the child. Again, this is not a question that children normally will pose to us, but it definitely is a question with which their very existence confronts us. Identity, we are told by philosophers, is dependent on acknowledgment, recognition, and acceptance from others. The human self is always relational.

Many philosophers and psychologists consider this kind of recognition and acceptance a purely mundane or secular process that has nothing to do with religion. Yet what does it really mean if the self is seen as the product of the affirmation afforded by other people? Does it mean that the identity of a child is ultimately dependent on his or her parents' recognition? From my point of view this is a very dangerous interpretation of self or identity. It turns parents and other adults into godlike figures of ultimate importance and power while reducing the identity of the child to a human product.

In a rarely quoted passage from his book *Identity: Youth and Crisis*, Erik Erikson seems to have had this in mind when he distinguished between the psychoanalytic *Ego* and what he calls the human *I* as the center of awareness:

> But "I" is nothing less than the verbal assurance according to which I feel that I am the center of awareness in a universe of experience in which I have a coherent identity . . . it means nothing less than that I am alive, that I *am* life. (Erikson 1968: 220)

And from such observations Erikson arrives at the conclusion that is of central importance for our present context, the child's right to religion:

> The counterplayer of the "I" therefore can be, strictly speaking, only the deity who has lent this halo to a mortal and is Himself endowed with an eternal numinousness certified by all "I"s who acknowledge this gift.

In everyday life the affirmation that is given by parents is certainly what we have to wish for a child. But whoever is interested in the child's autonomy must also wish for some other source of ultimate recognition that goes beyond parental affirmation. It is for this reason that I count the developing self among the issues that necessarily include a transcendent or religious dimension.

My fourth question is rather obvious. It has to do with children's exposure to other faiths and to other religions. In countries like Germany it is quite normal for children to encounter other children with different religious backgrounds in nursery school (and this includes children with no explicit religious background). It is for this reason that multi*cultural* education has rightfully become a central issue for many educational institutions. What has received far less attention is the *religious* dimension of multiculturalism. But culture cannot really be understood without reference to religion. And if it is true that multicultural society makes it inevitable to work toward the acceptance not only of the other but explicitly toward positive and accepting attitudes toward the stranger, this also must come to include the religion of the stranger. And it seems true that this actually is the most difficult part of this task – to accept the religion of the strangers, their strange beliefs and practices, their unfamiliar rituals, and possibly their different ethics.

In Germany with its large growing Moslem population, nursery-school children sometimes quarrel about whose God is better or stronger, the Christian God or Allah. Fortunately, this is not always the case. But this kind of argument clearly indicates that children need support in sorting out different religions and religious faiths.

With this, I come to my fifth and last question, which is about God. I am aware that children encounter the word "God" through adults and through their environment. The concept of God is not invented by children. In this sense this question does not arise from children's experience like the question of death and dying, which is more or less inevitable for all people.

Of course, it is possible to show that children almost automatically encounter the word "God" in Western culture even if they do not receive any religious education. "God" is presented to them in art and architecture, in music and literature, in history and politics. But do children really need a religious explanation for what they can observe here? Isn't it enough to just give them a historical explanation, for example, by pointing out that this is what people once believed?

This is where a reference to the experiences in early childhood must come into play. Psychoanalysts have pointed out that early childhood is connected to the experience of primal unity that can be seen as the psychological origin of all images of God (Rizzuto 1979). At that time children perceive their parents or caretakers as omnipotent sources of recognition and care. With them they find warmth, protection, and shelter. Such experiences in early childhood – or their lack – are much more than can be observed from the outside. They are experiences of ultimate importance and meaning, which gives them a religious dimension.

These early experiences are below the level of language, and they are not conscious in a way that could be connected to terms like "God." Nevertheless such experiences leave their traces in the life of the child. They remain present in the shape of hopes and longings but also as fears and disappointments.

Later on, these feelings form the background against which children will hear the narratives from the religious traditions that resonate with their early experiences. And what is even more important in our present context, these stories give children a language through which they can access and express the longings, fears, and hopes that are connected to their early childhood experiences. And with the help of this language such feelings can be communicated and shared with others. Unless this kind of communication is made possible through the acquisition of a language adequate for this task, the ambivalences and conflicts of early childhood experience cannot be accessed, let alone be resolved or healed.

Hope is the core and presupposition of all true education. Listening to some of children's deepest questions is one of the most important ways of securing this hope. In my understanding this is what the first Declaration of Children's Rights – the famous Geneva Declaration of 1924 – was referring to: children's right to spiritual development. The famous Polish Jewish educator Janusz Korczak (Korczak 1967: 40) takes this up with the formulation of three basic rights of children:

1   The child's right to his death, which in my view means the child's right to life;
2   The child's right to the present day;
3   The child's right to be like he is.
     And I add to this,
     the child's right to be a creature of hope!

References

Erikson, E. H. 1968: *Identity: Youth and Crisis*. New York: Norton.

Fay, M. 1993: *Do Children Need Religion? How Parents Today Are Thinking About the Big Questions*. New York: Pantheon.

Korczak, J. 1967: *Wie man ein Kind lieben soll*. Göttingen: Vandenhoeck & Ruprecht.

Rizzuto, A.-M. 1979: *The Birth of the Living God: A Psychoanalytic Study*. Chicago/London: University of Chicago Press.

Schleiermacher, F. 1799/1967: *Über die Religion. Reden an die Gebildeten unter ihren Verächtern*. Göttingen: Vandenhoeck & Ruprecht.

Schweitzer, F. 2000: *Das Recht des Kindes auf Religion*. Gütersloh: Gütersloher Verlagshaus.

—— 2002: *The Postmodern Life Cycle: Challenges for Theology and the Church* (in press).

Chapter 9

Children's Spirituality: A Bahá'í Perspective

IRAJ AYMAN

Fundamental Questions for the Study of Children's Spirituality

ANY STUDY OF children's spirituality is necessarily based on the answers to a number of questions such as:

- What do we mean by "spirituality"?
- What do we mean by "spirit" as the basis for spirituality?
- What is the relationship between spirituality and religiosity? Is it possible to develop and maintain children's spirituality without any relationship to religion?
- How do we define religion? What is the phenomenon of religion?
- What is faith? Is it a phenomenon independent from religion?
- Is it possible to develop and maintain spirituality that is not faith-based?
- How are religious concepts and beliefs conceived by children and transformed during their formative years of life?
- How can children's spirituality develop and be reinforced, applied, and sustained?

The answers to these and similar questions are in turn based on the perspectives used in undertaking such studies. This chapter attempts to answer some of these questions: by first presenting a short introduction of the Bahá'í perspective on children's spirituality based on the Bahá'í religion's scripture and belief system, then discussing the relationship between spirituality and education, and ending with an approach to faith-based education for the development of children's spirituality.

The Bahá'í faith is a global movement for unifying humankind and enhancing its spirituality. It is a new way of life. Among its fundamental beliefs are the following: the unity of God as the Supreme Source of Being; the essential reality of the human soul and its everlasting existence; the essential unity and developmental nature of religion; and the harmony of science, reason, and religion. Its aim is the establishment of sustainable world peace and the global prosperity of humankind. The Bahá'í faith emphasizes the vital importance and priority of developing spirituality in children through teaching them fundamental verities of religion in a way that does not result in fanaticism and prejudice.

The Spiritual Nature of the Human Being

The human being, from the Bahá'í perspective, is essentially a spiritual reality. This spiritual reality, however, is manifested in a physical form – born in this contingent world – for the purpose of developing qualities necessary for the emergence of an ever-advancing civilization in this world, and for empowerment to enjoy an everlasting existence in the non-contingent world beyond. Although in this world the nature and specifications of the world beyond are inconceivable for human beings, it is possible to understand the wisdom of such an arrangement.

In the words of Bahá'u'lláh, Prophet-Founder of the Bahá'í faith, "The world beyond is as different from this world as this world is different from that of the child while still in the womb of its mother" (Bahá'u'lláh 1952: 157). This concept is further elucidated by Ábdu'l-Bahá, authorized interpreter of the words of Bahá'u'lláh. He says:

> If a human life, with its spiritual being, were limited to this earthly span, then what would be the harvest of creation? . . . Were such a notion be true, then all created things, all contingent realities, and this whole world of being, all would be meaningless. . . . For just as the effects and the fruitage of the uterine life are not to be found in that dark and narrow place, and only when the child is transferred to this wide earth do the benefits and uses of growth and development in that previous world become revealed, so likewise reward and punishment, heaven and hell, requital and retribution for actions done in this present life, will stand revealed in that other world beyond. And just as, if human life in the womb were limited to that uterine world, existence there would be nonsensical, irrelevant, so too if the life of this world, the deeds here done and their fruitage, did not come forth in the world beyond, the whole process would be irrational and foolish. (Ábdu'l-Bahá' 1978: 185)

The same way that the uterine life exists in this world but the embryo cannot understand the nature and attributes of this world, the world beyond also exists in this world but it is beyond our comprehension.

God (the Supreme Source of Being) has created human beings as an act of love, the love to bring forth a creation capable of recognizing Him. He has endowed human beings with the capacity to reflect divine attributes and, in the words of Bahá'u'lláh, to "carry forward an everlasting civilization" (Bahá'u'lláh 1952: 215). Spirituality, therefore, is the reflection of such attributes. Spirituality can be achieved and manifested at both the individual and the societal levels. At the individual level, spirituality involves having a loving relationship with the Creator, and acquiring and manifesting spiritual values and moral attributes in our personal conduct. At the societal level it is the collective efforts of individuals to create a spiritual and moral environment able to facilitate and reinforce spirituality and moral behavior. It is important to note the mutual impact and the interdependency of these two levels of spirituality. One cannot be fully materialized without the other. Children have to receive the type of education and development that empowers them to manifest spiritual qualities both individually as well as collectively. This will be greatly reinforced if they live in a socially supportive environment. Parents and teachers can act as the best role models, demonstrating spirituality in their way of life.

The origin or the seed of spirituality is inherent in each individual. It only needs to be properly nurtured and developed. In the same way that the embryo does not acquire or receive various organs and capabilities but rather develops them from within, we do not acquire spiritual qualities and capabilities from outside, but develop them from within ourselves.

We not only need these virtues in order to become more valued and useful citizens, we also need them to be able to live a more rewarding and successful life in the world beyond. Again, in the same way that a handicapped baby cannot live a normal and successful life in this contingent world, a spiritually handicapped person cannot fully enjoy the opportunities available in the life after.

The Dual Nature of the Human Being

The human being has a dual nature: material and spiritual. Both of these pass through a developmental process that needs to be properly protected and guided. In the same way that physical education and proper health care improve and enhance qualities of physical existence, proper spiritual education and development heighten and elevate the spiritual reality of the human being. From this point of view, the human being is in the hierarchy of the contingent world, as stated by Ábdu'l-Bahá:

> in the highest degree of materiality, and at the beginning of spirituality –
> that is to say, he is the end of imperfection and the beginning of perfec-
> tion. . . . He has the animal side as well as the angelic side, and the aim of
> the educator is to so train the human souls that their angelic aspect may
> overcome their animal side. (Ábdu'l-Bahá 1981: 236)

The human being is endowed with free will, constantly making choices, directing his or her behavior to one or the other of the two ways of life. If prevented from achieving spiritual maturity, human beings proceed to the world after as handicapped beings. Bahá'í education prescribes a holistic and balanced development leading to the eventual maturity of the spiritual, intellectual, and physical dimensions in children as they pass through their formative age.

Spirituality and Education

Spirituality means emancipation from the bonds and limitations of the material side of life and realization of the virtues inherent in the reality of the human being. In the words of Bahá'u'lláh, the human being is "as a mine rich in gems of inestimable value. Education can, alone, cause it to reveal its treasures, and enable humankind to benefit therefrom" (Bahá'u'lláh 1952: 259). He also says that the human being is "as steel, the essence of which is hidden; through . . . good counsel and education, that essence will be brought to light. If, however, he be allowed to remain in his original condition, the corrosion of lusts and appetites will effectively destroy him" (Bahá'u'lláh et al. 1987).

Steel is hard, dark, and cold. However, it has the potential qualities of softness, light, and warmth. Such qualities may become manifested through the proper transforming processes in order for the steel to be turned into useful and beautiful items. Education may bring about the same transformation in children, evolving the best aspects of their characters and empowering them to attain sustainable spirituality. Therefore, what is needed is spiritualization of education. The three dimensions of education – physical, intellectual, and spiritual – are not completely independent of each other. Education is a comprehensive process encompassing all three aspects.

The Educational Process

Developing the intellectual powers of discernment, moral judgment, and personal conduct that will be individually healthy and socially acceptable may also be the aim of what is nowadays referred to as "secular education." However, spirituality is based on a God–person relationship. Sustainable spirituality is necessarily faith-based. No degree of intellectual conviction by itself can produce spiritual experience and guarantee ethical behavior at all times and under all adverse conditions. No amount of externally imposed codes of proper conduct will guarantee the prevention of wrongdoing or excessive materialistic tendencies, when such behavior serves one's personal interest and can be committed with impunity.

A sustainable inner spiritual conviction, self-confidence, and a sense of "constructive" freedom from the material aspects of life cannot be forced upon the individual. It is the natural outcome of a spiritually oriented educational process. There is need for an inner agent in the heart and soul of the individual that would control his or her behavior and prevent overstepping the limits of morality. History is full of examples of highly educated and intellectually developed individuals who have become victims of their own passions and worldly desires. In order to live a spiritual life one has to enter into a firm covenant with the Creator, a covenant that is based on love and trust and is free from feelings of guilt and fear of hellfire. Furthermore, one needs to have a set of guiding principles and undertake certain spiritual practices. They assist the individual to find the correct approach and to be empowered to make the right decision. This is the process of shifting responsibility from an external source that constantly watches over and controls behavior to the individual, so that everyone can control personal conduct in appropriate manner.

Individuals need to have an intellectually satisfying and personally encouraging understanding of the meaning and purpose of their lives and or their relationship with their fellow human beings. They should be clear about their responsibilities and prerogatives so that they can protect their own as well as others' best interests. In light of such an education and such a covenant, fear of God will become fear born out of love for the Creator, Supreme Source of Being, the same way that children's fear of parents could be so guided to be out of love and respect for them. Such consideration and fear has a preventive advantage. It keeps the individual from committing acts that are injurious to the self or to others.

Faith-Based (or Religious) Education

The basis of effective spiritual education is enabling the individual to appreciate spiritual values. This is a developmental process. Appreciation of higher-order values such as those of the arts, science, and religion needs an educational and developmental process that takes place gradually and over a long period of time. In the same way, appreciating the spiritual values such as worship and meditation, the concept of divinity, spirituality, the reality of everlasting life in the world beyond, care for others, and selfless deeds could also be learned through the gradual process of education. The earlier such education starts, the more effective and lasting the results will be. This will help children to add a spiritual dimension to their lives.

Bahá'u'lláh enjoined that spiritual and moral education should be accorded priority over other aspects of education. He said, "It is the bounden duty of the parents to rear their children to be staunch in faith . . . For every praiseworthy deed is born out of the light of religion, and lacking this supreme bestowal the child will not turn away from any evil, nor will he draw nigh unto any good" (Bahá'u'lláh et al. 1987). However, Bahá'u'lláh also cautioned that such an education should be provided in a manner that "it may not injure the children by resulting in ignorant fanaticism and bigotry" (Bahá'u'lláh et al. 1987). Religious education should not instill prejudice or a tendency toward discrimination. In other words, what is recommended is that the "schools must first train the children in the principles of religion" (Bahá'u'lláh et al. 1987).

Religious principles and moral teachings are common to all religions. They are mostly subscribed to by secular education as well. In this way the inner agent mentioned earlier would evolve and emerge within the heart and soul of a person, leading the individual to achieve and maintain spirituality.

This is the dimension of children's education that, at present, is either ignored or insufficiently attended to. Some parents are of the opinion that children should not receive religious education at all because it inculcates superstitions and limits freedom of choice. In this they are mistaken. Thus their children grow spiritually illiterate. The same way that an illiterate person cannot benefit from schooling, a spiritually ignorant person cannot understand and appreciate spiritual values and grow spiritually. As mentioned earlier, religious education must be provided in a manner that equips the child with an appreciation of spiritual and religious values, without teaching and inculcating superstition and vain imaginings. Such a religious education will equip children with the tools and facilities for attaining spirituality. In other words religious education will provide the means to an end – spirituality.

References

Ábdu'l-Bahá 1978: *Selections From the Writings of Ábdu'l-Bahá.* Haifa: Bahá'í World Centre.

—— 1981: *Some Answered Questions.* Laura Clifford Barney (trans.). Wilmette, IL: Bahá'í Publishing Trust.

Bahá'u'lláh 1952: *Gleanings From the Writings of Bahá'u'lláh.* Shoghi Effendi (trans.). Second revised edn. Wilmette, IL: Bahá'í Publishing Trust.

——, Ábdu'l-Bahá and Shoghi Effendi 1987: *Bahaá'í Education.* (Compiled by the Research Department of the Universal House of Justice). Revised edition, Haifa: Bahá'í World Centre.

Chapter 10

Communities of Character: Religion in the Moral Development of American and Korean Youth

PAMELA EBSTYNE KING

THE INFLUENCE of religion and spirituality in the lives of youth is gaining increased attention in the public and academic domain. Spiritual education has become mandated in the United Kingdom. In the United States President George W. Bush has established an Executive Office on faith-based initiatives. In the year 2000, *Newsweek* magazine featured the cover stories "Kids and God" and "What Teens Believe: God, Sex, Race and the Future." This trend is also evidenced in the increased frequency and depth of scholarship in the area of adolescent religion and spirituality in the social sciences (Benson, Donahue, and Erickson 1989; Jessor et al. 1995; Johnson et al. 2000; Johnson et al. 2001; Lerner and Galambos 1998; Resnick et al. 1997; Wagener et al., 2003).

An increasing number of studies in the 1990s document benefits associated with religion in three distinct ways. First, religious participation and religious salience act as a buffer against engaging in risky and potentially dangerous behaviors. This is evidenced by studies indicating that religious youth display lower levels of activities like substance abuse, sexual promiscuity, violence, and delinquency than their less religious peers (Amey, Albrecht, and Miller 1996; Benson, Donahue, and Erickson 1989; Donahue and Benson 1995; Johnson et al. 2000; McBride, Mutch, and Chitwood 1996; Wallace and Forman 1998). Secondly, being religious or participating in religious activities is associated with a number of prosocial outcomes, such as having social skills and coping skills, valuing diversity, and having access to developmental resources (Donahue and Benson 1995; Donelson 1999; Furrow and Wagener 2000). Thirdly, adolescent religiousness is associated with moral attitudes and actions. Religious youth are more involved with community service and are identified as having higher degrees of altruism and caring (Donahue and Benson 1995; Hart and Fegley 1995; Serow and Dreyden 1990; Youniss, McLellan, and Yates 1999).

While a positive contribution of religion to adolescent development can be documented, a theoretical understanding is needed to explain these effects. What is it about being religious or participating in religious activities that might promote positive development? Of specific concern in this chapter is the question of what aspects of religion are associated with moral development. Is it the values and behavioral sanctions? Is it transcendent experience? Is it the social support and social control?

Studies in moral psychology suggest that moral beliefs and behaviors are socially influenced. Based on a review of the literature on adolescent moral development, this paper proposes that faith communities promote a social context in which character can develop. It is suggested that faith communities can provide a unique fertile ground, in which seeds of character can be planted, nurtured, and will eventually flourish. It is the nutrients from the surrounding environment that enable the plants to mature. Specifically, the paper will put forth a theoretical framework for understanding how congregations and faith-based organizations cannot only be faith communities but communities of character as well.

Religious congregations have been recognized for their role in shaping the moral life of their participants. Berger and Berger (1983) describe congregations as *mediating structures* capable of this morally nurturing role. Essential to society, especially to democracy, mediating structures are institutional contexts, in which responsible individuals can develop and gain their moral bearings. Such institutions provide reliable social ties where moral attitudes and behaviors are acquired and maintained. The field of moral psychology also documents the social embeddedness of moral development. Personal relationships and social experiences play a pertinent role in shaping an individual's moral commitments, beliefs, and behavior (Colby and Damon 1995; Damon 1988; Hart, Atkins, and Ford 1998; Hart and Fegley 1995; Youniss, McLellan, Su, and Yates 1999; Youniss, McLellan, and Yates 1999). Specifically, these studies also reveal that religious and social influences play a significant role in the lives of highly moral individuals.

Social Capital

How can religion provide such a moral milieu – an environment conducive to nurturing moral commitment, attitudes, and actions? Is there something unique about a religious environment that fosters moral development? Despite the rapidly growing body of literature on religion and moral outcomes, little is understood about the psychosocial processes underlying religion's positive association with moral behavior. Drawing upon social capital theory, this paper proposes a theoretical framework for understanding the role of the religious social context in promoting moral development.

Social capital theory has its roots in the field of sociology and is used to conceptualize the links between individuals and their context. Since its inception in the 1980s, social capital has taken on many different meanings as it has been applied to different social issues. In general, social capital refers to benefits garnered through social ties. Social capital exists in relationships between persons – whether personal or associational relationships – and produces something of value for those involved. The first theorists to use social capital emphasized this relational and beneficiary nature of social capital (Bourdieu 1985; Coleman 1988; 1990). Although early theoretical development conceptualized social capital as an individual asset, more recent theorists have extended the concept to be a community or even a national resource (Putman 1993 and 1995).

In general, research on social capital and youth emphasizes the interpersonal nature of social capital, examining the benefits that accrue to young people through relationships. Scholars have demonstrated that youths with a greater number of, and deeper, social ties inside and outside the family reported higher levels of academic achievement and prosocial outcomes (Coleman 1988; Furstenberg et al. 1999; Kahne and Bailey 1999; King, Furrow, and Roth 2002). Coleman posited that developmental benefits are socially embedded, meaning that they take place and take shape in a network of personal relations. Coleman identified three forms of social capital that can be described as social trust, social networks, and social norms. According to Coleman, these forms are manifested in reciprocity exchanges and obligations, information channels, and shared norms and expectations, respectively.

Social capital provides a helpful lens for understanding how benefits are embedded in a social context and can be applied specifically to understanding the relevant social processes in the religious context. In doing so, we can begin to decipher how resources for moral development might be embedded in the social networks associated with religious participation. Just as relationships with parents mediate academic and prosocial benefits, relationships available through religious participation might mediate moral outcomes. This being the case, social capital provides theoretical insight into religion's association with moral outcomes.

While social capital offers insight into the potential richness of religious involvement, a specific formulation is needed in order to illustrate the interpersonal dynamics and benefits garnered through these dynamics. This chapter identifies three aspects of social capital that potentially affect the lives of children: social interaction, trust, and shared vision. Tsai and Ghoshal (1998) refer to these as the structural, relational, and cognitive dimensions of social capital. The structural dimension refers to social interaction that takes place in communication and shared activities. The relational aspect of social capital is indicated by trust, closeness, cohesion, and trustworthiness. The cognitive dimension is manifested in having a shared vision of mutually held beliefs, values, and goals. This chapter will use this three-dimensional conceptualization of social capital as a framework to understand how a religious social context might impact moral development in US and South Korean youth.

Social Capital and the Religious Context

The impact of social interaction, trust, and shared vision on children is evident in the religious context. Although social capital has not been explicitly examined in the church context, several studies illustrate the dynamics of social capital present in faith communities. The significance of social interaction is illustrated in the development of faith. Studies demonstrate that religious interaction, such as family devotions, family worship, conversations about faith or spirituality, and family service projects, predicts higher levels of reported adolescent religious saliency and commitment (Erickson 1992; King, Furrow, and Roth 2002; Lee, Rice, and Gillespie 1997; Roehlkepartain and Benson 1993). The relational dimension of trust also plays an important function in promoting religious development. For example, perceived parent-child closeness, warmth, and expression are associated with increased religiousness in youth (Pearce and Adinn 1998; Tamminen 1994; Wilcox 1998). Adolescents from families with higher levels of emotional closeness are more likely to share their parents' religious convictions over time (Ozorak 1989). The cognitive dimension, described as shared vision, is extremely relevant to the religious context. Social science research reveals the potential significance of shared religious beliefs between parent and child. Religious beliefs play an important supportive role in families, even where there is much stress, as a protective factor for developmental resiliency (McAdoo 1995; Walsh 1998). Shared religious beliefs between adolescent child and parent have an indirect effect on decreased levels of anomie (Bjarnason 1998).

Although the dynamics of social capital have not been explicitly studied in the religious context, religious participation is acknowledged as a source of social capital (Coleman 1988; Furstenberg et al. 1999;

Furstenberg and Hughes 1995; Hart and Fegley 1995; Stolle and Rochon 1998). Religion is noted to be one of the most effective structures in society that nurture social trust for shaping social norms, beliefs, and actions (Fukuyama 1995; Rahn and Transue 1998; Stolle and Rochon 1998). Social capital theory is a helpful organizing theory to apply to the religious social context because it begins to explain the relationships between interpersonal ties and benefits mediated through them. A three-dimensional model of social capital demonstrates how social interaction, trust, and shared vision might enable these social ties within the religious context to be associated with moral outcomes.

A Proposed Model

The purpose of this chapter is to propose a theoretical framework that offers insight into the positive association of religious participation and moral outcomes. In order to accomplish this, three underlying questions must be asked. First, how might the religious influence on moral behavior be understood in the social context of the adolescent? This question is based on the recognition that moral behaviors are socially influenced and that religion does not have to be conceptualized merely as beliefs but can also be understood in terms of a social context. The second question, which follows these assumptions, is to what degree are social resources mediated through the religious social context? Finally, to more fully understand the influence of the social context, this study asks and explores what social factors most influence moral behaviors in adolescents.

In short, the proposed model uses social capital to understand the dynamics in the religious social context that impact moral outcomes. Figure 10.1 demonstrates the relationship between adolescent religiousness, social capitol dimension, and moral behavior. It is suggested that religious participation provides access to social capital resources and that the presence of interactive, trusting, mutual relationships promotes commitment to a moral code and the presence of moral behaviors.

In addition, drawing upon an ecological understanding of human development (Bronfenbrenner 1979) and evidence of the power of combined contextual influences (Jessor et al. 1995; Lerner and Galambos 1998), this model addresses the relations most proximal to the lives of youth. Influences of parents, peers, and nonparental adults are taken into consideration. It is suggested that the confluence of multiple influences across relational domains will have greater influence on moral outcomes than the individual influences of parents, friends, and adults.

The proposed model suggests that social interaction, trust, and shared vision experienced in relationships with parents, peers, and adults will

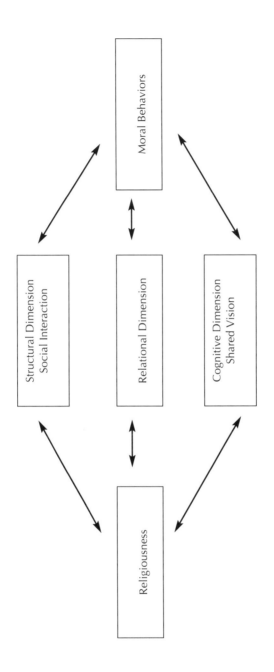

Figure 10.1 Relationship between Adolescent Religiousness, Social Capital Dimensions, and Moral Behavior

contribute to the presence of adolescent moral behavior. By integrating the concept of the confluence of relational influences, the three-dimensional model elucidates the social processes within religion that serve as a resource for moral outcomes for adolescents. Figure 10.2 illustrates the proposed model of the unique and combined influences of the parental, peer, and adult social capital dimensions and their effects on moral behaviors.

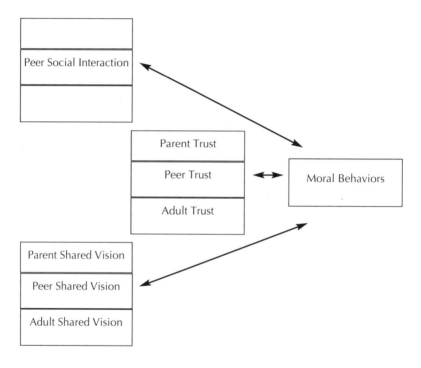

Figure 10.2 Relationship of Social Capital Dimensions and Relational Domains and Moral Behaviors

Two Samples Considered

This framework has been applied to two samples in distinct settings (see King 2000; King and Park 2002). The first sample consisted of American youth (N = 1524) from the Los Angeles metropolitan area with ages ranging from 13 to 19 (M = 15.89; SD = 1.24). Females represented 53 percent of the population with the majority of the students being Christian. The second sample was collected in the Seoul metropolitan area (N = 1204). The ages ranged from 12 to 18 years old (M = 15.32, SD = 1.30) and the sample was equally split between genders. Thirteen percent of the Korean sample reported being Buddhist, 43 percent Protestant, 11 percent Catholic, and 32 percent reported having no religion. Both samples represented the ethnic, socioeconomic, and religious diversity of those areas. Data was collected using a 190-item self-report questionnaire that measured both attitudinal and behavioral dimensions of religiousness; parent, peer, and adult social capital resources; and moral outcomes as indicated by altruism, empathy, volunteer service, and filial piety (Korean sample only).

In each sample analyses first explored whether a significant difference existed between religiously active youth and less religiously active youth. Second, the entire model (figure 10.2) was tested in each population in order to determine the social capital resources relevant to influencing moral behavior in a religious social context.

American Findings

One-way analysis of variance revealed that religious youth reported higher levels of all the social capital resources than their less religious peers – with one exception. Levels of reported parent trust were not significantly different in the religiously active and the less religiously active. With that exception in mind, youth who more frequently attended a religious congregation reported higher levels of social interaction, trust, and shared vision with their parents, peers, and other adults. Being religiously active seemed to provide access to more social capital resources for this group of youth.

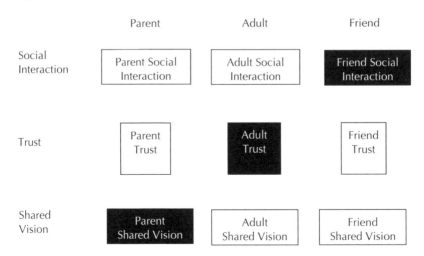

Figure 10.3   American Findings

Furthermore, the general model was validated among the American adolescents. Analyses revealed that social capital resources explained 24 percent of the variance of the moral outcomes. Social interaction, trust, and shared vision each significantly contributed to moral outcomes in youth. Additionally, parents, peers, and other adults each made unique contributions. However, not all influences were equal. The factors that most strongly influenced moral outcomes in this sample were having a sense of shared vision with parents, being in a trusting relationship with an adult, and engaging in positive communication and interaction with one's peers (figure 10.3).

Such findings affirm the presupposition that moral behavior is shaped by one's environment, suggesting that an optimal environment for nurturing moral development would include interactive, trusting, mutual relationships. Relationships in which youth have rich communication, meaningful interaction, an experience of trust, and a clear sense of shared values and expectations among their parents, friends, and other adults seem to be associated with positive moral outcomes. Such findings suggest that youth need a web of support that runs both wide and deep. The web must run wide across the important relationships in their lives. Much ink has been spilled debating whether parents or peers have more influence on adolescents (Harris 1998). These findings suggest that when it comes to developmental resources, more is more. Youth benefit from the positive influence of their parents, their friends, and significant adults in their lives. The web not only runs wide, but deep as well. Youth need more than spending time with these key people in their lives. In addition, they need to experience trusting, close relationships that encourage them to internalize explicit beliefs and values.

Given that the religiously active youth report more of such relationships, the findings suggest that religious settings provide unique opportunities for these connections to take place. Perhaps the existence of intergenerational relationships, the intention of following a moral code as a community of believers, and the presence of trusting relationships create opportunities for youths to form moral commitments in the religious context. That being said, most congregations, religious schools, and character education programs overlook the crucial role of the social context. Limiting moral education to cognitive abstractions of religious beliefs, family values, or ethical standards is to miss the nurturing role of the moral milieu – at least in American youth.

Korean Findings

The findings within the Korean population presented a different picture. When looking at the Korean sample as a whole, frequency of religious attendance does not serve to show a clear pattern of those who report higher levels of social capital resources than others (see King and Park 2002). Perhaps the religious diversity of Korea contributes to these finding in two ways. First, the largest religious group represented followed Buddhism, which does not emphasize religious services, meetings, or fellowship in the same way that Judeo-Christian traditions do. Consequently, religion is experienced less in explicit social gatherings. Second, the prevailing religious diversity within Korean culture and the relatively new introduction of Christianity to 5,000-year-old cultural patterns might prohibit religious institutions from affecting the social structure and social relations of Korean society (Song, Smetana, and Kim 1987). This would be in sharp contrast to the United States, which has a fairly homogeneous religious population. Until the more recent past, the local synagogue and church have been woven into the social fabric of American society.

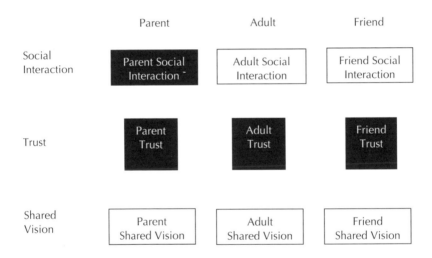

Figure 10.4   Korean Findings

These social differences are apparent in the findings when looking at the model as a whole. The American sample supported the general model – affirming the significance of social interaction, trust, and shared vision as well as the importance of parents, peers, and other adults. However, the Korean sample's results were not as conclusive. What is most evident among the Korean youth sampled is the role of trust (figure 10.4). Within this sample of Korean youth, trust overwhelmingly plays the most significant role in predicting the moral outcomes.

Trusting relationships with parents, friends, and other adults were each important. In addition to trust, communication and shared activities with parents were also significant predictors of the outcomes. Perhaps the most surprising finding was the insignificant role of shared vision across each relational domain. This provides a sharp contrast to the American population where shared vision with parents was the most influential factor.

The findings suggest that these interpersonal factors of social capital modestly predict the moral outcomes in Korean culture, explaining only 17 percent of the variance. The model seems to be missing significant factors that influence moral behaviors in Korean youth. Reflection on Korean social dynamics suggests that perhaps cultural capital, rather than social capital, may be more helpful for understanding influences on moral behaviors in Korean youth. Cultural capital refers to resources or influences embedded not in interpersonal relations but in society at large. In ecological terms, these are macrosystemic issues, such as cultural values. Korean culture has been grounded in the ethics of Confucius for the last 5,000 years. The Confucian ethical maxims of duty, loyalty, obedience to authority, and care have laid the foundation for social interactions not just for centuries but for millennia. Given the pervasiveness of these cultural norms, it is not surprising that interpersonal factors do not impact behaviors that have been proscribed by a traditional ethical code. Given the power and influence of these traditions, having beliefs and goals in common with your parents may in fact not have much influence on one's duty towards them as displayed in filial piety. Filial piety is more of a cultural mandate than a social option.

The different findings in the two samples affirm the role of contextual influences on moral behavior. Moral behavior in American youth appears to be explained to a larger extent by interpersonal factors. Moral behavior in Korean youths, however, is less effectively predicted by social capital but perhaps is more a product of cultural capital. Shweder and colleagues (1987) have acknowledged such cultural differences. He explains that in Western cultures moral development occurs at the individual level. In contrast, in other cultures such as that of Korea, the community carries the burden of moral education. The findings of this Korean sample are consistent with Shweder's understanding, demonstrating that interpersonal relations do not impact on moral behavior in youth to the same extent as they do within a Western context.

Implications for Moral Education

The theoretical framework posited in this paper suggests that moral development is nurtured in the presence of interactive, trusting, and mutual relationships. The insights gained from social capital highlight places of developmental leverage within the religious social context. Although faith communities are often first spiritual groups and exist to promote and sustain the religious life of their members, they are concerned with the entire well-being of their parishioners, including their moral well-being.

The findings based on the empirical work with Korean and American youth reveal the cultural particularities of social influences on adolescent moral development. It is important to recognize the cultural differences both in the religious context and in moral development. Furthermore, it is noted that cultural values may also vary in their conceptualization of moral constructs such as altruism and may not reflect the particularities of differing traditions (Carlo et al. 1999).

That being said, the structure of the theoretical framework might provide insights into the social process of particular developmental leverage within different social contexts. Furstenberg and Hughes (1995) suggest that social capital processes vary in different cultural, social, and economic groups. For instance, within the American group, parent shared vision, adult trust, and social interaction with friends were most influential factors in predicting moral behaviors. The trust variables across the three relational domains, however, were the most effective among the Korean youth. Such findings suggest that the framework is useful for evaluating or discussing potential developmental resources within different contexts.

Social capital provides a model for evaluating faith-based social programs that seek to increase positive moral outcomes among youth. The three-construct model provides a framework that could be used to assess the ways in which programs promote a durable network across the domains of parents, peers, and nonparental adults. Intervention programs that assume the importance of parent involvement but do not take into account fostering shared goals and values between parent and child may find that they are successful in creating greater social engagement without nurturing moral development.

Mind the Gap!

This next section attempts to jump the epistemological gap between empirical research and the realities of spiritual and moral education of children and adolescents. I will attempt to leap from the banks of positivism, which are supported and maintained by reductionism and empiricism, to the banks of postpositivism, where one is free to wrestle with the particularities of peoples and places. The findings resulting from the particularities of the two cultures send my theoretical framework into a positivist tailspin. Where are the universals? What generalities can I make? That being said, the empiricist in me is not dismayed but rather asks what we can learn. What can we learn from this project that will promote moral lives for young people? I believe there are several potential lessons to be learned.

Based on experience in ministry and informed by the findings of research, I propose a practical model that can serve religious and spiritual educators concerned about nurturing character and caring in their students. I propose that a helpful way of thinking about moral development in the context of religious or spiritual education is to seriously consider the role of the social context. The period of adolescence is strongly characterized by its social susceptibility (Damon 1983; Feldman and Elliott 1990). To an adolescent, relationships are not just something, they are everything. In addition, theoretical and empirical work on moral development strongly suggests the potency of social influences. I believe the framework presented here provides the religious and spiritual educator with a practical means of creating a social environment conducive to moral development.

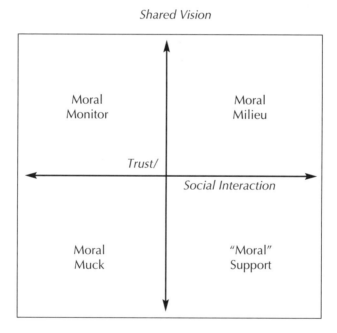

Figure 10.5   Types of Moral Nurturing: Social Contexts

As the findings from the two samples considered here suggest, there is no single best way to promote moral behaviors in adolescents. Figure 10.5 represents four descriptions of social contexts that have the potential to promote moral development. They are based on the social capital resources of social interaction, trust, and shared vision. For the sake of practicality, the typology uses relational and cognitive dimensions to summarize the social capital resources. The vertical axis represents the relational dimension integrating the constructs of trust and social interaction. This axis indicates the level of relational support, experienced in terms of physical presence and interaction (for example, communication and participation) as well as emotional support (for example, trust and respect). The horizontal axis represents the cognitive dimension or shared vision and indicates the degree to which values, goals, and expectations are communicated and shared.

Moral milieu. It is proposed that a social environment that is high both in relational support and in clear goals and expectations serves as a moral milieu – an environment conducive to nurturing adolescent moral development. In this environment individuals in a youth's life are physically present, are perceived as trustworthy and respectful of the youth and have clearly articulated moral values and goals. Young people share a sense of moral goals and feel supported by adults and peers in their lives. This situation is depicted in the upper right quadrant of the figure.

Moral monitor. The figure's lower right quadrant is characterized by an atmosphere in which moral values and expectations are clear. This environment may be demanding in terms of moral standards and values but does not provide the trusting, empowering relations often needed for the internalization of moral commitment. This environment acts as a "moral monitor," where ethical maxims regulate individual moral actions without the presence of inductive relationships. Such a social context is conducive to nurturing moral development in individuals who do not need relational support.

Moral support. The upper left quadrant in the figure, high in relational support but low in moral vision, is referred to as having "moral support." This label is tongue-in-cheek, using the term to refer to the emotional encouragement associated with the popular use of the term "moral support" as opposed to a literal meaning. Such "moral support," although relational and kind, lacks explicit moral substance because clear expectations and values are not communicated. This is only effective for moral development in young people who have a strong internal sense or individual clarity of moral convictions and respond well to affirmation and social approval.

Moral muck. The last quadrant of the figure, which is low in both relational support and moral vision, is referred to as "moral muck."

Although hardly academic, the term evokes an image of a place lacking in solid ground on which to stand. Environments that do not provide clear moral standards, goals, values, or expectations for youth do not provide the foundations that enable them to internalize the ideologies necessary to develop purpose and meaning in life, which is so vital to navigating the pitfalls of adolescence. Moreover, such an environment is devoid of the relational support needed for nurturing moral commitment.

Conclusion

In sum, moral action is associated with nurturing relationships that help clarify beliefs and encourage moral behavior; experiences that bring about the transformation of personal goals; and a transcendent system of beliefs that give personal clarity of ideals, meaning, and hope. In some cultures, such as that of the United States, the religious context provides such relationships, experiences, and a moral code in which moral behavior can be nurtured. In other cultures, where religious institutions are not as woven into the social fabric of society, such as South Korea, religion and the interpersonal relationships associated with religious participation only partially explain the presence of moral behavior. Social capital as conceptualized by social interaction, trust, and shared vision provides a helpful lens through which to view the various relational influences that shape moral development.

References

Amey, C. H., Albrecht, S. L., Miller, M. K. 1996: Racial Differences in Adolescent Drug Use: The Impact of Religion. *Substance Use & Misuse* 31: 1311–32.

Benson, P. L., Donahue, M. J., and Erickson, J. A. 1989: Adolescence and religion: a review of the empirical literature 1970–1986. *Social Scientific Study of Religion* 1: 153–81.

Berger, B. and Berger, P. 1983: *The War Over the Family: Capturing the Middle Ground*. Garden City, NY: Anchor Press.

Bjarnason, T. 1998: Parents, religion and perceived social coherence: A Durkheimian framework of adolescent anomie. *Journal for the Scientific Study of Religion* 37: 742–54.

Bourdieu, P. 1985: The Forms of Capital. In J. G. Richardson (ed.), *Handbook of Theory and Research for the Sociology of Education*. New York: Greenwood.

Bronfenbrenner, U. 1979: *The Ecology of Human Development: Experiments by Nature and Design*. Cambridge, MA: Harvard University Press.

Carlo, G., Fabes, R. A., Laible, D., and Kupanoff, K. 1999: Early adolescence and prosocial/moral behavior II: the role of social and contextual influences. *Journal of Early Adolescence* 19: 133–47.

Colby, A. and Damon, W. 1995: The Development of Extraordinary Moral Commitment. In M. Killen and D. Hart et al. (eds.), *Morality in everyday life: Developmental perspectives*. New York: Cambridge University Press.

Coleman, J. S. 1988: Social capital in the creation of human capital. *American Journal of Sociology* 94: S95–S120.

—— 1990: *Foundations of Social Theory*. Cambridge, MA: Harvard University Press.

Damon, W. 1983: *Social and Personality Development*. New York: W. W. Norton & Company.

—— 1988: *The Moral Child: Nurturing Children's Natural Moral Growth*. New York: Free Press.

Donahue, M. J. and Benson, P. L. 1995: Religion and the well-being of adolescents. *Journal of Social Issues* 51: 145–60.

Donelson, E. 1999: Psychology of religion and adolescents in the United States: past to resent. *Journal of Adolescence* 22: 187–204.

Erickson, J. A. 1992: Adolescent religious development and commitment: a structural equation model of the role of family, peer group, and educational influences. *Journal for the Scientific Study of Religion* 31: 131–52.

Feldman, S. S. and Elliott, R. 1990: *At the Threshold*. Cambridge, MA: Harvard University Press.

Fukuyama, F. 1995: *Trust: The Social Virtues and the Creation of Prosperity*. New York: The Free Press.

Furrow, J. L. and Wagener, L. M. 2000: Lessons Learned: The Role of Religion in the Development of Wisdom in Adolescence. In W. S. Brown (ed.), *Understanding Wisdom: Sources, Science, and Society*. Philadelphia: Templeton Foundation Press.

Furstenberg, F. F., Cook, Thomas D., Eccles, J., Elder, G. H. Jr. and Sameroff, A. 1999: *Managing to Make It: Urban Families and Successful Youth*. Chicago: University of Chicago Press.

——, Jr. and Hughes, M.-E. 1995: Social capital and successful development among at-risk Youth. *Journal of Marriage & the Family* 57: 580–92.

Harris, J. 1998: *The Nurture Assumption: Why Children Turn Out the Way They Do: Parents Matter Less than You Think and Peers Matter More*. New York: Free Press.

Hart, D., Atkins, R., and Ford, D. 1998: Urban America as a context for the development of moral identity in adolescence. *Journal of Social Issues* 54: 513–30.

Hart, D. and Fegley, S. 1995: Pro-social behavior and caring in adolescence: relations to self-understanding and social judgment. *Child Development* 66: 1346–59.

Jessor, R., Van Den Bos, J., Vanderryn, J., Costa, F. M. and Turbin, M. S. 1995: Protective factors in adolescent problem behavior: moderator effects and developmental change. *Developmental Psychology* 31: 923–33.

Johnson, B. R., Li, S. De, Larson, D. B., and McCullough, M. 2000: A systematic review of the religiosity and delinquency literature. *Journal of Contemporary Criminal Justice* 16: 32–52.

——, Jang, S. Joon, Larson, D. B., and Li, S. De. 2001: Does adolescent religious commitment matter? A reexamination of the effects of religiosity on delinquency. *Journal of Research in Crime and Delinquency* 38: 22–44.

Kahne, J. and Bailey, K. 1999: The role of social capital in youth development:

the case of "I Have a Dream" programs. *Educational Evaluation and Policy Analysis* 21: 321–43.

King, P. E. 2000: *Adolescent Religiousness and Moral Outcomes: A Proposed Model of Social Capital Resources and Moral Behavior.* Doctoral dissertation, Fuller Theological Seminary, School of Psychology, 2000. *Dissertation Abstracts International*, 0371.

——, Furrow, J. L., and Roth, N. H. 2002: The influence of family and peers on adolescent religiousness. *The Journal for Psychology and Christianity* 21, 2: 109–20.

——, and Park, S. 2002: Culture as Developmental Context: Social Capital and Moral Outcomes among American and Korean Youth. *Biannual Meeting of the Society for Research on Adolescents.* New Orleans.

Lee, J. W., Rice, G. T., and Gillespie, V. B. 1997: Family worship patterns and their correlation with adolescent behavior and beliefs. *Journal for the Scientific Study of Religion* 36: 372–81.

Lerner, R. M. and Galambos, N. L. 1998: Adolescent development: challenges and opportunities for research, programs, and policies. *Adolescent Development* 49: 413–46.

McAdoo, H. P. 1995: Stress levels, family help patterns, and religiosity in middle- and working-class African American single mothers. *Journal of Black Psychology* 21: 424–49.

McBride, D. C., Mutch, P. B., and Chitwood, D. D. 1996: Religious Belief and the Initiation and Prevention of Drug Use among Youth. In C. B. McCoy, L. R. Metsch, et al. (eds.), *Intervening with Drug-Involved Youth.* Thousand Oaks, CA: Sage Publications, Inc.

Ozorak, E. W. 1989: Social and cognitive influences on the development of religious beliefs and commitment in adolescence. *Journal for the Scientific Study of Religion* 23: 448–63.

Pearce, L. D. and Adinn, W. G. 1998: The impact of family religious life on the quality of mother–child relations. *American Sociological Review* 63: 810–28.

Putman, R. D. 1993: The prosperous community: Social capital and public life. *The American Prospect* 13.

—— 1995: Bowling alone: America's declining social capital. *Journal of Democracy* 6: 65–78.

Rahn, W. M. and Transue, J. E. 1998: Social trust and value change: the decline of social capital in American youth, 1976–1995. *Political Psychology* 19: 545–65.

Resnick, M. D., Bearman, P. S., Blum, R. W., Bauman, K. K., Harris, K. M., Jones, J. I., Tabor, J., et al. 1997: Protecting adolescents from harm: findings from the National Longitudinal Study on Adolescent Health. *Journal of the American Medical Association* 278: 823–32.

Roehlkepartain, E. C. and Benson, P. L. 1993: *Youth in Protestant Churches.* Minneapolis: Search Institute.

Serow, R. C. and Dreyden, J. I. 1990. Community service among college and university students: individual and institutional relationships. *Adolescence* 25: 553–66.

Shweder, R. A., Mahapartra, M., and Miller, J. G. 1987: Culture and Moral

Development. In J. Kagan and S. Lamb, *The Emergence of Morality in Young.* Chicago: University of Chicago Press.

Song, M.-J., Smetana, J. G., and Kim, S. Y. 1987: Korean children's conceptions of moral and conventional transgressions. *Developmental Psychology* 23: 577–82.

Stolle, D. and Rochon, T. R. 1998: Are all associations alike? Member diversity, associational type, and the creation of social capital. *American Behavioral Scientist* 42: 47–65.

Tamminen, K. 1994: Religious experiences in childhood and adolescence: a viewpoint of religious development between the ages of 7 and 20. *The International Journal for the Psychology of Religion* 4: 61–85.

Tsai, W., and S. Ghoshal. 1998: Social capital and value creation: The role of intrafirm networks. *Academy of Management Journal* 41 (4): 464–76.

Wagener, L. M., J. L. Furrow, P. E. King, N. Leffert and P. Benson. 2003: Religion and developmental resources. *Review of Religious Research* 44 (3): 271–284.

Wallace, J. M., Jr., and T. A. Forman. 1998: Religion's role in promoting health and reducing risk among American youth. *Health Education and Behavior* 25 (6): 721–41.

Walsh, F. 1998: Beliefs, spirituality and transcendence: Keys to family resilience. In M. McGoldrick (ed.), *Revisioning family therapy: Race, culture and gender in clinical practice,* pp. 62–77. New York: The Guilford Press.

Wilcox, W. B. 1998: Conservative Protestant childrearing: Authoritarian or authoritative? *American Sociological Review* 63: 796–809.

Youniss, J., J. A. McLellan and M. Yates. 1999: Religion, community service and identity in American youth. *Journal of Adolescence* 22 (2): 243–253.

———, J. A. McLellan, Y. Su and M. Yates. 1999: The role of community service in identity development: Normative, unconventional and deviant orientations. *Journal of Adolescent Research* 14 (2): 248–261.

Chapter 11

Using Children's Literature for Spiritual Development

ANN M. TROUSDALE

I WAS ONE OF THOSE fortunate children born into a family of story-
tellers. On summer evenings we would gather on the screened porch
under a lazy ceiling fan, in winter around the fireplace in the living
room, and the grown-ups would tell stories – stories about the day's
events, about local characters, stories about a recent hunting or fishing
trip, anecdotes, jokes . . . stories told for amusement primarily, or to pass
along information about what had taken place in town that day. But
occasionally the stories had a deeper impact.

Every year when the pecan crop came in, my father's friend King
Stubbs would bring over a sack of pecans from the Stubbs pecan
orchard, and then in the evenings we would crack the pecans while the
grown-ups talked. Daddy would tell the story of how King's father,
whom we called Uncle Guy, had had a dream of developing a pecan
orchard, how he saved every penny he could to buy more land to plant
trees. Pretty soon he had a good bit of acreage – and then the Great
Depression hit. Everybody was hurting financially, of course, and just
to keep things going, to fertilize and harvest, and to keep his family in
food and clothing, Uncle Guy had to borrow money against the crop.
And Daddy told how every year, when the crop came in, the first thing
Uncle Guy did, before he brought any money home, was to go to every
person in town who had loaned him money and pay them back. Then
he would take what was left home for his family's needs. That's all. He
just told the story. But the impact on me was tremendous. Oh, I thought,
that's who we are. We're people who pay our debts. We're people who
honor the trust other people have placed in us. And we do that before
we attend to our own wants and needs. No amount of preaching or
sermonizing could have made that truth, that principle, more deeply
implanted in my soul. A story did it.

Why do stories affect us so profoundly? According to Jerome Bruner, there are two primary modes of human thought, two "distinctive ways of ordering experience, of constructing reality" (Bruner 1986: 11). One is the paradigmatic mode, which operates on a vertical axis, if you will, describing and explaining phenomena according to categories, which are related to one another to form a system. This mode of thought, which Bruner also calls the logico-scientific mode, deals in general causes and is concerned with verifiable empirical truth. The second mode of thought is the narrative, formed along a horizontal axis, a mode of thought that seeks not to establish formal and empirical truth but verisimilitude, likeness to life. Bruner comments upon the "heartless-ness" of logical thought, whereas, he says, "narrative is built upon concern for the human condition" (1986: 14).

The human impulse toward story reaches as far back as we can remember, perhaps even farther. In describing the origin of story, the great storyteller Ruth Sawyer (1962) would take us back to prehistoric days, when our ancestors lived in caves or trees, clad if at all in rough skins, when their only concern was the urgent everyday need to hunt for food in order to survive – or to defend themselves from being hunted for food in order to survive. Some who study the history of language have suggested that human language was developed by these early hunters to communicate where the wild boar was lurking in the under-brush or on what branch of the tree crouched a panther.

Sawyer says that the first primitive efforts at conscious storytelling likely began as impromptu first-person chants exulting in some act of bravery or accomplishment. Gradually these chants developed into prose narratives, and the narrow focus on one's own accomplishments broadened to include family, tribe, and others; thus the third-person narrative came into being (Sawyer 1962). If the rudiments of language – grunts and gestures, perhaps the first words – were developed for basic communication, surely the beauty of language, the poetry of language, the subtleties of language, were developed for story.

Stories of great exploits, deeds of great daring or courage, were told and retold, and an appreciation for courage was passed along. Yes, courage was good. As stories of extraordinary kindness or generosity were told, an appreciation for generosity, for kindness, was passed along. A mother interposed herself between a hungry lion and her child, giving her life for the life of her child, and the value of self-sacrificial love was recognized. And so cultural values were developed and passed along through story.

Did such concepts come first, with story being developed to illustrate them, to give them shape? Or did story come first, the relating of people's deeds giving rise to an understanding of such values as courage or sacrificial love? In whatever way the relationship between values and story developed, the relationship is there. It is something every great teacher, every great spiritual leader, has understood.

Let us consider the time when our ancestors, having the leisure to pause for a few moments, sat back on their heels, lifted their heads, and looked about themselves. A few questions must have come to mind.

Who am I?

What is this place that I live in, and how did it come to be?

Look how the sun goes across the sky every day and then leaves us in darkness until it comes again. Why does it do that?

Is there some force beyond what we can see that makes it do that? If there is such a force, what is it like?

Then, perhaps casting an eye on its offspring as well as on others in the group, wondering, How am I to relate to these other people? What about this world we live in: is it friendly, or hostile? How am I to understand my relationship with it?

And, ultimately, noting the cycles of birth and death, asking, What does my life mean?

These are the great questions that have been intriguing the human race ever since. What was humankind's first response to these questions? Was it to develop compasses and gyroscopes, measuring rods and telescopes, to study and understand such phenomena? No, it was to develop stories. Stories that explain how we came to be here, how to understand the natural phenomena around us, to explain what force or forces control and uphold the universe. These are the stories we know as myth; every culture has developed them.

If one had been able to go from clan to clan, from continent to continent, to hear these early stories, one would likely have been struck by basic similarities among them, as well as by differences, shadings in values or understandings. And so children grew up, their perceptions of the world influenced by the stories of their culture. As we hear these stories today, we become aware of the many connections we have with people of other cultures, of how similar we are in our basic impulses and desires.

Today we more often encounter story in the written mode, but the power of story is in no way diminished in contemporary times. As one of my seminary professors put it, there's something almost hypnotic, almost trancelike that happens when one is reading a good book. The story takes you to another world, and when you finish the story and look around you, your world is different somehow. You are different. The story has affected how you see the world. When a story does that, it has transformational power. It has revelatory power.

Why should story affect us on such deep levels? Why should a story bring home to me the value of honesty, of meeting one's obligations, in a way that preaching about it never would have? Do we refrain from killing because the law says, "Do not kill"? Or because when we read stories about killing, we see what it means to kill; these are the consequences?[1] Narrative somehow has an inner persuasiveness, as Bakhtin has pointed out; it works in us on a level that authoritative discourse, discourse that seeks to tell us what or how to think, simply cannot attain (cited in Rosen 1986).

In recent years literary theorists have brought forth various explanations for what happens when readers engage with literary texts. Such reader-response theorists as Louise Rosenblatt (1978) and Wolfgang Iser (1978) have taken us beyond the view that a work of literature has one meaning that every reader should arrive at. According to Rosenblatt, the meaning of a literary work does not reside on the pages of the text but comes into being in the transaction that occurs between the reader and the text. What the reader brings to the text – life experiences, present preoccupations, purposes for reading, even the setting where the reading takes place – all influence the meaning the reader will make of the text.

Iser points out that an effective writer or storyteller leaves gaps, or blanks, in the text, when information is not made explicit, perhaps the character's motivation or emotional response to an event. The reader fills in those gaps, is drawn into the text by supplying what is meant by what is not said. The text continues to guide, to confirm, or to correct the reader's inferences, as the reader continually casts forward toward a future horizon of possibilities, while retaining the "past horizon that is already filled" (Iser 1978: 111). Thus in reading a work of literature, the reader is "composing" the story in his or her own mind; the story is in effect being "rewritten by the reader, rewritten so as to allow play for the reader's imagination" (cited in Bruner 1986: 35).

For me, it is the filling in of these gaps – the making of inferences, the act of interpreting – that gives story its power. It is the coming to sudden realizations, seeing the connections between motivations and actions and consequences, making judgments, drawing conclusions, that allow us to connect with the story in a way that is relevant and authentic for our own lives. My father's story about Uncle Guy held up a possible model for me and allowed me to judge, to decide whether it was a model I wanted to follow. I decided it was.

Here studies in reader response to literature urge a word of caution, however; no matter how profoundly we feel that we have understood the meaning of a story, we must not assume that others find the same meaning, that the story has struck the same chord in someone else. Once, at a storytelling festival, I listened to a beautifully told story that was speaking directly to an issue in my life at that moment. The story was having revelatory power for me. The storyteller finished the story.

"Ah," I sighed, satisfied – and enlightened. Then he spoke again, to add the "moral" of the story, which was not at all what the story had said to me; in fact the moral he attached to the story seemed rather glib, relating to the most superficial level of the story's events. For me the spell the story had cast had been broken, the purity of its message distorted.

Many of us have had the experience of walking out of a movie with a friend and beginning to discuss it, only to find that the two of us seemed to have seen two different movies, or different versions of the same story. Or we have had the experience of reading a book or a poem and having it speak very powerfully, and then months or years later reading it again only to find that it had somehow lost its punch, its immediacy. I propose that this is because our transaction with the text is affected by who we are and what we bring to the present encounter. My male friends often focus on a different aspect of a story than I do, and the response of adults and children to the same story is often very different.

How tempted we are to read or tell a story to a child and then explain to the child what the story means, to trot out a "moral lesson" that we want the story to teach the child. What is the result? The meaning the child has made of the story – likely different from ours but equally valid – has been violated, denied. It gives the child the message that the meaning she has found in the story is somehow "incorrect." This is not only disempowering, it turns what had been a pleasurable experience into a slightly unpleasant, troubling one. And, finally, it is probably useless.

For years adults have known – or claimed to know – what meanings fairy tales hold for children. My own dissertation research (Trousdale 1987) was a study of young girls' responses to fairy tales, and what I found was that the meanings the stories held for the children were in no way those that adults had claimed they would hold. The children's "morals" or meanings were not at all abstract, but very concrete and rooted in their own experiences. *Snow White* was not about "the evil consequences of narcissism for both parent and child," as Bruno Bettelheim claimed (1977: 203); nor was it a story "about a jealous queen whose vanity destroys her and almost destroys our heroine," as Shelley Duvall (1983) has claimed. For two of the children in my study the moral lesson was a warning against cruelty to others, because of the consequences of being caught (Trousdale 1987: 161), something a child has likely learned the hard way. For the third child it was a lesson never to "trust your eyes. Don't ever trust your eyes like Snow White, 'cause she trusted the wicked queen and she was gonna kill her" (Trousdale 1987: 161). A slightly more sophisticated response, and perhaps not one an adult would derive, but a valid one indeed.

If our approach in using story is not to impose a particular meaning on children's understanding, how then may story be used to foster children's spiritual development? The answer goes back to what our conception of education includes: is it primarily to indoctrinate, or does it also mean "to lead forth"? If it is simply to tell the child what to think, we would do better with catechisms and creeds. If it is to lead forth from a child insights and glimmerings of understanding that are ready to be articulated and explored, then story's our medium.

Let's return to those first questions that our ancestors must have asked. If we may encapsulate them into three, they might be:

Who are we?
Is there a power beyond what we see; and if so, what is it like?
What is our relationship with others and with Creation to be?

These questions are the foundations of the fields of anthropology, theology, and ethics. It seems to me that these are three basic questions we have about life. They are the questions that prompt our spiritual searching. They are the questions that religions seek to answer. There are many children's books that raise these questions in ways that children might consider. In the following section I discuss several examples of these types of stories.

Universal Concerns

In *Old Turtle* (1992) Douglas Wood takes the reader back in history to the days when all animals and beings can speak and understand one another. But an argument begins. The breeze says that God is a wind who is never still; the stone says that God is a great rock that never moves. The fish says that God is a swimmer; the antelope, a runner. Their perceptions of God are rooted in and limited to their own natures. The argument grows louder and louder until finally Old Turtle, who seldom says anything, speaks.

Old Turtle encompasses all the creatures' understandings of God and goes beyond them, into the realm of mystery. The arguing ceases. Then God creates another species, humankind, and the pattern, of course, is repeated, until the humans begin to lose a sense of who they had been created to be and who God is. They misuse their power and begin to hurt each other and to harm the earth. Again Old Turtle stops the argument, and now the creatures – the stone, the breeze, the antelope, the fish – speak of their broadened perceptions of God. And after a long time the people listen and begin to understand.

Old Turtle offers explorations of all three questions: the nature of humankind, the nature of the Divine, the nature of our relationship to one another and to the earth. It is a story that can be understood by adults on whatever level of experience or understanding they bring to it and understood by children on whatever level of experience or understanding they bring to it.

I suggest that after reading such a book to children, it is not the time to instruct children about the "meaning" of the story but to ask them what they think. This is the time to listen to the child's ideas, to draw them forth, and to engage with the child on the child's level. We will learn a great deal about what our children are thinking – and we will almost certainly discover new levels of meaning we had not considered!

In *Stormy Night*, Michele Lemieux explores a child's nighttime thoughts and questions: Where do we come from? Who decided what the first human would look like? Who am I? Is my whole life already worked out in advance, or will I have to find my way all by myself? I'm afraid that nobody loves me! Are things better after death than in life? (Lemieux 1999.) The book, which is appropriate for children age 10 and up, raises troubling questions but ends on a peaceful and hopeful note.

The human propensity to judge and stigmatize others, and its hurtful effects on those who are so judged, is captured in Max Lucado's *You Are Special* (1997). In this toy fantasy young Punchinello learns that the stigmas don't stick if he checks in daily with his creator, who knows and cares for him just as he is.

The human need for hope, for a vision to follow, is explored in *The Spyglass* (2000) by Richard Paul Evans. The story functions almost as an elaborated parable, for it has a specific point. Here we see through a fictional story the observation in Proverbs 19:18, "Where there is no vision the people perish."

In *The Hunter* (2000), a Chinese folktale retold by Mary Casanova , the value of self-sacrificial love is explored. It invites comparison with stories on similar themes from other spiritual traditions.

Spiritual Quest Books

There are a number of outstanding books that present characters on a spiritual quest, a quest for meaning, for self-understanding, for connection with the universe, or to know what lies "beyond."

John Steptoe's retelling of *The Legend of Jumping Mouse* (1993) is an excellent example for young children. Jumping Mouse has a dream: to see the far-off land. Bravely he sets out for the unknown. Helped on his way by Magic Frog, Jumping Mouse learns the value of friendship, of self-sacrifice, and of hope.

For older children there is Gary Paulsen's *The Island* (1988). In this story Wil Neuton discovers an island on a lake near his home and is drawn to return to the island again and again. There for the first time he observes the natural world closely, discovering hidden truths about nature, about life, about his connection to other living things. He begins to draw and write about what he sees: to dance with the birds, to swim with the fish, to meditate. Through Wil's experience, young people may come to see the possibilities of the richness of a life lived close to nature.

One can hardly discuss children's books that deal with the spiritual lives of children without mentioning Katherine Paterson, an American author who has won both the John Newbery Medal in the United States and the international Hans Christian Andersen Prize for her international contributions to children's literature. Paterson treats children's spiritual concerns with understanding and respect. In *Jacob Have I Loved* (1980), Louise struggles with and finally rejects the narrow and legalistic religion of her family. Robbie, in *Preacher's Boy* (1999), has a hard time with his father's rather liberal understanding of how the Gospel of Christ is to be lived out. For a time Robbie decides to become an "apeist" until he finds his own way to belief. Paterson seems to believe that children's spiritual quests are to be taken seriously and often involve struggle and questioning.

In Sonya Levitin's *The Singing Mountain* (2000), Mitch, a Jewish teenager living in California, has gone to Israel with a group of school friends. He becomes enthralled with the Jewish faith and wants to stay to study in a yeshiva. His parents, who are not observant Jews, fear that he has become involved in a cult. It is hard for his mother and his cousin, who go to Israel to bring him home, to realize that Mitch is on an important journey.

Lois Lowry's Newbery Medal-winning novel *The Giver* (1993) is set in a world that denies a spiritual dimension in life. It is also devoid of color, of emotion, of imagination, of sexuality, of choice. When 12-year-old Jonas is chosen as the Receiver of Memories, he begins to experience for the first time pain, fear, love, a life beyond this bland and carefully controlled dystopia, and when he comes to understand what the euphemism "release" means – killing the elderly and any less-than-perfect infants – he reaches a spiritual crisis and must make a radical, life-changing decision.

Social Critique

Other stories invite us to critique society or prevailing cultural values. An economic structure based on greed and self-aggrandizement is indirectly critiqued in *The Great Kapok Tree* (1990) by Lynne Cherry and more directly challenged in *The Lorax* (1981) by Dr. Seuss. Both books, written for young children, stress humankind's relationship with the earth.

On another level of social critique, the rich and fully realized characters in Mildred Taylor's *Roll of Thunder, Hear My Cry* (1976) offer children a vicarious experience of the effects of racial oppression and injustice.

Conclusions

Mary Elizabeth Moore describes narrative method as "relational teaching." As she points out, "sharing stories grounds people in their heritage and gives expression to their present situation"; it "binds people together even across ideological divides." Stories have the capacity to "enflesh social critique" and to give hope for the future (Moore 1991/1998: 131). Ched Myers has pointed out that for two centuries modernism has waged war on narrative as a way of knowing; Myers makes the plea that we must recover the power of narrative if we are to reconstruct a more humane culture (Myers 2000: 4).

These and other children's books offer tremendous potential for exploring important spiritual questions. But let us remember that while it can be helpful and informative to discuss such books with children, there are times when it is more appropriate to read the story and let it be. To pass along a saying I learned in the storytelling world, let the story expand in the silence that follows.

Note

1 I thank Professor Roy C. Heller of the Perkins School of Theology for these insights.

References

Bettelheim, B. 1977: *The Uses of Enchantment: The Meaning and Importance of Fairy Tales*. New York: Alfred A. Knopf.

Bruner, J. 1986: *Actual Minds, Possible Worlds*. Cambridge, MA: Harvard University Press.

Duvall, S. 1986: *Snow White and the Seven Dwarfs* (videotape). Hollywood: Platypus Productions.

Iser, W. 1978: *The Act of Reading: A Theory of Aesthetic Response*. Baltimore: The Johns Hopkins Press.

Moore, M. E. M. 1991/1998: *Teaching From the Heart*. Harrisburg, PA: Trinity Press International.

Myers, C. 2000: The church, stories and lower education. In *The Witness* 83, 2: 4–5.

Rosen, H. 1986: The Importance of Story. In *Language Arts* 63, 3: 226–37.

Rosenblatt, L. 1978: *The Reader, the Text, the Poem*. Carbondale, IL: Southern Illinois University Press.

Sawyer, R. 1962: *The Way of the Storyteller.* New York: Penguin Books.

Trousdale, A. M. 1987: *The Telling of the Tale: Children's Responses to Fairy Tales Presented Orally and Through the Medium of Film.* Doctoral dissertation, The University of Georgia.

Children's Books

Casanova, Mary (Reteller) 2000: *The Hunter: A Chinese Folktale* (Ed. Young, Illus.). New York: Atheneum.

Cherry, Lynne 1990: *The Great Kapok Tree: A Tale of the Amazon Rain Forest.* San Diego: Harcourt Brace Jovanovich.

Evans, Richard Paul 2000: *The Spyglass* (Jonathan Linton, Illus.). New York: Simon & Schuster.

Levitin, Sonya 2000: *The Singing Mountain.* New York: Aladdin.

Lemieux, Michele 1999: *Stormy Night.* Niagara Falls, NY: Kids Can Press.

Lowry, Lois 1993: *The Giver.* New York: Bantam Doubleday Dell.

Lucado, Max 1997: *You Are Special.* (Sergio Martinez, Illus.). Wheaton, IL: Crossway Books.

Paterson, Katherine 1980: *Jacob Have I Loved.* New York: HarperCollins.

—— 1999: *Preacher's Boy.* New York: Clarion.

Paulsen, Gary 1988: *The Island.* New York: Orchard Books.

Steptoe, John (Reteller) 1993: *The Story of Jumping Mouse.* New York: Scholastic.

Dr. Seuss 1981: *The Lorax.* New York: Random House.

Taylor, Mildred 1976: *Roll of Thunder, Hear My Cry.* New York: Bantam Books.

Wood, Douglas 1992: *Old Turtle* (Cheng-Khee Chee, Illus.) Duluth, MN: Pfeifer-Hamilton Publishers.

Chapter 12

Modalities of
Theological Reasoning

HOWARD DEITCHER AND JEN GLASER

D ISCUSSIONS ABOUT GOD are culturally sensitive, reflecting the way in which religious traditions give expression to immanent and transcendent relationships – relationships that in turn provide parameters for the way children raised within religious traditions think through theological issues.

This essay explores two issues relating to theological understanding:

1   The way individuals characterize "knowledge of God," and the relation between "knowledge of God" and "feeling God's presence";

2   The way in which cultural context and religious tradition shape young people's thinking about God.

Within the essay we draw upon an interview with Maya, a 14-year-old girl from a traditional Sephardic Jewish Israeli family.[1] We have chosen to explore these issues in our reflections on this interview because we believe that Maya's spontaneous, raw articulation of theological sensitivities and commitments offers rich insight into our thinking about modalities of theological reasoning; insights that tend to be distorted or lost when viewed through the adult lens of traditional theistic categories.

In analyzing sections from this dialogue, we will draw upon the important work of Michael Polayni (Polayni 1974; Polayni and Prosch 1975). Significantly, in this essay we are not seeking to make generalizations about children's theological positions but rather to explore possibilities concerning the structural and cultural basis of Maya's thinking.

We believe this research has important implications for the way educators explore students' beliefs and their claims to knowledge, and for the way we explore aspects of spirituality and belief in teaching and learning.

Awareness, Knowledge, and Inference

In addressing fundamental questions of knowledge – what do we know and how do we know it? – Michael Polayni points to two forms of awareness that play a role in knowing something: focal awareness and subsidiary awareness. These two forms of awareness, and the distinct forms of knowing that are attached to them, are illuminated sharply when we think of what it takes to perform a skilled task.

Take the skill of hammering a nail into a wall. When driving in the nail, I have my attention fixed on the nail and (I hope) on the fingers of my left hand. With my attention thus fixed, I reach back with the hammer and swing it toward the nail. As I watch the effects of my strokes, my *focal awareness* is of driving in the nail – this is the direct object of my attention. But clearly this is not all that I am aware of. I am also aware of my grip on the hammer. I am aware of the amount of force exerted – the difference between a gentle tap and a powerful swing. Polayni argues that I am aware of the grip and the force in a way different from the way in which I am focally aware of driving in the nail. I am aware of them not as direct objects of my attention, but in a subsidiary way as they functionally contribute to driving in the nail. We might say that *knowing how to drive in a nail* is in part constituted by a subsidiary functional knowledge of the pressure of my grip, the tension in my muscles, and the motion of the swing (and so on) as I attend to this task. It is the kind of tacit, sensory knowledge that comes into play as we attend explicitly to something else.

Polayni's claim is that *all* knowing involves some form of subsidiary, or tacit, knowledge that is grounded not in theoretical constructs or principles of argumentation but in sensory awareness. He describes this form of knowledge as arrived at through *in-dwelling* – a subsidiary bodily or sensory knowledge we employ as we attend to other things. Take the case of playing the piano. Think of the change that occurs when our focal attention shifts from the music we are playing to our fingers as we play it. In focusing directly on our fingers, we lose the kind of sensory awareness we had of them as we experienced them function-ally in relation to the music. When our focus was on the music, our knowledge of our fingers was not as something *watched* in themselves but was a functional knowledge of them as they contribute to the object of our focal attention, the music.

An important feature of this subsidiary form of knowledge is that it is not something that we can hold up for examination by making it the direct object of our attention. If we do this, we lose the very sensory quality of in-dwelling as it appears functionally in establishing the object of our focal attention. As Polayni points out (Polayni and Prosch 1975: 38), "we can paralyze the performance of a skill by turning our attention away from its performance and concentrating instead on the several motions that compose the performance."

In brief, what Polayni is challenging here is the split between cognitive and affective domains whereby the cognitive is associated with claims to knowledge, and the affective is linked to the realm of sensory experience and personal judgment.[2] Polayni challenges this split not by rejecting the distinction between categories but by suggesting that *all* knowledge claims involve both cognitive and affective dimensions. The important distinction for Polayni is not between cognitive and affective domains but between focal and subsidiary awareness (focal attention and in-dwelling) as they play out in our everyday engagement with the world and find articulation in our knowledge claims.[3]

But what does this focus on two modes of knowing contribute to our understanding of theological reasoning? For Polayni, as for ourselves, the importance of drawing attention to this distinction is in order to clarify the difference between two kinds of inference that each play a role in knowledge claims: explicit and tacit inference.

Explicit inference is the kind of inference in which we draw conclusions by an explicit deduction. Here the inference itself occupies the focal target of our activity; it is the direct object of our attention. Functionally, in Michael Scriven's words, explicit inferences seek to "get from old truths to new truths, from the known to the unknown, from the accepted to the debatable (in order to make it less debatable), and so on . . . " (Scriven 1977: 57). We might see the traditional rational proofs of God's existence fitting into this category. Such proofs strive to provide knowledge of God by reasoning from premises to conclusion, where the premises are themselves the focal target of the reasoner's attention. We also find this approach in Simone De Roos's recent study exploring young children's descriptions of God in which the research questions posed to the children included such queries as "What does God look like?" "Is God a man or a woman or something else?" and "What is God able to do?" Such questions seek to arrive at an understanding of children's theological reasoning by leading children to articulate propositionally what they know about God when God becomes the direct object (focal object) of their attention (De Roos, Iedema and Miedema 2001: 19–30).

The kind of inference associated with subsidiary knowing is different. Rather than connecting two things (premise and conclusion), such inference plays a tacit integrative function, integrating elements that we are subsidiarily aware of as we attend to something else (the focal object). Good illustrations of tacit integration can be found in optical puzzles. In Ames's skewed-room experiment we are asked which of the two people in the room is taller, the boy standing at the back of the room, or the man standing at the front. As long as we remain focused on the people and only subsidiarily aware of the room, the boy will look taller than the man. The illusion is caused by the skewed construction of the room in which the walls angle slightly toward the back, the floor slopes upward, and the ceiling gets lower from front to back. In focusing our attention on the people, we integrate our subsidiary experiencing of the room as if it has greater depth than it indeed has. Such integration involves seeing the receding floor line as a factor of distance and adjusting our expectations of height relative to distance accordingly. We do this as we look at the people. Importantly, the patterning such integration takes will depend on our previous experiences of integrating just this sort of sensory information into judgments of perspective (Polayni and Prosch 1975: 41–3).[4] In the case of the Ames room, correcting the illusion requires us to turn our attention to the structural way in which the room has been skewed – a process that involves transforming the object of our subsidiary awareness into the focal target of our attention. With the focus thus shifted, we process the information in a different light and come to a different conclusion about the height of the man and boy. This tacit integrative function has a bearing on the way we give meaning to what we focally see or experience. Usually we only become aware of this integrative function when the tacit inference turns out to be mistaken; for instance, when we see a person out of the corner of our eye and think we recognize someone we know, only to realize it is a total stranger when we turn and look at the person directly.

What we are suggesting is that the role this tacit integrative function might play in religious reasoning is very different from the kind of role inference plays in explicit theological argumentation. We might see the way such tacit integration is present in theological reasoning through the philosophy of Martin Buber. For Buber, God's presence is experienced as a form of subsidiary awareness of "being in relation" as we focally attend to the world around us. It is this "knowledge of God" as an in-dwelling – as a subsidiary sensory awareness of "being in relation" as we attend to something else – that is functionally integrated into our theological understanding and into our relationship with others and the world.

Such a view of religious knowing challenges the idea often put forth that children's first encounter with God is through words, a claim that seeks to differentiate children's understanding of God from their understanding of other abstract concepts. The claim here is that while children's cognitive understanding of everyday concepts (concepts of family, death, love) generally emerge in relation to prior experiential encounters with the phenomena that these concepts name, knowledge of God is gained solely through the linguistic domain, through children's encounters with God talk.[5] However, once we allow subsidiary awareness to play a significant role in coming to know, we raise the possibility that children might first learn to identify something they come to understand as "God's presence" through an experience of indwelling as they attend to something else, and only later do they come to identify that experience with the concept of God.

In raising the question of subsidiary awareness and knowledge, our concern lies not with the question of whether tacit integration may at times be mistaken (for clearly it can be) but with illuminating the difference between these two kinds of inference. Explicit inference involves moving from premise to conclusion whereby the inference itself is the object of our attention, whereas subsidiary inference involves the way we tacitly integrate information as we functionally attend to something else.

The way these two forms of inference – and two forms of knowledge to which they give rise – surface in the following dialogue is very illuminating and, we believe, challenges the way adults often relate to children's theological talk. In applying Polayni's distinction between focal and subsidiary knowing, it seems to us that there is a real possibility that what appears at first as incoherent and relativistic may in the end be seen to operate according to a meaningful logic expressive of these two forms of knowledge.

> **14. Maya:** It's really funny to hear people who don't believe in God and they exist and breathe and laugh. And they say to me, if the Holocaust happened, where was God? People, as if, it is really really not the point. It's stupid.
>
> . . . .
>
> **17. Amir:** *If Yifat asks from where do you know this?*
>
> **18. Maya:** Look. Everyone has his own thoughts. Right? Like I said to you I have two girlfriends who think . . . I don't argue with them as you say. They want to believe? So they should believe. I have my own beliefs, end of story. They don't want to believe. Look, to explain – I explained, it didn't help. Look, that is their life, they will believe in what they want to believe. I go on my path/way. But they are my friends. I don't argue with them and don't quarrel with them about such a thing.
>
> **19. Amir:** *Have those friends ever asked you from where you know?*
>
> **20. Maya:** From where do they know? That's it. That is my feeling. I don't know. I don't speak with God or something like that. But to know, I know for sure. I haven't seen him and not that in truth. But, what I feel? No one is able to change my opinion.
>
> *(The numbers here refer to the sequence of comments in the interview. Gaps in*

*the number sequence point to comments that have been omitted in the quoted
section of transcript. Comments have been transcribed as recorded.)*

What do we learn about Maya's theological reasoning to this point?
First, we learn that Maya's knowledge of God is strongly connected to,
even emerges out of, her feelings (comment 20). We also learn that while
Maya is certain enough of her own feeling to say no one will change her
mind, she is also accepting of her friends' differing positions – she
knows what she knows, and they believe what they will believe
(comment 18).

How might we interpret such a position? We could read it as non-
rational and relativistic, reinforced by the judgment that this issue is not
important enough to warrant a fight with her friends: "They want to
believe? So they should believe." To read it this way trivializes the
centrality of theology in Maya's life and discounts the cultural
patterning of her relationships; belief comes across as something to be
grounded in whimsical choice. In trivializing the sophistication of
Maya's response her reasoning also comes across as unthinking and
dogmatic: "But to know, I know for sure. . . . No one is able to change
my opinion."

Could there be another way to read it? This is where Polayni's insight
opens up alternate possibilities. "It's really funny to hear people that
don't believe in God, and they exist and breathe and laugh. And they
say to me, if the Holocaust happened, where was God? People, as if, it
is really, really not to the point." For Maya, existing, breathing, laughing
give testimony to God's existence even as people evoke the Holocaust
as a counter proof. It might be that for Maya such counter arguments
are "really not to the point" because invoking them confuses two kinds
of question: the question of God's existence as given through experience, and the question of God's existence as given through explicit
proof. Might we then understand Maya to be making a claim of knowledge of God's existence based on her experience of God as she lives,
breathes, and laughs? A "kind of knowing" that she accepts cannot act
as evidence for people who seek proof of God's existence by focusing
on God as the direct object of their attention? Knowing that she has not
seen God or spoken with God, she is unable to provide the kind of proof
that holds weight if we are looking for *that* kind of knowledge, but her
own subsidiary experience of God does leave her with certainty.

To understand Maya's response fully, we also need to understand her
cultural context. Within Israeli society the Sephardic community is
known to have a liberal attitude toward religious difference as played
out in Jewish commitments and practice. Traditionally, the Sephardic
responsa to questions of Jewish law reflect an acceptance of difference as
a positive value. High importance is given to the value of extending

one's self as much as possible to be inclusive and respectful of differences of belief and practice among members of the Jewish community (Zohar 2001). Maya's claim may not be so much a flippant attempt to avoid the issues but rather an expression of inclusivity, a preparedness to live with the tensions associated with differences of belief.

> **21. Amir:** *You used the word 'feeling'. If Yifat asks you what do you mean when you say 'feeling', how would you describe the feeling?*
> **22. Maya:** To feel. The truth? Every day that I get up in the morning my feeling is excellent. That I am a living breathing creature. God above guards me from above. Feeling simply excellent that you know that someone guards you and furthermore, from above. And I don't know . . . there is this thing that you travel to far places there is the prayer of the road/way. Correct? All these things. And also when you travel to some place. You have no idea. I always know that there is someone. There isn't . . . always in every situation in every place there is someone. Even [if it's] not my parents. There is someone.

Waking in the morning, Maya is aware of *feeling excellent*; this is the direct object of her attention. But there is a subsidiary in-dwelt awareness too, a subsidiary awareness of *being in relation*. We might say that, for Maya, God's presence is experienced functionally as she attends to something else (feeling excellent). It is this subsidiary experience that gives rise to the tacit knowledge that "always in every situation in every place there is someone."

If this interpretation is at all plausible, then it might give a clue to Maya's first comments about how she negotiates between her own belief and the lack of belief amongst her friends. The problem Maya has discovered is that there are some things you know obliquely that are just not convincing when addressed frontally. The experience of God's presence – and the tacit knowledge of God to which it gives rise – can no more be passed on to her friends through rational debate than she is able to pass on to them the knowledge of the piano she experiences through her fingers in the act of playing music. She knows this doesn't work because she has tried. "Look, to explain – I explained, it didn't help" (comment 18). It didn't *help*. This is an interesting choice of word. Rather than seeing this passage as a tribute to relativism, we might see it as Maya's acknowledgment of the limitations of scientific explanation. Forms of explanation that are convincing when the object under investigation is the focal target of our attention turn out not to be that helpful when applied to knowledge arrived at through in-dwelling.

Maya's tacit knowledge that "always, in every situation . . . there is someone" points to the primacy of relationship. Rather than approaching knowledge of God in Cartesian terms of doubt and "proof," Maya starts with the experience of relationship and care and infers from this the existence of one who cares. Annette Baier (1995), John MacMurray (1961), Nel Noddings (1984) and many others have walked this road before when they have taken the primacy of relation as the foundation for moral knowledge.[6] Given this experience of relationship, what is so striking about Maya's response is that she has drawn theological, rather than moral, conclusions.[7]

Maya's awareness of the differing criteria for establishing focal knowledge and subsidiary knowledge is further borne out by the way she responds to Amir's questions. Aware that Amir's concern for proof is a concern with focal knowing, she tries to respond to him on his own terms. Without withdrawing her claim to be subsidiarily aware of God's presence, Maya repeatedly makes the point that, without explicit evidence of God as focal object we can have no proof in the sense that Amir seeks it; that is, we can have no certainty of God as focal object. For proof of this kind we need to turn back to the period of the Bible or forward to the time of the Messiah, back or forward in time to those periods when God is set to appear in history as the object of our focal attention.[8]

> **23. Amir:** *Do you live with a feeling that someone takes care of you?*
> **24. Maya:** Yes.
> **25. Amir:** *Is that a thing that you can give a proof of?*
> **26. Maya:** To prove? Look, a period we once went through.
> **27. Amir:** *There were times when it was possible to prove it?*
> **28. Maya:** I saw many verses and story in the Bible. Many many things that interested me. I saw many films. On Passover there was Moses in the basket and all sorts of things. They showed this and simply I absorbed this. I love to see this. It is really interesting. And of course Bible lessons I also like. I love stories and all the stubborn . . . I like everything, all the Bible. I think that, I don't know, simply I enjoy it. Look, [if] I enjoy something I continue on with it. To prove? So far I don't think it is possible.
> **29. Amir:** *In the era of the Bible was it possible?*
> **30. Maya:** I think [so]. I am not certain.
> **31. Amir:** *How would they prove it in the era of the Bible?*
> **32. Maya:** That – he spoke with God.

While Maya is not herself certain that the Bible "proves" God's existence, when invited to think of how it might count as proof, she draws on the way in which human characters relate to God in the biblical narrative as the explicit object of their attention. Speaking to God in the biblical sense is to encounter God as focal object. In the Bible, God's presence is not only experienced through subsidiary inner feelings of transcendence and relationship but is also experienced by direct encounter in speech and physical manifestation. God appears in a burning bush, is witnessed by the masses at Sinai, and is a force to be negotiated with in the service of justice.⁹ It is this explicit manifestation that Maya takes to be necessary in order to satisfy Amir's need for proof.

> **33. Amir:** *Today there isn't anyone who speaks with God?*
> **34. Maya:** Really no. I don't think so. Maybe yes, maybe the really religious people who go every day and put on tefillin. Perhaps they speak with God. Perhaps their feeling, like I say, their feeling. But like in the past, I don't think.
> **35. Amir:** *Do you think that the religious people are able to prove that there is God?*
> **36. Maya:** Look, they say that the Messiah will come. Correct? They wait. Like I said, the religious people go, pray, do as they say [regarding] their thing – put on tefillin, go to synagogue everyday, go on Friday to pray. Correct? We will wait . . . . But to think again that someone speaks with God? That not. Once again, I say feeling can be certain. That is their feeling. But thus? I don't think so.
> **37. Amir:** *The coming of the Messiah will prove it?*
> **38. Maya:** I think so. Will prove it to any person.

In Maya's terms, to the extent that contemporary people might speak *to* God, they do not speak *with* God in the way people did in the Bible. God does not appear as the focal object. If we can speak of "speaking to God" at all today, this experience of dialogue is experienced as a feeling of in-dwelling as they participate in religious practice.

> **43. Amir:** *How certain are you of the existence of God? Very certain, very sure, not so much?*
> **44. Maya:** How would I say? I said to you, not certain. And also I think that it comes as a question. I am still alive and breathing, I wait, I do not hurry to any place. It will come, that someone will come – the Messiah, or suddenly someone will come with . . . what will come will come. I cannot say with certainty because I am not God and not the Messiah. I am simply a 14-year-old girl. So perhaps, it is a question.
> **45. Amir:** *Are there people who don't believe?*
> **46. Maya:** Very many people.
> **47. Amir:** *Is it possible that they are right?*
> **48. Maya:** It is possible. No one is perfect. It's possible that they are right. And people like religious people, or like me, or other people who believe in God are wrong. It's possible.
> **49. Amir:** *What would Yifat say in order to show you that there is no God?*
> **50. Maya:** Like I said to you, they ask "why was there a Holocaust?" She would surely say to me . . . every human being that I know who doesn't believe always comes to me and attacks me in a sentence. I don't have anything to answer him. Because I wasn't in the Holocaust and I didn't suffer. But I've also seen pictures, a four-hour movie, something like that. And I also saw . . . Every ceremony or something like that I simply cry. It is really moving. And it is not possible to say it doesn't concern me or

something like that. But with respect to Yifat's position, if she thinks in her opinion why was there a Holocaust. I will tell her perhaps I am wrong and she is right, perhaps I am right. Simple.

Maya's repetition of her point to Amir (comment 44) expresses her feeling of frustration at his inability to grasp that her certainty of indwelt feeling does not, and cannot, translate into certainty of God as focal object. The capacity to know is bounded by who we are: as Maya points out, she is not God (omnipotent) but a 14-year-old girl, and the nature of her knowledge is appropriate to the capacity of a 14-year-old girl. She feels God *subsidiarily* as she lives and breathes, but for certainty of the type Amir wants she, like the rest of us, must wait for history to play itself out. From her point of view the appearance of the Messiah is that point in history, a point when God becomes tangible and overt. That her imaginary landscape is bounded by the biblical era on one hand and the messianic era on the other is an important cultural point. Within the Sephardic tradition these serve as points of reference from which we orient ourselves in history.[10]

It is important to note that, for Maya, to know God contingently *is* to have knowledge, and her commitment to this knowledge is just as certain as focal knowledge. The remarkable point here lies in Maya's ability to accept the contingency, and the potential fallibility, of her own position, and yet despite this to remain committed to this position as strongly as she does. To show such commitment in the face of contingency expresses an ironic or philosophical sensibility.

Here too we must point to the cultural context in which Maya's thinking operates by reflecting on the way the Holocaust is integrated into her negotiation with the world. We see this here in comment 50 and also earlier in the dialogue in comment 14. Within Israeli education the Holocaust occupies a privileged position. Even though much of the population of Israel, including Maya's family with its Eastern (Sephardi) origins, didn't experience the Holocaust firsthand, its centrality in Israeli life and education cannot be overstated (Segev 1993).[11] The Holocaust not only acts as a national reference point in regard to justification of the creation of the state; it also acts as a paradigmatic symbol of evil. In addition, it is often a focus around which to discuss theological issues (Segev 1993: 477–86). Despite being born 50 years later, "close to nine out of every ten students said that they identified with the holocaust's victims" (Segev 1993: 483). In Israeli schools this identification is strongly affective, and students see the adequacy of their response to the Holocaust in affective terms. This is clearly the case with Maya, who feels compelled to defend her own theological conclusions (comment 50) by describing the strength of her own affective response to her encounters with the Holocaust through films and ceremonies. To continue to believe in God despite the Holocaust is not to trivialize the enormity of the evil and suffering it represents.

By paying careful attention to one child's thinking we have been convinced of the importance of listening carefully to children on their own terms. Their theological reasoning – and the imaginary landscape in which it plays out – provide a rich resource for thinking about modalities of religious experience and the construction of meaning. The educational implications of this await further exploration.

Notes

1   This essay contains an accurate transcript of this interview; however, the participants are given pseudonyms. The interviewer is a Ph.D. student at the School of Education, Hebrew University. We thank him for making this interview available. Sephardic Jews include those whose roots can be traced to Spain or regions around the entire Mediterranean Sea coast. Sephardic Jewry developed its own cultural expressions and norms. See Zohar 2001.

2   We might see such a distinction when people use the term "spirituality" when speaking of our affective awareness of immanence, and the term "God" when exploring our theoretical understanding of transcendence. It is also played out in Piagetian accounts of religious development that track this development through the child's cognitive understanding. For an example of this, see Hyde, 1990, ch. 3.

3   This focus on in-dwelling forms part of Polayni's larger agenda. In claiming that subsidiary in-dwelling underpins all claims to knowledge, Polayni seeks to challenge the perceived "objectivity" of scientific knowledge.

4   See reference to Ames's room experiment on p. 42. The film version of *Alice in Wonderland* makes clever use of just such a skewed room. Alice finds herself in a long corridor, and as she walks down it after the rabbit, she appears to grow taller and the corridor grows smaller until she is twice the size of the door into Wonderland.

5   See Hyde 1990, ch. 5 and note 3.

6   We might say that this view instantiates a feminist ethic that builds on the primacy of relationship.

7   Friedrich Schweitzer noted in chapter 8 of this volume that while many describe the self in relational terms, this is generally not seen to have spiritual import. Yet this is precisely what Maya does. For Maya, relational awareness is the foundation of theological knowledge.

8   We say "allegedly" here because in both cases Maya "thinks, but is not certain," that God is literally seen or heard.

9   For instance, Genesis 18 (Abraham's intervention in the destruction of Sodom and Gomorrah), Exodus 32 (the intervention of Moses preventing the destruction of the Israelites after the building of the golden calf), Job 10 (Job petitions God to explain the absence of justice in determining his fate).

10 See Zohar 2001.

11 See in particular ch. 7.

References

Baier, A. 1995: *Moral Prejudice*. Cambridge, MA: Harvard University Press.

De Roos, S. A., Iedema, J. and Miedema, S. 2001: Young Children's Descriptions of God: Influences of Parents' and Teachers' God Concept and Religious Denomination of Schools. *Journal of Beliefs and Values* 22: 1–19.

Hyde, K. E. 1990: *Religion in Childhood and Adolescence*. Birmingham, AL: Religious Education Press.

MacMurray, J. 1961: *Persons in Relation*. London: Faber & Faber.

Noddings, N. 1984: *Caring: A Feminine Approach to Ethics and Moral Education*. Berkeley: University of California Press.

Polayni, M. 1974: *Personal Knowledge*. Chicago: University of Chicago Press.

—— and Prosch, H. 1975: *Meaning*. Chicago: University of Chicago Press.

Scriven, M. 1977: *Reasoning*. New York: McGraw Hill College.

Segev, T. 1993: *The Seventh Million: The Israelis and the Holocaust*. New York: Hill and Wang.

Zohar, Z. 2001: *The Luminous Face of the East: Studies in the Legal and Religious Thought of Sephardic Rabbis of the Middle East*. Tel Aviv: Hakibbutz Hameuhad (Hebrew).

Part III

Cultural and Critical Perspectives

P ART III ADDRESSES questions of power and authority in spiritual
and ethical education. Drawing on the resources of neo-Marxism,
post-modernism, human rights theory, cultural anthropology,
relational ethics, and discourse criticism, the essays in this section challenge many of the assumptions of spiritual education that are grounded
in political liberalism and Enlightenment morality. Most of them tend
to be less religiously "tethered" than those in **Part II** (Alexander and
McLaughlin 2003). They argue that more than faith, spiritual education
should emphasize the plight of the oppressed and the disenfranchised,
in economics, politics, public ceremonies, and classroom discourse. To
do this, however, may require realignment of the inner voice of the child
with the authority of tradition or alternatively abandonment of spiritual
education as it is commonly understood altogether.

Part III opens with a passionate argument by Clive Erricker that spiritual education ought to transcend liberal preoccupations with
theological diversity in favor of promoting awareness among students
that hidden global agendas seek to disenfranchise individuals and
communities. Ethics not only precedes epistemology in education, as
Alexander and Ben-Peretz have argued (2001), epistemology serves
free-market capitalism – the dominant ideological paradigm of our time
– by cloaking injustice in a "spell of progress and prosperity" that are
"passed off" as necessary to a civilized and just society. Business and
education collude, Erricker holds, to prevent a spirituality of dissent
(Gearon 2001) by pursuing liberal values within the context of "democratic" schooling. His response to this "manifest deceit" is a radical
oppositional pedagogy he dubs "spiritual activism," which calls on the
"counter-will" of those concerned with the spiritual development of
young people, regardless of faith.

This is followed by Buckley and Erricker's critique of the British citizenship education, which, in their view, co-opted spiritual and moral
education to a modernist agenda that is out of step with postmodern
"moments" that are challenging and redefining contemporary culture.

Citizenship education, they contend, is an outgrowth of the "moral panic" that ensued when secularism, pluralism, and relativism challenged accepted social values. It is a vehicle to reintroduce clear moral standards by replacing religion with reason as the primary source of moral authority. Yet this modern desire for universal rational values conflicts with modernity's commitment to heteronomy and the autonomous rational self. Education is drafted to play down this conflict by producing the rational subject that will embrace what Lyotard (1992) called the meta-narrative of Enlightenment rationality. However, today's young people are growing up with the experience of post-modern "moments" that eschew meta-narratives. This leads to a lack of fit between the educational system that promotes modern rational citizenship and the students being "educated" by that system. They propose an alternative that empowers students to take a more critical stance toward the status quo.

Liam Gearon understands spirituality as associated as much with "ultimate worldview," which can be secular, as with "ultimate experience," which tends to be religious. The inward turn toward personal experience and away from social and political consciousness is, therefore, the wrong direction for spiritual education. This approach is too self-centered and overemphasizes religion at the expense of secularism. Secular models of spirituality stress relation and community but often lack ethical frameworks for action. Secular spiritual education, if it wishes to move beyond "self-indulgence and narcissism," must be "tested in the world" by engaging social justice. The human-rights agenda, "for all of its many organizational and human failings," can fill this gap because it remains crucial "to life on a planet with such a diversity of cultures and worldviews."

An example of spiritual education that embraces "spiritual activism," critical citizenship, and human rights can be found in Zvi Bekerman's ethnographic depiction of Palestinian–Jewish education for coexistence through school ceremonies. The context is a bilingual (Arabic-Hebrew) bi-national (Palestinian–Jewish) school in the Jerusalem area for Jewish and Arab citizens of Israel. This in itself is unique in that there are four independent Israeli school systems: one for secular Jews; a second for modern Orthodox, Zionist Jews; a third for ultra-Orthodox, non-Zionist Jews; and a fourth for Arabs. None educate the children of Palestinian and Jewish Israelis together. Grounded in a theory emphasizing the transformative power of public rituals (Geertz 1973, Handelman 1990), the paper describes a syncretic school ceremony called "The Festivals of Light" that brings together celebrations of the Jewish holiday of Hanukkah with Christmas and Eid al Fitr – the climax to the holy Moslem month of Ramadan. By giving the ceremony this name, the organizers verbally challenged "the standard hegemonic celebration of

Hanukkah," which is the national Jewish winter holiday in Israeli schools. Although Arab schools do not necessarily celebrate Jewish festivals, other elements of the Zionist narrative that do not reflect their own national or religious aspirations are found in Palestinian (Arab) Israeli schools. The study describes how, by de-emphasizing nationalist interpretations of their respective holidays and conceiving a common celebration, this school educates toward coexistence. It also discusses some of the cultural problems and tensions that emerge.

If the previous authors in **Part III** connect spiritual education to social justice and political critique, Moshe Re'em discusses how authoritative discourse in classrooms can have a corrosive authoritarian influence on teaching that undermines what Bakhtin (Sidorkin 1999: 29) calls the polyphonic character of spiritual truth. Authoritative discourse is monological and characterized by direct or didactic instruction. Student questions do not challenge the nature of this discourse, since the point is to receive static knowledge. Clearly, this form of ideological discourse fits authoritarian religious instruction. An alternative can be found in what Bakhtin (1981: 341) dubs internally persuasive discourse, which, like Buberian dialogue, allows disruption and disagreement. This alternative allows for shared knowledge that can reflect the polymorphous or multilayered character of textual interpretations and knowledge claims. Re'em illustrates these concepts with excerpts from Philip Roth's wonderful story "The Conversion of the Jews" (Roth 1969).

Part III concludes with an essay that challenges the very notion of spiritual education. Writing within the neo-Marxist tradition that inspired Erricker, and with the concern for social justice, coexistence and dialogue that motivated other authors in **Part III**, Ilan Gur-Ze'ev argues forcefully that Judeo-Christian notions of spirituality and spiritual education do more to enslave than liberate students. In his view, education as commonly understood is a normalizing institution that "subjectifies" students by transforming them into the sort of people that will accept the dictates of Enlightenment rationality, or religious irrationality, or some other externally-imposed narrative. This constitutes an act of violence against a child's individuality. Neither "spiritual activism," nor critical citizenship, nor human rights, nor coexistence ceremonies, nor persuasive discourse is sufficient to resist the inherently anti-human character of such violence. We require counter – not new forms of – education that struggles to resist all forms of normalization. This calls for counter-spirituality – not spiritual education – that liberates the child from the national and religious meta-narratives used by adults to manipulate and control. Counter-spirituality of this kind is the only genuine way to reveal the unique quality of openness and readiness for relation that is the essence of children's spirituality.

What can we learn from these essays about the questions of ontology, ethics, naturalism, development, pedagogy, and hermeneutics with which we began? These authors connect spirituality and spiritual education to a profound concern for social justice and liberation of the oppressed. The abuse of power is quintessentially opposed to any possible sense of transcendence, natural or supernatural, secular or religious. Spiritual education in this view cannot only be about attention to a moment of innocence, or relatedness, or possibility. It must also call us to action, to the defense of human rights, to the liberation of children from the violence of normalizing education. Spiritual potential can be found in the child's vulnerability that leads – and all too often even invites – abuse, not only in the promise of his or her creativity.

Spiritual development of this kind is more pessimistic and tragic than that discussed in **Parts I** and **II**. It is born of suffering and violence and oppression that strives toward but that does not always achieve liberation. Even Gur-Ze'ev is aware, for example, that counter-spirituality becomes a normalizing force with which we must continue to contend. The pedagogy of this sort of critical spirituality is grounded as before in a discourse of dialogue, storytelling, and *midrash*. But the narratives here are darker. They confront injustice but rarely overcome it. Meaning is found in continuing to struggle against, not by conquering, evil.

There is something to be said for living with the tensions between an optimistic, liberal and a pessimistic, tragic account of spiritual education, as there is for striking a balance between exegesis and eisegesis. At the very least, the dialogue among these disparate views can help to reveal the strengths and weakness of each, which, at the end of the day, is what scholarship in spiritual education ought to be about.

References

Alexander, H. A. and Ben-Peretz, M. 2001: Towards a Pedagogy of the Sacred. Erricker, Jane, Ota, Cathy and Erricker, Clive (eds.), 2001: *Spiritual Education: Cultural, Religious, and Social Differences – New Perspectives for the 21st Century.* Brighton & Portland: Sussex Academic Press, pp. 34–47.
—— and McLaughlin, T. H. 2003: Education in Religion and Spirituality. In N. Blake, P. Smeyers, R. Smith and P. Standish (eds.), *The Blackwell Guide to the Philosophy of Education.* Oxford: Blackwell.
Bakhtin, M. 1981: Discourse in the Nove in M. Holquist (ed.), *The Dialogic Imagination.* Austin, TX: University of Texas Press.
Gearon, L. 2001: The Corruption of Innocence and the Spirituality of Dissent: Postcolonial Perspectives on Spirituality in a World of Violence. In J. Erricker, C. Ota, and C. Erricker (eds.), 2001: *Spiritual Education: Cultural, Religious, and Social Differences – New Perspectives for the 21st Century.* Brighton & Portland: Sussex Academic Press, pp. 143–55.
Geertz, C. 1973: *The Interpretation of Cultures.* New York: Basic Books.
Handelman, D. 1990: *Models and Mirrors: Towards an Anthropology of Public Events.* Cambridge: Cambridge University Press.

Lyotard, J.-F. 1984: *The Postmodern Condition: A Report on Knowledge*. Manchester: Manchester University Press.

Roth, Philip 1969: The Conversion of the Jews. In *Goodbye Columbus*, 2nd edn. New York: Bantam Books.

Sidorkin, A. M. 1999: *Beyond Discourse*: *Education, Self, and Dialogue*. Albany: State University of New York Press.

Chapter 13

A Manifesto for Spiritual Activism: Time to Subvert the Branding of Education

CLIVE ERRICKER

THIS ESSAY DRAWS attention to the influence of corporatism within global capitalism: behaviors of nations in seeking economic and political power and the resultant suppression of academic and educational freedom. It argues that spiritual education needs to identify itself with particular values that oppose current global trends.

Furthermore, it argues that theoretical constructs of the spiritual, whether theologically or academically constructed, are of little use unless their aim is to activate change through critical dissent.[1]

The role of the spiritual educator therefore transcends liberal preoccupations with drawing attention to diversity and inclusivity and opposes exclusivist theological definitions of spirituality in favor of a form of "conscientization" that eschews any spurious claims to neutrality or objectivity in advocating the promotion of student awareness of hidden global agendas that seek to disempower both individuals and communities.

Concerning spiritual education in particular, and education in general, the distinctive lines need to be drawn not on the traditional basis of religious and secular but on the values basis of justice.[2] As Alexander and Ben-Peretz have argued (2001), epistemology is not the foundation of education, but rather education proceeds according to ethical and theological orientation. The subterfuge that results from the deceit of the epistemological supposition is part of what I wish to uncover in this paper. My argument substantially rests on showing that "epistemology" is framed within particular paradigms and that when we ask what epistemology serves, we have to investigate its logic within the dominant paradigm of the time. In this case I shall argue that the dominant paradigm of our time is an economic one that serves free-market capitalism. Free-market capitalism, however, is the ideological base behind the economic paradigm. The superstructure, as Marx would have it, is a decorative edifice of moral or values rhetoric that seeks to cloak injustice by weaving the spell of progress, prosperity and lifestyle – the point being that progress and prosperity (the economics) are passed off as the necessary basis of a civilized and just society and a pleasurable individual lifestyle. It then becomes implausible to question the economic paradigm and, by virtue of that, the ideology that drives it, since by doing so you are perceived to be seeking to subvert the pursuit of justice, happiness, and so on. To challenge this monstrous fallacy is, therefore, to subvert it. To suggest that we ask children to be aware of this fallacy and challenge it must therefore be something not far removed from child abuse. Nevertheless, my argument is that this is precisely what we need to do.

How Did We Get Here?

When we speak of branding we are not dealing with something trivial, even if what we are dealing with is something that most obviously operates at an unconscious level and is literally related, in the corporate sphere, to such mundane items as clothes, shoes, and coffee. We are dealing with a phenomenon that can legitimately be said to relate to the spiritual. We long to live with certainty. At a transcendent level certainty is not available to us, but ideologically or corporately we can buy into its historicized simulacrum.[3] This simulacrum, surprising as it may seem, offers itself as a spiritual panacea. The Starbucks coffeehouse chain, for example, according to its marketing director, Scott Bedbury, states that they want to be aligned "with one of the greatest movements towards finding a connection with [the] soul" (Klein 2000: 138). What Bedbury means by this is unclear, but its consequences and motivation I intend to expose in this study. The problems with such counterfeits are to be found in the lack of authenticity of such vacuous pronouncements as the above. But it is not the vacuity itself within which the real problems lie. The vacuity is merely an aspect of the decorative rhetoric that trivializes the spiritual and cloaks injustice. Beneath it we find the significant issues to address, the issues that the rhetoric is meant to camouflage.

We can trace the development to the present from the industrial age, which allowed the situation we are now witnessing to evolve. As Walter Benjamin observed, it was given its "cue in the advent of machines" out of which emerged "the amorality of the business world and the false morality enlisted in its service" (Benjamin 1999: 5). In his commentary on this, Benjamin refers to Fourier and his utopia of the phalanstery, conceived as a socialist community paralleling the emergence of the mechanistic age with a psychology of relationship in which "this mechanism made of men produces the land of milk and honey, the primeval wish symbol that Fourier's utopia has filled with new life" (Benjamin 1999: 5). It was in the Paris Arcades, observes Benjamin, that "Fourier saw the architectural canon of the phalanstery. . . . Whereas they originally served commercial ends, they become, for him, places of habitation" (Benjamin 1999: 5), places that "restore human beings to relationships in which morality becomes superfluous" (Benjamin 1999: 5). Fourier's vision – that overcoming conditions of scarcity through production would bring about a society in which not only material want would be erased but, as a result, so would the dysfunctions of human relationships – now appears naive in the extreme. It suggests a blindness to the inherent greed that afflicts us. But Fourier's naïveté is surpassed by our own, more than 170 years later (Fourier wrote *Nouveau Tableaux de Paris* in 1828). Our naiveté consists in thinking that, despite the history of exploitation that has permeated the period from the Industrial Revolution to the present, we are in the midst of increasing progress toward an ever better future. Such is the pervasive force of the economic paradigm within which we live.

Prophets of the past like Benjamin, who contrarily judged that the World Exhibitions of the mid-nineteenth century, proffering the same allure as the Arcades in their display of merchandise and achievement, were "places of pilgrimage to the commodity fetish" (Benjamin 1999: 7), identified the march of the future more correctly. In fact, Benjamin's observation on commodity fetishism is precisely what we witness at a more sophisticated level in the metamorphosis from commodity manufacturing to branding. Perversely, branding allows commodity fetishism to act as a simulacrum, or replacement, for the spiritual and a license for amorality at the same time. It is able to do so because of our willingness to believe in the economic paradigm of free-market capitalism, and its false promises, that underpin corporate practices. Following Benjamin, both Guy Debord and Jean Baudrillard later take up this theme with the identification of the spectacle that commodity fetishism has turned into. "The life of the consumer becomes increasingly absurd, . . . able to find identity only in the act of pointless consumption" (Plant 1992: 25; see Debord 1977) as "the circulation of commodities almost becomes an end in itself, quite regardless of the subjects who buy, sell and produce them" (Plant 1992: 35; see Debord 1977 and Baudrillard 1968).

Just as Fourier underestimated the capacity of capitalism to harness industrial innovation to its own ends, so too, in our age of technological and digital advance, it is possible to believe that innovation will necessarily herald the introduction of a more democratic society. Kevin Kelly, a countercultural activist and writer, made the assumption in the 1990s that *networks*, created through online communication and the Internet, would connect everything to everything else, making possible the distribution, uncontrollable by governments, of knowledge and power. The complex organism of the network would enable "utilizing the timeless, anti-hierarchical principles of distributed intelligence" through the facility of the free market (Frank 2001: 57–8). What is interesting in both Fourier's and Kelly's views is the presumption that new technology will transform society by virtue of the possibilities that the technology itself offers. There is no consideration of how that technology might be harnessed by those who seek power in order to dominate rather than liberate. Such naiveté can also be found in the writings of Adam Smith:

> Servants, labourers and workmen . . . make up the far greater part of every great political society. But what improves the circumstances of the greater part can never be regarded as an inconvenience to the whole. No society can surely be flourishing and happy, of which the far greater part of the members are poor and miserable. It is but equity, besides, that they should feed, clothe and lodge the whole body of the people, should have such a share of the produce of their own labour as to be tolerably well fed, clothed and lodged. (Smith 1976: 78–9)

The ethical expectations expressed above derive from Smith's earlier work on moral sentiments. In support of his view of the benign landlord and the rich, he resorts to the "invisible hand" of "Providence":

> They are led by an invisible hand to make nearly the same distribution of the necessities of life, which would have been made, had the earth been divided into equal portions among all its inhabitants. . . . When Providence divided the earth among a few lordly masters, it neither forgot nor abandoned those who seemed to have been left out in the partition. These last too enjoy their share of all it produces. (Smith 1937: 184)

And, in support of such a view, there were merchants who shared its utopian spirit:

> Methinks I wou'd not have you not only learn the Method of Merchantize . . . merely as a means of getting Wealth: it will be well worth your pains to study it as a Science, to see how it is founded in Reason, and the Nature of Things; how it promotes Humanity . . . by mutual Benefits diffusing mutual Love from Pole to Pole. (Lillo 1731)

Thus, the "trickle down" theory, so important to statements made by Tony Blair and other Western leaders today, was, for Smith, understood as dependent upon a moral sentiment dependent in turn on the

invisible workings of Providence. It was not an economic law of capitalism and unrestricted free trade. It was a sentiment of the times born
of a certain worldview to which Smith subscribed. That sentiment no
longer holds sway as it did for Smith; thus the distribution of such
wealth can no longer be expected. Indeed, writing later in 1844, Marx
exposed its lack of effect on entrepreneurial practice: "The alienation of
the worker is expressed thus: the more he produces, the less he can
consume; the more value he creates, the less value he has. . . . Labour
produces fabulous things for the rich, but misery for the poor.
Machines replace labour, and jobs diminish, while other workers turn
into machines . . . " (Marx 1977: 69–70). And it was Engels who spelled
this out in illustrative detail in *The Condition of the Working Class in
England* (Engels 1987).

The significance of observing this shift in expectation and practice is
that it alerts us to the following:

- the importance of spiritual and moral sentiment and conviction in
  determining the use of capital;
- that capitalism, as an economic system is, in itself, amoral;
- that sentiment can be preserved as a rhetorical device, adapted to
  the spirit of the age, in order to cloak and protect unjust entrepreneurial practice, rather than underpin it;
- that we cannot presume that an economic system, of itself (qua
  economics), will result in any prescribed outcomes in relation to
  humanitarian concerns (for example, the prevalent notion that since
  prosperity will inevitably and eventually lead to prosperity for all,
  we must pursue wealth creation as efficiently as possible).

Given this analysis, we might expect that, for the majority of the
world's population, a deregulated free-market economy would lead to
a Hobbesian existence. This, of itself, would be nothing new, since
according to recent statistics, if you have food in the refrigerator, clothes
on your back, a roof overhead, and a place to sleep, you are richer than
75 percent of the world's inhabitants. However, we might expect such
a situation to deteriorate rather than improve.

Thus we come to the question of how domination comes about and is
maintained in relation to technological innovation.

The Present State of Affairs

The right to domination is never advertised as such in democratic
societies; rather domination is gained by appeal to its very opposite,
liberty. This play on paradox is at the heart of strategies employed by

those who have gained influence over today's global economy. In attempts to immunize themselves against charges of injustice, their claim is that they are just responding to the demand expressed by the will of the people. Thus those who seek domination are precisely those who suppress that will through regulation: governments, trade unions, and liberal intellectuals. These are the elite figures and bodies used to exercising power and influence, the suppressers of the popular will (Frank 2001: 45–7).

As Frank records in dwelling on the statements made by Jeffrey Bell, a former aide to Ronald Reagan, in Bell's book *Populism and Elitism* (Bell 1992: 3), "' Elitism' . . . was a term correctly applied to those who believe in 'the decision making ability of one or more elites, acting on behalf of other people'; [thus] . . . Ronald Reagan, whose deregulatory and tax-reducing fervour could be portrayed as faith in the public's ability to manage their own money, came out populist; while Michael Dukakis, along with anyone else who believed in regulation, was an elitist" (Frank 2001: 45).

As Frank mentions, this was a "clever inversion device" (Frank 2001: 45) since it inverted the term's meaning as used in the populist move-ment of the 1890s in the United States and removed the significant issue of relative wealth, which was central to the populist cause. This new "populism" acted as an energizing focus for corporate and multina-tional companies as it constructed a climate of moral injustice within which business Goliaths could be seen to be acting benevolently for the common person rather than, as had been incorrectly perceived previ-ously, out of self-interest. Thus a double injustice had to be rectified and the previous delusions as to the character and purposes of capital dispelled.

Frank's analysis of how this was implemented depended upon the upturn in the financial market in 1999, when the Dow Jones Industrial Average crossed the 10,000 mark. Such a bull market led to the invest-ment fairy tales so common now in any subway advertisement. The idea was that any ordinary person could invest in the stock market and receive a share of its riches as a result. This way you could fulfill your dreams and prove the populist power of deregulated democracy at the same time. The two were not incompatible after all. It was the "inalien-able right" of "every man and woman . . . to make money – and lots of it," declared *Individual Investor* magazine, in copies of an "Investment Manifesto" handed out around Manhattan (Frank 2001: 90). Thus, entre-preneurs and financiers were depicted in various manifestations of spin as the inaugurators of a populist revolution that bore the values of Woody Guthrie: this land becomes your land through your investments (see Frank 2001: 91).

Frank's analysis is complemented by those of others, notably Klein

(2000) and Monbiot (2000). Inside the front cover of Klein's book is recorded the observation of Indonesian writer Y. B. Mangunwijaya on July 16, 1998: "You might not see things yet on the surface, but underground, it's already on fire" (Klein 2000).

The fire metaphor, as it can be applied to the present state of global affairs, does not relate to the flames of revolution against corporate practices but, contrarily, to the stoking up of bonfires of human suffering located and fuelled by the corporate will. On the surface we do not see them. What we see is what we desire to see: the commodities that serve our lust for a distinctive and admired sense of individual identity. How does this strange state of affairs arise? Klein begins to chart it when she observes and reports on the "underground" by visiting the Asian sweatshops herself. In one report, from Jataka, she remarks:

> By now these Indonesian workers were used to people like me: foreigners who come to talk to them about the abysmal conditions in the factories where they cut, sew and glue for multinational companies like Nike, the Gap and Liz Claiborne. . . . Here they were all young, some of them as young as fifteen . . . (earning) the equivalent of US $2 per day . . . being forced to work long hours of overtime but (not) being paid at the legal rate for their trouble. . . . In this part of the world, hundreds of workers every year burn to death because their dormitories are located upstairs from firetrap sweatshops. (Klein 2000: xv–xvi)

The late twentieth century outcome of what Benjamin observed concerning the Paris Arcades and the commodity fetish is recorded by both Klein and Monbiot. But the shift from marketing manufactured hardware to marketing spiritual software based on identity and image was the crucial one: branding. Branding operates at the microcosmic level of the individual and the macrocosmic level of global identity. IBM's campaign entitled "Solutions for a Small Planet" is an example of the latter: Its therapeutic message of technology bringing about a harmonious and humanitarian global society provides the façade behind which it hides its increasing control and extortionate profits. Further such profits are presented as justified in the light of IBM's potential to succeed in its utopian vision. Such a campaign is a barely concealed manifesto for control, feeding off the democratic sensibilities of liberalism, again part of the decorative values rhetoric. There is, of course, an inherent duplicity employed as a tactic in these branding games. The slogans themselves are imbued with a particular values message that the company wishes to convey, which at the same time promotes its own sense of concern for individuals and community *and* extends the influence of capitalism's values orientation: individualism, choice, and competition.

Klein refers to this vision of choice as follows, in order to evidence the corporate restriction within which it is envisaged and the community destruction on which it depends: "Everyone has, in one form or another, witnessed the odd double vision of vast consumer choice coupled with Orwellian new restrictions on cultural production and public space. We see it when a small community watches its lively downtown hollow out, as big box discount stores with 70,000 items on their shelves set up on their periphery, exerting their gravitational pull to what James Howard Kunstler describes as 'the geography of nowhere'" (Klein 2000: 130).

Corporatism, Values, and Education

John Ralston Saul (1997) offers one of the most incisive analyses of the effect of corporatist "philosophy" on education. He argues for a radical reform of an education system that has increasingly turned toward a utilitarian function, neglecting, in the process, to address the significant values questions related to individual identity and human society. Having been "co-opted into the corporatist system, becoming obsessed with operating as businesses rather than with instilling deeper philosophical values" (Daniel Britten 1998: 18), the education system rejects the importance of self-understanding and is uncomfortable with, if not (paradoxically) hostile to, noncomformity.

The means of reorienting education to a free-market economy are manifestly bureaucratic as Yeats has argued (Yeats 2001) and as Clarke and Newman explain:

> Management . . . is the force elected by the New Right to carry through the restructuring of the welfare state. It is the agency which inherits the dismantling of old regimes and provides a new regime (a new mode of power) around which organisations can be structured. (Clarke and Newman 1992: 6, quoted in Gewirtz, Ball, and Bowe 1995: 115–16)

The institutional conflict this new agency generates is one that divides across understandings of democracy embedded in differing foundations: communitarian and free market. The former is identified as outmoded and the latter as open to change and opportunity.

The term "outmoded" used here is, of course, another example of rhetoric rather than argument. It has nothing to do with "time" as such, but with "mode" or fashion; thus old-fashioned is a pejorative term requiring no further justification within the paradigm of the new model. It renders the old model manifestly implausible. The purpose of this, as the above authors go on to expose, is that, just as we can observe in corporate business practice, the opportunity for choice is the selling point for these operations. But "as far as equity is concerned, choice is a dangerous irrelevance" (190).

This new model of democratic education, based on instrumentalist restructuring and lacking any fundamental educational philosophy, has important implications for business. Businessmen have long been well aware of this, as is evidenced in the following statement that "a democratic system of education . . . is one of the surest ways of creating and greatly extending markets for goods of all kinds and especially those goods in which fashion may play a part" (Rorty 1934, quoted in Klein 2000: 87).

However, the new model of democratic education only fulfills its potential once closer partnership with business ensues. Witnessing the shortfalls in government funding set against schools' growing needs, especially in relation to ICT (Information Computer Technology) resources, required by curriculum changes introduced by government education agencies operating with the "new model" may appear to throw education into crisis. But what hasn't yet been taken into account is the role businesses can play. This role is unlikely to be that of the neutral benefactor. Examples from the United States illustrate how corporations can, by the back door, attempt vital changes affecting the values of schools and higher education, using such institutions to affirm their own business practices and their value to a democratic society. One way to accomplish this is by contracts ensuing from sponsorship deals, as the following report reveal. "At South Fork High School in Florida, [where Pepsi has introduced "Pepsi Achievement Awards"] there is a blunt hard-sell arrangement: the school has a clause in its Pepsi contract committing the school to "make its best effort to maximize all sales opportunities for Pepsi-Cola products" (Klein 2000: 91).

At the university level a similar form of agreement can also operate. "The University of Kentucky's deal with Nike . . . has a clause that the company has the right to terminate the five-year, £25 million contract if the 'University disparages the Nike brand . . . or takes any other action inconsistent with the endorsement of Nike products'" (2000: 97).

The impact of such agreements on everyday decision-making regarding what can and cannot be allowed is signaled in the following two examples. In a school in Evans, Georgia, that had decided to have a Coca-Cola Day and invite representatives of that company, one student came wearing a Pepsi-Cola t-shirt when students all had to wear Coca-Cola t-shirts. He was suspended (2000: 95). More worrying still, Kent State University's Amnesty International chapter wanted to bring a Free Nigeria Movement speaker to the campus. In April 1998 they applied to the student council for funding. Coca-Cola had exclusive vending rights on the campus. The chapter members were asked whether the speaker would say negative things about Coca-Cola "because Coca-Cola does a lot of positive things on our campus like helping organizations and sports." They said he would in relation to the company's involvement in Nigeria. Funding was denied (2000: 97).

In summary, these corporate interventions in the education system desire nothing less than to change the policies and values operating within educational institutions to serve their own advantage. The "new model" of democratic education is an attempt to ensure that such economic opportunities as the above can be made available to these corporations. In order for that to happen, the old values must be swept away by new management initiatives. A more philosophical interrogation of how this collusion is affecting the humanities curriculum in higher education is made below.

De-Centering Education

Spanos's *The End of Education* (1993) set out to de-center the approach to higher education. His claim was that after the Vietnam War and the publication of the Harvard Core Curriculum Report in 1978, the aim in higher education in the universities of the United States was to ensure the restoration of the humanities curriculum by basing it upon the world's great literature, thereby protecting it from the "self-destructive" course it had followed in the 1960s with the disruptive introduction of theoretical discourse in literary studies (Spanos 1993: 1–2). This reclamation of legacy, "the great task of transmitting a culture to its rightful heirs" by those who responsibly care, amounted to the "reclamation of 'our' cultural heritage" (1993: 2). These are the phrases of the report itself. The connection with the Vietnam War was made using the metaphors of health: "the recuperation of the good health the nation apparently lost during the turbulent decade of the Vietnam War" (1993: 1) and the "healing of the wound" (1993: 3) caused by the civil-rights, feminist, and student protest movements. Spanos identified in this book the attempt to generate a national consensus by appealing to a generalized "we" that included not only academics themselves but the readers of the *Wall Street Journal* (1993: 3) among others who could be counted upon to support it. It is the genealogy of this naturalized "we" that he set out to pursue and, in doing so, advance a contemporary counter memory to demystify the Harvard construction of humanist modernity by investigating its method, content, and *"especially . . . what it leaves unsaid"* (1993: 3). In this his guiding principle was that *"identity is the condition for the possibility of difference."* My understanding of this principle is that the individual articulation of identity, arising from experience (thus it is ontological, or onto-theo-logical to use Spanos's term), stands against a classically epistemological model (which privileges the consensus of inquiry and thus generalized and universalized claims to knowledge). Thus the former provides the possibility of difference (its articulation) that the method of the latter denies. The method of the latter privileges "consultation" and "consensus" precisely because such methods are means to its own ends, in political terms the power of government and the construction of a homogenized heritage. At the same time it pushes difference to the margins. The center is presented as the model for progress and civilization by virtue of it being the center (occupied by the agreed will). By default, in this *pharmakonic* strategy, the margins are occupied by those who oppose the march of civilization and accompanying progress.

Contrarily, Spanos quoted Heidegger in repositioning these boundaries and articulating a differing mapping of ontological standpoints: "The de-struction [Dekonstruktion] . . . should stake out the positive possibilities of the tradition, and that always means to fix its *boundaries*. . . . Its criticism concerns 'today' and the dominant way we treat the history of ontology. . . . It has a *positive* intent" (1993: 5; quoting Heidegger 1962: 44).

Thus we may conclude that, contrary to the idea that the late 1960s bought to bear a new destructive critique of an age-old classical tradition enabling the involvement of the humanities in the project of civilization and progress, we have witnessed the marginalization of radical critical method within the processes of education on the basis that it is politically unacceptable to the economic and imperial interests of the age – characterized by what Michel Foucault has called "the disciplinary society" (Foucault 1977).

At this point it is useful to investigate the difference between "postmodern" writers such as Spanos and Foucault and the phenomenon of "postmodernity" in order to ensure that there is no confusion between the two and that we can identify the way in which postmodernism, as a critique of modernist discourse, is being marginalized, while postmodernity is accommodated. Postmodernism is not the same as postmodernity principally because the former is an articulation of difference by subverting the dominant mode of discourse; the latter is a state of affairs ready to be accommodated by the dominant mode. As an example, the display of difference is not the same as the articulation of its voice. Tommy Hilfiger sweatshirts, originally worn by blacks articulating dissent and difference, become "cool" for white teenagers who want to identify with the style of the original wearers. Identifying with the style does not amount to being imbued with the values of the original. Thus postmodernity, as the display of difference, is happily accommodated within the modernist practices of capitalism because it is no more than identification with that which one is not. It is the superficial accommodation of the majority to a branding operation that allows them the simulacrum (replacement) for a more-rooted spiritual and values identity. As Frank records one chief executive of a company recognizing, in the Spanish Civil War soldiers would die with Stalin's names on their lips, but one cannot imagine them having the same devotion to a brand name. Similarly, when we turn to education, the simulacrum is easily sold in the context of a lack of *critical* investment in the questions of identity and values. If postmodernity is no more than the modernist accommodation of difference in lifestyle, a rebranding of modernism itself that actually serves the deregulatory desires of corporations, postmodernist writers and thinkers are attempting to allow for the articulation of difference at the level of identity and values by undermining the modernist model and its methods.

Conclusion

My argument has been that late capitalist operations in both business and education collude to ensure that there is no, as Gearon (2001) puts it, spirituality of dissent against the dominant values. These values (exploitative and unjust) are glossed over by the strategies employed by government agencies designed to ensure that we still understand ourselves to be pursuing the liberal values of "objectivity" within the context of democratic education. My response is that such a manifest deceit should be disclosed by pursuing a radical oppositional pedagogy, which I have called spiritual activism. Such an activism calls on the counter-will of those concerned with the spiritual and values development of young people, regardless of specific faith commitments. In conclusion, I have tried to express the amorality of our present educational system, which colludes in the immorality of capitalist exploitation, as starkly as I can.

Notes

1   Here I use the term in a similar sense to Derrida (1991: 47) when he announces, following Heidegger, "The world is always a *spiritual* world." Here he is examining Heidegger's use of "Geist" and suggests "if the thinking of *Geist* and of the difference between *geistig* (the spiritual) and *geistlich* (that which is spiritual) is neither thematic nor athematic and if its modality thus requires another category, then it is not only inscribed in contexts with a high political content. . . . It perhaps decides as to the very meaning of the political as such. In any case it would situate the place of such a decision, if it were possible" (1991: 6). In other words, I am picking up the reference to the relationship between spiritual and political as the context that we have to inquire into. I should add that my translation of the German terms is somewhat misleading because it is far too simplistic to do

justice to the way in which Derrida looks into the complexity of their meanings in Heidegger.

2   The notion of justice operates, of course, within different models of knowledge. Here I approach justice as a matter of inquiry, a process or movement
toward justice. For Lyotard it is a matter of "a calculating reason, as in
strategy; it is a mode of strategy, but one in which the issue is not how to
conquer but how to achieve parity between people. . . . In every instance
one must evaluate relations: of force, of values, of quantities, and of qualities " (Lyotard and Thebaud 1985: 27). However, while Lyotard's principle
of parity offers guidance, his understanding that there are no criteria, only
opinions (1985: 27) in a practical political sense reduces the political force
of his critique. In this respect John Ralston Saul's presentation of different
political structures provides a helpful corrective to, or augmentation of,
Lyotard's position. Saul argues that we are in the grip of a particular self-
interested model of operation, one of "the group." The ideology of the
group is manifest in corporatism and the manner in which it sets about
"reducing . . . the individual to a state of passivity . . . the state of a subject.
That is, he is subjected to the will of one or more of these other legitima-
cies" (Saul 1997: 33). The other legitimating models are God and king, i.e.,
states of theocracy and monarchy respectively. Saul's point is that the
model for legitimacy and thus justice is owned by such groups and that
society is seen as the sum of all the groups rather than as the collective of
individual citizenry with a concern for the public good. Power in the hands
of the groups results in a passive acceptance of the way in which they shape
globalization to their own ends and reduce the human to a measurable
value (Saul 1997: 34–5). While not wishing to suggest that Lyotard and Saul
are ultimately compatible in their thinking (that, after all, goes against my
mode of inquiry), I am suggesting that they both help us forward in
presenting an oppositional understanding of justice in relation to the "soft
pretensions to democracy " (Saul 1997: 34) that we are presently experiencing.

3   Simulcrum: a replacement that has a shadowy likeness to, or a pretence of,
the real thing (*OED*).

References

Alexander, H. A. and Ben-Peretz, M. 2001: Towards a Pedagogy of the Sacred:
Transcendence, Ethics and the Curriculum. In C. Erricker, J. Erricker, and C.
Ota (eds.), *Spiritual Education: Cultural, Religious and Social Differences – New
Perspectives for the 21st Century,* Brighton & Portland: Sussex Academic Press.
Baudrillard, J. 1968: *Le Systeme des objets.* Paris: Denoel-Gonthier.
Bell, J. 1992: *Populism and Elitism: Politics in the Age of Equality.* Washington D.C.:
Regnery.
Benjamin, W. 1999: *The Arcades Project.* Cambridge, MA and London: The
Belknap Press of Harvard University Press.
Britten, D. 1998: Free to do as we're told. *The Observer Review,* 14 June: 18.
Clarke, J. and Newman, J. 1992: Managing to Survive: Dilemmas of Changing
Organisational Forms in the Public Sector. Paper presented at Social Policy
Association Conference, University of Nottingham, July.

Debord, G. 1977: *The Society of the Spectacle*. Detroit: Black and Red.

Derrida, J. 1991: *Of Spirit: Heidegger and the Question*. Chicago: Chicago University Press.

Engels, F. 1987: *The Conditions of the Working Class in England*. London: Penguin.

Foucault, M. 1977: *Discipline and Punish: The Birth of the Prison*. London: Penguin.

Fourier, C. 1828: *Nouveau Tableaux de Paris: Vol. 1*. Paris: publisher unknown.

Frank, T. 2001: *One Market Under God*. London: Secker and Warburg.

Gearon, L. 2001: The Corruption of Innocence and the Spirituality of Dissent: Postcolonial Perspectives on Spirituality in a World of Vilence. In C. Erricker, J. Erricker and C. Ota (eds.), *Spiritual Education: Cultural, Religious and Social Differences - New Perspectives for the 21st Century*. Brighton & Portland: Sussex Academic Press..

Gewirtz, S., Ball, Stephen J., Bowe, R. 1995: *Markets, Choice and Equity in Education*. Buckingham: Open University Press.

Heidegger, M. 1962: *Being and Time*. New York: Harper and Row.

Klein, N. 2000: *No Logo: Taking Aim at the Brand Bullies*. London: HarperCollins.

Lillo, 1731: *The History of George Barnwell, or, the London Merchant* (publisher and date unknown).

Lyotard, J.-F. and Thebaud, J.-L. 1985: *Just Gaming*. Manchester: Manchester University Press.

Marx, K. 1977: *Economic and Philosophic Manuscripts of 1844*. Moscow: Progress Publishers.

Monbiot, G. 2000: *Captive State: The Corporate Takeover of Britain*. London: Macmillan.

Pilger, J. 2001: Spoils of a Massacre. In *The Guardian Weekend*. London and Manchester: Guardian Newspapers, 14 July: 18–28.

Plant, S. 1992: *The Most Radical Gesture: The Situationist International in a Postmodern Age*. London and New York: Routledge.

Rhys, J. 1968: *Wide Sargasso Sea*. Harmondsworth: Penguin.

Rorty, J. 1934: *Our Master's Voice*. New York: The John Day Company.

Saul, J. R. 1997: *The Unconscious Civilization*. London: Penguin.

Smith, Adam [1759] 1976: *The Theory of Moral Sentiments*. Oxford: Clarendon Press.

—— 1937: *The Wealth of Nations*. New York: Random House.

Spanos, W. V. 1993: *The End of Education*. Minneapolis and London: University of Minnesota Press.

Yeats, P. 2001: Postmodernism, Spirituality and Education in Late Modernity. In C. Erricker, J. Erricker, and C. Ota (eds.), *Spiritual Education: Cultural, Religious and Social Differences – New Perspectives for the 21st Century*, Brighton & Portland: Sussex Academic Press.

Chapter 14

Citizenship Education in the Postmodern Moment

Jane Buckley and Jane Erricker

THE INTRODUCTION of citizen education in Britain can be seen as an attempt to address issues such as a perceived erosion of moral standards and a lack of participation in democracy. The process of secularization in Britain and the subsequent decline in participation in religious organizations (Davie 1994) and by implication, in religious beliefs, together with a decrease in community involvement, have contributed to a general belief that values in society have also declined. There is a sense of moral panic, generally conceived to be due to the lack of a clear framework of values in society. The secularization and pluralism of modern society have resulted in a move toward a perceived relativism in which people are unsure of their responses, with no absolute sense of what is right and wrong.

The solution to this situation, it appears, is a return to a clear standard of values and the inculcation of those values through the curriculum. Citizenship education is seen as the vehicle with which to inculcate these values, while at the same time giving students a knowledge base that will lead to a desire to involve themselves in public life.

Background: Reasons for the Introduction of Citizenship Education

The *National Curriculum* document for England and Wales (DfEE 1999) states that at the forefront of the purposes that underlie the curriculum is the belief that education is a route to the all-round development of the individual, including moral, cultural, and social development. "Education should also reaffirm our commitment to the virtues of truth, justice, honesty, trust and a sense of duty" (DfEE 1999: 10). The *National*

Curriculum also accepts that the curriculum cannot remain static but must be responsive to changes in the economy and within society, and in line with this, the subject of citizenship education will be introduced in secondary schools in 2002.

The official curriculum framework has been subject to revision since 1988, and the development of the goals of the National Curriculum has involved both public consultation and significant political input while citizenship education itself has generated a great deal of discussion and controversy (Kerr 1999).

The National Foundation for Educational Research (NFER) found that, to a very large extent, the focus of citizenship education is "often dependent on the views of the dominant social or political group at the time" (Kerr 1999: 5). During the 1980s and early 1990s, the Conservative government emphasized the individualism of the free market to such an extent that Mrs. Thatcher was prompted to comment "There is no such thing as society; there are individual men and women and there are families" (*Woman's Own,* October 10, 1987, quoted in Eyre 1991: 45). The market economy, and the new culture that it heralded, was presumed to give individuals more control over their lives together with more choice and opportunity (Jonathan 1999) and was backed up by policies that encouraged greater private ownership and consumer rights in all areas, including education (Kerr 1999). The stress of the Conservative government on the individualism of the free market emphasized the importance of civic obligation or "active citizenship" (Kerr 1999: 5). For the Conservatives the term "active citizen" was part of a wider philosophy "based on the privacy of the rights and responsibilities of the individual over those of the state" (Kerr 1999: 5). The promotion of active citizenship was a response to the economic situation at the time and the perceived decline in a sense of individual obligation to the community, both local and national. The Conservative emphasis was on the citizenship of duty and responsibility through an increasingly prosperous society that encouraged and rewarded individual effort and self-reliance (Parsons 1994). "Both the rationale for that political programme, and the moral acceptability of its social consequences, have generated heated debate, not least in relation to education" (Jonathan 1999: 68).

The Education Reform Act of 1988 extended the rights of the consumer into education and proposed that "citizenship should form part of what schools should seek to convey" (National Curriculum Council 1990: 1). The National Curriculum Council (NCC) report *Education for Citizenship,* published in 1990, sought to provide a framework for citizenship education that would establish the aims and objectives and give "guidance for schools . . . on how to develop essential components of education for citizenship" (Kerr 1999: 21).

The NCC identified the aims of education for citizenship as establishing "the importance of positive, participative citizenship . . . [which would] . . .provide the motivation to join in [and] help pupils to acquire and understand essential information on which to base the development of their skills, values and attitudes towards citizenship" (NCC 1990: 2).

The objectives of education for citizenship were identified as knowledge, attitudes, moral codes, and values, thereby placing spiritual and moral education explicitly within its scope. Attitudes to be encouraged included "a constructive interest in community affairs . . . [and] . . . appreciation of the paramount importance of democratic decision-making" (NCC 1990: 3). This report places great value on the democratic system in this country and suggests that a moral consensus may be reached through the comparison of values and beliefs and the identification of common ground so that differences can be discussed and conflict resolved (NCC 1990). The NCC stated that a pluralist, democratic society "is based on shared values, and a variety of cultures and lifestyles can be maintained within the framework of its laws" (NCC 1990: 6). The framework for citizenship education does not go into detail regarding these shared values; neither does it state exactly what these shared values may be, nor which parties have agreed or outlined them.

Dr. Nicholas Tate was "closely involved in developing the National Curriculum Council document on Citizenship Education" (Tate in Crewe et al. 1997: 17), and he has been rather more forthcoming regarding his view of the necessary values and morality that he understands to be important in the development of citizenship education. In a commentary during an event hosted by the Citizenship Foundation on May 21, 1996, (Crewe et al. 1997), Dr. Tate suggested that civic education requires the promotion of core values and virtues and the transmission of ethical values through spiritual and moral education. Dr. Tate went on to say that according to his understanding, "existing civil society is permeated by the excesses of individualism . . . and by the results of consumerism and moral relativism and of the decline of religion" (Tate in Crewe et al. 1997: 18). Dr. Tate had previously identified relativism in postmodernity as undermining "our surviving moral language. . . . If ever a dragon needed slaying, it is the dragon of relativism" (Tate 1996: 5–6). Dr. Tate has also suggested that intrinsic motivation is brought about by values and attitudes, which he outlined as "the promotion of values that emphasise concern for others, compassion, self-discipline, restraint, concern for the truth, and also enterprise" (Tate in Crewe et al. 1997: 18). It is interesting to note that some of Dr. Tate's views appear to be contradictory to the political climate at the time, while his support for self-discipline and enterprise backed up prevailing political views.

Dr. Tate states that education "is about promoting the moral and spiritual well-being of society . . . .There is evidence that one of the key factors distinguishing successful urban schools . . . is their explicit and sustained commitment to a set of core values" (Tate 1996: 3). There is little doubt, therefore, that Dr. Tate believes that the moral well-being of society rests not only with the family and society itself but is an intrinsic part of the education system. "Citizenship is about values" (Tate 2000: 69), and these values should be transmitted through citizenship education. Citizenship education, Dr. Tate proposes (2000), is not morally neutral about the kind of society that we wish to establish, or about the fact that we want a participative democracy, or about "what it is to be a fully developed and good human being" (Tate 2000: 69). Within this view, it would appear that citizenship education bears a heavy responsibility. It should not only teach the political knowledge necessary to understand how the democratic system in this country operates, but it should also impart the moral values seen by some as a necessary part of that system.

By 1997 there had been public discussion and the presentation of outlines for citizenship education. In May 1997 the Labour Party came to power. The question for "New Labour" was how to reconcile individual choice with collective interest, and how citizenship rights could be a means of offsetting the unequal outcomes of market forces.

"New Labour" placed the emphasis on "civic morality," which is based on "the civic responsibilities of the individual in partnership with the state" (Kerr 1999: 5). The answer, then, was to emphasize "the importance of educating individuals into a sense of communal national responsibility" (Crewe et al. 1997: 3), thus developing caring individuals "aware of the needs and views of others and motivated to contribute positively to wider society" (Kerr 1999: 5).

The Labour Government Education White Paper (1997), *Excellence in Schools*, announced the setting up of an advisory group on citizenship that produced the Crick Report in September 1998. "The Group's final recommendations form the basis of the proposals for the formal inclusion of Citizenship in the revised National Curriculum in schools from 2002" (Kerr 1999: 24). According to Kerr (1999), the group was deliberately nonpartisan, an approach that he considers vital if citizenship education is to be effective. The debates prior to the setting up of the advisory group had incorporated a large number of nongovernmental agencies, including youth agencies and children's rights organizations, national organizations concerned with equal opportunities and racial equality, together with citizenship organizations (Kerr 1999). It was subsequently felt by some members of these groups that the debates had become dominated by "narrow concerns about the shape of the school curriculum, to the exclusion of wider issues" (Kerr 1999: 12). The advisory group for *Education for Citizenship and the Teaching of Democracy in Schools* (the Crick Report) had, according to Kerr, "a carefully chosen, balanced membership" (Kerr 1999: 23).

The Summary of the Final Report "identifies three strands which should run through all education for citizenship" (www.qca. org.uk/citizenship – summary.htm: 4). These three strands are outlined as social and moral responsibility, community involvement, and political literacy. Considering the first of these strands, which is social and moral responsibility, the report believes that this is "the heart of the matter . . . Guidance on moral values and personal development are essential preconditions of citizenship" (Qualifications and Curriculum Authority (QCA) 1998: 2.10–2.11).

If guidance on moral values is a prerequisite of citizenship, then this appears to assume that people are not naturally moral and need education in moral behavior. This attitude has echoes of Thomas Hobbes, who believed that in a natural state, humanity would be at constant war because, without laws to restrain them, people would seek only their own ends and "in the way to their end, which is principally their own conservation, and sometimes their delectation only, endeavour to destroy, or subdue one another" (Hobbes 1946: 81). In short, for Hobbes, in the state of nature, humanity would live in "continual fear, and danger of violent death; and the life of man (sic), solitary, poor, nasty, brutish and short" (Hobbes 1946: 82). It appears, then, that social and moral responsibility need to be inculcated through citizenship education in order that individuals may learn to follow the rules of society and thereby live together in some sort of harmony, free from continual fear.

In the Crick Report (QCA 1998), civic education is understood as being "about the civic virtues and decent behaviour that adults wish to see in young people . . . Active citizens are as political as they are moral; moral sensibility derives in part from political understanding; political apathy spawns moral apathy" (Hargreaves quoted in QCA 1998: 2.6). This rather surprising quote appears to suggest that a person cannot be moral without political literacy, and therefore an active citizen must be both political and moral. The aim of citizenship education therefore, according to this report, is to identify and relate the "legal, moral and political arena of public life" (QCA 1998: 2.7) and induct young people into this arena. In addition to understanding, "citizenship education should foster respect for law, justice, democracy and nurture common good at the same time as encouraging independence of thought" (QCA 1998: 2.7). No mean feat for a subject that should take up "no more than five percent of curriculum time" (QCA 1998: 4.5). The report does suggest that citizenship education should be cross-curricular, combining elements of citizenship with other subjects. It also recommends that schools should "consider the relation of citizenship education to whole school issues" (QCA 1998: 4.7).

From the mid-1990s, controversy over citizenship education has "centred on the moral, spiritual and social dimensions in education and modern life" (Kerr 1999: 22), and part of the rationale behind the introduction of citizenship education appears to be the desire to halt the perceived erosion of the social, political, and moral fabric of society in England, which is partly attributed to rapid economic and social change (Kerr 1999). Crick suggests that the present consensus that citizenship education should be introduced has come about because there has been a "general questioning of whether our old institutions serve the purposes of society and worries about the alienation of young people from public values" (Crick 2000: 78). The Crick Report itself identifies the high abstention rate from voting among the 18–24 age group as a major concern together with alienation from society, indicators of which can be found in "truancy, vandalism, random violence, premeditated crime and habitual drug taking" (QCA 1998: 3.6). This is interesting when one considers the inclusion of members of the Prison Service and the Parole Board on the committee and their role in formulating citizenship education. Both the Prison Service and the Parole Board become involved when members of society do not follow the rules laid down for them. This appears to suggest that the role of morality in citizenship education is to teach young people to follow those rules. The report further suggests that "a main aim for the whole community should be to find or restore a sense of common citizenship" (QCA 1998: 3.14). Common citizenship could be understood in this context as citizens capable of following these rules; it does not appear to allow for discussion among students as to what common citizenship might mean to them.

The questions of the direction of spiritual and moral education and whether schooling actually contributes to better public behavior become confused when the problem of spiritual and moral education focuses on issues of discipline and control (Carr 1999). Through the emphasis on morality that runs through the report, it becomes clear that one of the purposes of citizenship education is to assist in halting the perceived moral decline of the young. A further purpose of motivating the younger voter out of a perceived political apathy is also apparent. Whether this is practical or possible remains questionable. Whether any system of education or a single subject within a system of education can achieve this seems unlikely. The rationale behind citizenship education appears to be an attempt to address these problems through the education system.

Spiritual and Moral Education as Modernist

If one of the aims of citizenship education is an attempt to address perceived problems in society through spiritual and moral education, then it becomes necessary to consider where society finds itself and whether education can address these problems. There are those who argue that we are in the "postmodern moment" (Usher and Edwards 1994; Marshall 1992), although postmodernity is itself a contested concept. If education is founded in modernity (Usher and Edwards 1994), and if society then finds itself in the postmodern era, the question is whether citizenship education, within the present curriculum, can address society's problems, including that of spiritual and moral education.

We claim here that spiritual and moral education, as suggested within citizenship education, is by its nature modernist. This is not to condemn it, nor to make a value-judgment, but to suggest that it therefore is not an appropriate form of education for this moment – the postmodern moment.

The first step is therefore to understand what modernity is, or rather what the characteristics of modernity might be. Osborne suggests that modernity came to be universalized as a way of differentiating "between itself and other 'times' . . . within a single temporal scheme of 'progress,' 'modernisation' and 'development'" (Osborne 1992: 34). He suggests that this became a universalizing discourse and, after Habermas (1990), referred to this discourse as "the philosophical discourse of modernity" (Osborne 1992: 35) whose task has been to unify and legitimate regional theories into the universal and the unifying. Central to the philosophical discourse of modernity is "the conception of the autonomy of reason" (Osborne 1992: 35), which in itself is central to the concept of enlightenment. For Kant, reason "must be able to validate its own laws to itself, within the present without reference to history or tradition" (Osborne 1992: 35). Lyotard (1992) suggests that the term "reason" is vast and so he restricts its use to what has been defined by science. Within these boundaries he refers to reason as "the collection of rules that a discourse must respect when it sets out to know an object . . . and make it known" (Lyotard 1992: 73). Kant's definition of enlightenment is the ability to use reason without direction from another; he suggests that the only thing required for enlightenment is the freedom to use reason, and the courage to use it without guidance (Kant 1997). Kant searched for the rules that reason must follow, for the transcendental reason for duty. Duty, for Kant, arises from reason, and duty recognizes that reason has rules that apply universally. For Kant (1997) the categorical imperative stood above emotion and apart from empirical motives.

Modernity, then, can be understood in one sense as the search, through reason, for the unifying and universal, for the unconditional or categorical imperatives that can serve as laws for humanity (Heelas 1998), where humanity can be understood as a center from which knowledge emanates and "to which absolute Truth may be made known" (Marshall 1992: 2). It could be argued, therefore, that if truth can be known through reason, it can be taught.

According to Usher and Edwards, modernity "is characterised by a hermeneutic search for an underlying and unifying truth and certainty that can render the world, experiences and events (including the self and its experiences) coherent and meaningful" (Usher and Edwards 1994: 12). It can be argued that a characteristic of modern life has been the development of the "individual" whose life is fragmented into many functions (Bauman 1992). Modernity has seen the division of labor, the separation between the public and the private, between the religious and the secular, and the separation of science from the religious life (Heelas 1998). This separation can be understood as differentiation in modernity. However, if modernity can also be understood as the search for the unifying, or de-differentiation (Heelas 1998), then it can be argued that modernity faces aporia, a contradiction that cannot be resolved or overcome. This aporia arises out of the contradiction between modernity's search for the unity while presiding over the fragmentation of the individual and society.

Bauman argues that modern legislators and thinkers attempted to "compose and impose . . . a cohesive code of moral rules which people could be taught and forced to obey" (Bauman 1993: 6). It was believed, argues Bauman (1993), that these rational rules would fill the void that had been left by the Church; in other words, it was thought that reason would replace belief in regulating moral conduct. Modernity then finds itself in the aporetic situation in which autonomous rational individuals and heteronomous rational management are "locked together for better or worse, bound to clash and struggle without end" (Bauman 1993: 7). Bauman suggests that a defining characteristic of modernity is that the aporia is "played down" (1993: 8) and that modernity admits to no conflict that cannot be resolved through reason. It can be argued therefore that modernity seeks closure, a resolution of conflict brought about by reason, and does not accept that there is no resolution or that there is conflict that cannot be overcome.

Modernity can be understood as attempting to present final and decisive explanations and theories (Usher and Edwards 1994), referred to as "metanarratives" by Lyotard (1984). These metanarratives, Lyotard argues (1992), are the mark of modernity, the progressive emancipation of reason and freedom and the search for the universal. Lyotard also argues (1992) that the project of modernity is the realization of universality, and so "education's historical role to enlighten and emancipate . . . is at the very heart of the project of modernity" (Usher and Edwards 1994: 125).

If the role of education is to enlighten, then it must be assumed that there is a subject, capable, through rational thought, of becoming self-motivated and autonomous, a "subject with inherent characteristics and potential" (Usher and Edwards 1994: 25). The task of education seems to be that of fulfilling this potential "in the forming and shaping of subjectivity and identity, . . . making people into particular kinds of subjects" (Usher and Edwards 1994: 25).

It is possible to argue that educational theory and pedagogy are founded in the modernist tradition. "Education is very much the dutiful child of the Enlightenment and, as such, tends to uncritically accept a set of assumptions deriving from Enlightenment thought" (Usher and Edwards 1994: 24). Enlightenment ideals and modernity itself can be understood to include the concept of critical reason, which seeks rational ways of solving humankind's problems while at the same time understanding humankind as responsible and intellectual beings. Modernity appears to believe that progress will emancipate "the whole of humanity from ignorance, poverty, backwardness, despotism. . . . Thanks to education in particular, it will also produce enlightened citizens, masters of their own destiny" (Lyotard 1992: 97). The enlightened citizen can be seen as the goal of citizenship education, and this goal, it can be argued, is founded in modernist ideas.

The Postmodern Moment

We would like to claim here that we are living in a postmodern moment though it is possible to suggest that the postmodern is not a distinct "time" in the chronological sense. Lyotard argues that "neither modernity nor so-called postmodernity can be identified and defined as clearly circumscribed historical entities, of which the latter would always come 'after' the former" (Lyotard 1992: 25). Marshall suggests that the postmodern "does not refer to a period or a 'movement'. . . . It's a moment, but more a moment in logic than in time . . . a space where meaning takes place . . . a moment of rupture, of change" (Marshall 1992: 5). Usher and Edwards argue that there are "enough glimpses of the postmodern moment or condition in our everyday lives for it to be something which is not . . . alien and incomprehensible" (Usher and Edwards 1994: 13). Marshall also argues that the postmodern has become an increasingly familiar term although "we are not living in a period identified 'totally' as postmodern . . . . The postmodern moment is not something that is to be defined chronologically; rather it is a rupture in our consciousness.

Its definition lies in change and chance, but it has everything to do with how we read the present, as well as how we read the past" (Marshall 1992: 5).

It could be argued that rather than "following on" from modernity, postmodernity could be understood as coming "out of" modernity. Lyotard argues that "modernity is constitutionally and ceaselessly pregnant with its postmodernity" (Lyotard 1991: 25). Bauman (1992) argues that features of the postmodern condition such as institutionalized pluralism, ambivalence, and contingency were understood by modernity to be failures. "The postmodern condition can be therefore described, on the one hand, as modernity emancipated from false consciousness; on the other, as a new type of social condition marked by the overt institutionalization of the characteristics which modernity . . . set about to eliminate and, failing that, tried to conceal" (Bauman 1992: 187–8).

The postmodern can be understood as embracing the aporetic situation in which modernity found itself. Postmodernity does not seek closure in the same way as modernity but embraces contingency and contradiction and celebrates differences. Postmodernity can be understood as a condition in which resolution of conflict, and the answers, are themselves contingent and open to change. Postmodernity could then be seen to provide temporary answers that may change with circumstance and perspective. It can be argued that postmodernity was always inherent in modernity and is a realization that universal "truth" was not something that, once discovered, would remain the same. Postmodernity then is not new but is a different way of looking at the world; it can be understood as a new understanding. Bauman suggests that an "adequate theory of postmodernity may be only constructed in a cognitive space organized by a different set of assumptions" and that while the postmodern condition may be "a site of constant mobility and change" (Bauman 1992: 188-9), it has no clear direction of development.

As an extreme simplification, Lyotard defines the postmodern as "incredulity towards metanarratives" (1984: xxiv), in which the concept of the inevitable progress of humanity has been called into question. To identify a clear direction of progress therefore returns to modernity. The postmodern questions the legitimacy of a center where action and belief are grounded, and therefore it undermines the certainty of modernity (Usher and Edwards 1994). For Usher and Edwards (1994), postmodernity describes a world that is complex, with many meanings, a world that legitimates local narratives in which individuals "make their way without fixed referents and traditional anchoring points. It is a world of rapid change, of bewildering instability, where knowledge is constantly changing and meaning 'floats'" (Usher and Edwards 1994: 10). In a postmodern culture "the question of the legitimation of knowledge is formulated in different terms. The grand narrative has lost its credibility" (Lyotard 1984: 37). However, Usher and Edwards understand that, significantly, "in postmodernity uncertainty, the lack of a centre and the floating of meaning are understood as phenomena to be celebrated rather than regretted" (Usher and Edwards 1994: 10). Marshall suggests that the postmodern moment "is an awareness of being within a way of thinking. . . . Crucial to an understanding of the postmodern moment is the recognition that there is no 'outside' from which to 'objectively' name the present. The postmodern moment is an awareness of being-within, first, a language, and second, a particular historical, social, cultural framework" (Marshall 1992: 3).

In a postmodern world, or in a postmodern moment in the modern world, the subject of educational activity has become a different subject that Usher and Edwards describe as "the *inscribed* subject, the subject constructed by discourses and signifying systems, 'de-centred' through language, society and the unconscious . . . [who] . . . thus seems to contradict the very basis of educational activity" (Usher and Edwards 1994: 25). As the postmodern moment appears to challenge existing structures and hierarchies of knowledge (Usher and Edwards 1994), education finds itself in a difficult position. Education, argue Usher and Edwards (1994), is "intimately connected with the production and dissemination of foundational knowledge and therefore with the re-creation and reproduction of the differential valuations and hierarchies of knowledge" (Usher and Edwards 1994: 25).

To apply these ideas directly to young people's education, we must look at what, specifically, within the experience of young people today, leads us to believe that they are existing within a postmodern moment. In other words, how can the above be directly related to their lives? First, young people are existing without metanarrative. There is no coherent "story" that tells them how they should live. Religions no longer fulfill that role, and the explosion of communication means that they know too much about other possibilities. They have choice, and who tells them how to choose? Second, young people often have multiple identities, existing within the pluralism, contingency, and complexity identified above. Again, they know this because they are told this. They know that they can choose who they want to be because every magazine and television program tells them so. Thus their context is giving them one message, while their citizenship education is committed to another – a rational, coherent message of shared values and aspirations.

Conclusions

It is possible to argue, therefore, that there is no "fit" between the system – education – and the student – the subject. As Usher and Edwards put it, "Education does not fit easily into the postmodern moment because educational theory and practice are founded in the modernist tradition" (Usher and Edwards 1994: 24). If this is the case, then the present education system is not able to speak directly to the student in a way that the student understands, and the world of education, the school, is no longer in tandem with the world of the student.

If the reason that education does not speak to the student is because it is founded in the modernist tradition and students find themselves in a postmodern world, then the outcome can be understood as the objectification of education in general and citizenship education in particular. If citizenship education is seen as a means to an end, then citizenship education has become the method of producing citizens. The product of citizenship education, as it appears in the Crick Report (QCA 1998), seems to be citizens who abide by the rules of society and are moral according to the definition of morality in the report. This definition of morality appears to be citizens who abide by the rules and who participate in democracy by voting. It could be argued that citizenship education is the means to this end, and this implies that the citizen has already become a commodity by Marx's definition. "The commodity is . . . a thing which through its qualities satisfies human needs of whatever kind" (Marx 1976: 125). It has been argued that the work of thinking has become separated from the product of thought, that is, ideas (Lukács 1971). If ideas have become alienated from the thinker, then thought has become objectified in the same way as labor has. In the context of citizenship education, individuals' thoughts on citizenship, and their work, become alienated from them. Citizenship education then becomes objectified, taken away from the student and handed back as a mark, which identifies how far the student has come on the route to becoming the "citizen." The outcome of "citizen" has already been decided, and citizenship education is the means of achieving the goals of "active citizen" and "civic morality" (Kerr 1999: 5).

The significance of the dichotomy between a modernist perception of citizenship education and the postmodern moment experienced by the students lies in this objectification. Is it possible for citizenship education imposed upon future citizens to achieve any of its aims if the understandings of the very concepts employed are not shared by the curriculum, the teachers, and the students?

We have argued that the final report of the Advisory Group on Citizenship, *Education for Citizenship and the Teaching of Democracy in*

Schools (QCA 1998), assumes a consensus on what morality is and assumes that this morality can be inculcated through citizenship education. The report further assumes that the inculcation of this morality will lead to specified outcomes, which will become evident in society.

We have called into question whether teaching morals will lead to a difference in behavior, and furthermore whether teaching a modernist version of morality will have any relevance to students in a postmodern moment. If this version of morality is somebody's metanarrative and therefore somebody else's power, it raises the question whether it is in fact moral to teach it and perpetuate that power.

We have also argued that the assumptions in this report have led to a definition of moral citizenship that is both static and narrow and does not take into account the difficulties and complexities of either the term "morality" or the term "citizenship"; furthermore, it does not allow for discussion of what a citizen might be.

> In order for democracy to work, people must be educated and then trusted to act morally, in the best interests of themselves and others. This has always been the uncomfortable part of democracy, and thus also the uncomfortable part of citizenship. (Erricker and Erricker 2000a: 104)

We would suggest that this trust in people to act morally is the difficulty that spiritual and moral education finds itself in and that it is the aporia of spiritual and moral education that cannot be resolved. This aporia would suggest that neither citizenship nor morality is static but changes with time and circumstance. The attempt to impose a morality for citizenship can be interpreted as a desire for a citizenry and a democracy that are static and unchanging, that do not build on what exists but attempt to preserve it unchanged. Spiritual and moral education within citizenship appears to be a process of solving society's problems without addressing the complex and dialectical nature of citizenship.

We argue that an open-ended and more flexible definition of the term "citizen" might allow for discussion and reflection on what being a citizen means to individuals and how these individuals might affect the world in which they live. Individuals reflecting on themselves and their world might lead to a desire to change this world, or not. However, by applying learning outcomes and a specified goal of being a citizen, we suggest that the goal has become commodified.

A Solution?

A citizenship education that draws on disciplines and experience from across the curriculum that address morality as a holistic experience intertwined with individual growth, would arguably have more chance of relevance. "Placing citizenship within the framework of achievable outcomes for all children implies a false universality of children's current experience and future expectations" (Rumsey 1999: 4). Applying standard definitions of attainment targets to this subject means that success is measured by learning outcomes. We suggest that learning outcomes are not relevant to individual growth and self-understanding, which appear to be a necessary part of the moral individual who exists in community.

As you might expect, we would argue for a citizenship education based on active participation and on a narrative pedagogy.

The problems for the citizenship curriculum are those of content and process. What should we teach, and how should we teach it? These decisions have, of course, already been made. The curriculum is in place, and the teaching methods expected are not controversial. It contains direction to teach about civics, but also the government has obviously expected it to be a form of moral education as the connections between the two have been clearly expressed. "Active citizens are as political as they are moral; moral sensibility derives in part from political understanding; political apathy spawns moral apathy" (Hargreaves quoted in QCA 1998: 2.6).

However, there is also evidence that moral instruction does not produce a moral person. Hartshorne and May,[1] as far back as 1940, conducted a study into behavior that raised questions about the assumption within moral education that teaching the difference between right and wrong would result in modification of behavior. Their findings indicate that there is no correlation between character training and actual behavior. Moral behavior is not consistent in one person in different situations, and there is not necessarily a relationship between what people may say and their actions (Duska and Whelan 1977).

So what do we have? A curriculum for citizenship that aims to produce moral, active citizens by teaching children about how their government works and telling them how to behave. Simple, straightforward, and, we might suggest, pretty useless. It's a curriculum that seems to take no account of the complex, daunting world that these children inhabit, a world that puts tremendous pressure on young people. Can we suggest a curriculum (or a subversion of this curriculum) that:

- tells young people how their government works;
- allows them to practice the democratic process by involvement in decision-making in their class and in their school;
- gives them the critical awareness that democracy and capitalism are

not the only ways that society can be organized and may not be the best way;

- helps them see how they might be manipulated by government agencies and by corporate advertising;
- makes sure they know their own rights;
- teaches them how people in other parts of the world are fighting for their rights;
- develops their emotional literacy and helps them deal with the stresses of life;
- Makes sure they know where and when to get help;
- and above all, shows them that they are important and should be listened to.

The assumptions contained within the new curriculum for citizenship training represent a missed opportunity to make citizenship education relevant and effective. On both philosophical and practical grounds this curriculum falls short of what might have been achieved and therefore cannot produce the desired outcomes.

Note

1   The three volumes of *Studies in the Nature of Character* (1940) by Hartshorne and May are missing from the British Library, so we have used Duska and Whelan 1977, who summarize their findings.

References

Bauman, Z. 1992: *Intimations of Postmodernity*. London: Routledge.
—— 1993: *Postmodern Ethics*. Oxford: Blackwell.
Carr, D. 1999: Cross Questions and Crooked Answers: Contemporary Problems of Moral Education. In J. M. Halstead and T. McLaughlin (eds.), *Education in Morality*, pp. 24–43, London: Routledge.
Carr, W. and Kemmis, S. 1986: *Becoming Critical*. Lewes: Falmer Press.
Crewe, I., Searing, D., and Conover, P. 1997: *Citizenship and Civic Education: A Presentation of the Findings of a Comparative Research Programme into Aspects of Citizenship in Britain and the United States*. London: The Citizenship Foundation.
Crick, B. 2000: The Citizenship Order for Schools. In N. Pearce and J. Hallgarten (eds.), *Tomorrow's Citizens: Critical Debates in Citizenship and Education*, pp. 77–83, London: Institute for Public Policy Research (IPPR.)
Davie, G. 1994: *Religion in Britain Since 1945*. Oxford: Blackwell Publishers.
Department for Education and Employment (DfEE) 1999: *The National Curriculum*. London: DfEE and QCA.
Duska, R. and Whelan, M. 1977: *Moral Development: A Guide to Piaget and Kohlberg*. London: Gill and Macmillan.
Erricker, C. and Erricker, J. 2000a: *Reconstructing Religious, Spiritual and Moral Education*. London: Routledge Falmer.
Erricker, J. 2000b: A Collaborative Approach to Researching Teacher Work in

Developing Spiritual and Moral Education. In R. Best (ed.), *Education for Spiritual, Moral, Social and Cultural Development*, pp. 185–98, London: Continuum.

Eyre, A. 1991: Charity, Faith and the Free Market. In P. Gee and J. Fulton (eds.), *Religion and Power, Decline and Growth*, London: British Sociological Association, Sociology of Religion Study Group.

Habermas, J. 1990: *The Philosophical Discourse of Modernity*. Cambridge: Polity Press.

Heelas, P. (ed.) 1998: *Religion, Modernity and Postmodernity*. Oxford: Blackwell.

Hobbes, T. 1946: *Leviathan*. Oxford: Basil Blackwell.

Jonathan, R. 1999: Agency and Contingency in Moral Development and Education. In J. M. Halstead and T. McLaughlin (eds.), *Education in Morality*, pp. 62–78. London: Routledge.

Kant 1997: *Foundations of the Metaphysics of Morals*, 2nd ed. New Jersey: Prentice-Hall.

Kerr, D. 1999: *Re-Examining Citizenship Education: The Case of England*. Slough: National Foundation for Educational Research.

Lukács, G. 1971: *History and Class Consciousness*. London: Merlin Press.

Lyotard, J.-F. 1984: *The Postmodern Condition: A Report on Knowledge*. Manchester: Manchester University Press.

—— 1992: *The Postmodern Explained to Children: Correspondence 1982–1985*. London: Turnaround.

Marshall, B. 1992: *Teaching the Postmodern*. London: Routledge.

Marx, K. 1976: *Capital*, vol. 1. London: Penguin.

National Curriculum Council 1990: *Curriculum Guidance 8: Education for Citizenship*. York: NCC.

Osborne, P. 1992: Modernity is a Qualitative, Not a Chronological, Category: Notes on the Dialectics of Differential Historical Time. In F. Barker, P. Hulme, and M. Iverson (eds.), *Postmodernism and the Re-Reading of Modernity*, pp. 23–45. Manchester: Manchester University Press.

Parsons, G. (ed.) 1994: *The Growth of Religious Diversity: Britain from 1945*, vol. II. London: Routledge.

Qualifications and Curriculum Authority 1998: *Education for Citizenship and the Teaching of Democracy in Schools: Final Report of the Advisory Group on Citizenship*. London: QCA.

Rumsey, H. 1999: "Perspectives on a Paradox: Teaching Children Citizenship," Paper for School of Social Studies, University College Chichester.

Tate, N. 1996: "Education for Adult Life: Spiritual and Moral Aspects of the Curriculum." Speech at a conference organized by the School Curriculum and Assessment Authority. Queen Elizabeth II Conference Centre, London, 15 January 1996.

—— 2000: Citizenship Education in a Liberal Democracy. In N. Pearce and J. Hallgarten (eds.), *Tomorrow's Citizens: Critical Debates in Citizenship and Education*, pp. 64–73. London: IPPR.

Usher, R. and Edwards, R. 1994: *Postmodernism and Education*. London: Routledge.

Chapter 15

Hope against Devastation: Children's Spirituality and Human Rights

LIAM GEARON

T HE HISTORY OF THE twentieth century has created a sense of moral vacuity, a sense of emptiness and even absurdity about the human condition; and with this came a deep-seated sense of human isolation in the universe, fundamental meaninglessness, *anomie*. In Europe during the same period the philosophical novel became, for many, the medium of this existential estrangement. European philosophy became unstructured and, when confronted with horror – mass death, genocide, the devastation of whole peoples and cultures, systematized cruelty – ideas about existence took on self-consciously challenging forms.

In one of the defining texts of French existentialism and twentieth-century literature, *L'Etranger* (*The Outsider*) by Albert Camus, Mersault's mother dies. He is uncertain whether it was today or yesterday, but he knows that she has died. In his court case, where he is found guilty of murdering an Arab man, the prosecution highlights the fact that a day or so after his mother died he was seen attending a local cinema for entertainment. This fact was meant to signify his callousness, his incapacity for moral sensitivity. Not without its postcolonial critics (Said 1994) for making the murdered Arab an anonymous, nameless figure, *The Outsider* came to define the alienation felt in the face of failed systems of belief, politics, religion, and science. At the conference in Israel from which this chapter arose, I was struck by its political resonance today. In the passage where the murder scene is so powerfully described, Mersault's first bullet kills the Arab man and, leaving no further trace, his four additional bullets are shot into a lifeless body, "like four sharp knocks at the door of unhappiness."

I revise this paper in London as planes are diverted away from their usual course over the center of the city. It is the morning after the devastating events in the United States of September 11, 2001. In 1942 too, in a cumulative senselessness, ethical codes that attempted to make sense of and control human action all seemed to be in a state of collapse. Today, of course, murder and violent conflict, which remain at the extremes of ethical consideration, also challenge our sense of meaning. To return to the past, within six years of the publication of *The Outsider*, the world itself, after two global conflicts, needed to renew its sense of moral identity. Thus in 1948 the United Nations General Assembly proclaimed the Universal Declaration of Human Rights as a global ethical standard for all peoples, almost, without forethought, a new morality. The history of the past few decades since the Universal Declaration tells us of course that declarations do not present easy solutions in practice.

Within this very specific historical context, this chapter presents an initial assessment of the potential relationship between children's spirituality and human rights as a critically important dimension of spirituality and ethics in education. Summarizing selected studies of spirituality in education over the past few decades, I argue that the *historical* and *political* contexts have been neglected. In order to counterbalance such a perceived neglect, it is argued that work on children's spirituality can benefit from a consideration of issues raised by human-rights education. In particular, I set out how and why our discussions of children's spirituality need to be closely connected with the human-rights agenda that, for all its many organizational and human failings (Ryan 2000), remains important, even crucial, to life on a planet with such a diversity of human cultures and worldviews.

Children's Spirituality and Worldview

Spirituality has become associated as closely with ultimate worldview as with ultimate experiences. It is thus for good reason that spirituality, while still often associated with religious traditions, is now commonly given secular interpretations, especially in education. But as William James pointed out in *The Varieties of Religious Experience*, the historical transmission of traditions of religious experience actually depends upon the successful adaptation of these beliefs in the world itself. In other words, the success of a spiritual tradition is measured by how effectively spiritual experiences (of transcendence and so forth) relate to the world of *other* experiences. Here William James talks of the material effects of spiritual or religious beliefs (James 1925: 325–31). And it is this testing of the spiritual in the material world that ensures the abiding relevance of human-rights education to children's spirituality.

Spirituality in education has in this respect taken a series of wrong turns that have led it to remain too focused on inwardness and personal experience at the expense of social and political consciousness.

My former tutor at Lancaster University in England, the late Ninian Smart, pioneered the phenomenological approach to the study of religion in universities and, more indirectly, in schools (Smart 1969; 1989, and so forth). The most significant influence on Smart's foundational and seemingly noninclusive text, *The Religious Experience of Mankind* (Smart 1969), was the great religious philosopher Rudolf Otto. In Otto's famous text, *The Idea of the Holy* (Otto 1950), the root of religious traditions is said to be the experience of the numinous, the most intense form of experience of the holy. Smart's interest, seeing what a myriad of public forms resulted from this experience in all its cultural and historical diversity, was how one could set aside one's own worldview prejudices in order to study religion and spiritual experience from a disengaged perspective. It is thus familiar to scholars of religion that Smart used a phenomenological method deriving from Husserl to approach the spiritual and religious experiences of others through six dimensions: ritual, mythical, doctrinal, ethical, social, and experiential (Smart 1969). In a later book (Smart 1989) the approach had a new and more inclusive title, *The Religions of the World*, and Smart added a further dimension, the aesthetic.

This approach has had a tremendous effect upon school religious education (Copley 1997; cf. Copley 2000). But the approach has been criticized on a number of fronts, implicitly but most fundamentally in school religious education in England and Wales (QCA 1998; QCA, 1998a; QCA 1998b). It is suggested here, and often by faith communities themselves, that the approach imposes artificial structures and conceptual categories that religious communities themselves don't recognize. For example, not all religions place the concept of God and theology at their heart. It is ironic that Smart's brand of phenomenology was also criticized by those who claimed that such an approach tended to neglect the *experiential* dimension – what resulted from the mid-1980s came (at least in the UK) to be recognized as a neglect of the spiritual in education. The debate went on in this period in the special spirituality issues of the 1984 and 1985 editions of the *British Journal of Religious Education*. In the UK it was a debate that John Hammond et al. provoked further with their volume *New Methods in Religious Education: An **Experiential** Approach* (my emphasis) (1990).

Interest in the spiritual in education within this context came to further prominence with Mark Halstead's 1993 National Conference on Spiritual, Moral, Social, and Cultural Development at the University of Plymouth, England, and with the development of the journal *SPES*. Various journal articles followed in the 1990s, and indeed the

International Journal of Children's Spirituality, edited by Clive and Jane Erricker and Cathy Ota, appeared in the later part of this decade as well. Andrew Wright's attempt (1998; 2001) to bring philosophical hermeneutics to bear on the subject managed to fault the experiential approach for its lack of conceptual clarity, just as Adrian Thatcher critiqued this trend for a lack of tradition (Thatcher 1991). If David Hay and Rebecca Nye's work on "relationality" in spirituality (Hay and Nye 1998) opened up another dimension beyond the self-reflective, this has not as yet gone as far as taking relational consciousness into political engagement. But any model that incorporates religious and secular ideas of spirituality exposes the very lack of (religious, ideological) grandnarrative in secular notions of spirituality, something treated by David Carr's important work in the journal *Philosophy of Education* (Carr 1996). We see these tensions in relation to worldview in Coles's work on *The Spiritual Life of Children* (1992). This remarkable book, based on 30 years of study and research by an American developmental psychologist, presents the importance of children's growth in understanding of key concepts in their tradition. In the work of the Chichester-based Children's Worldview Project (for instance, Erricker, Ota and Erricker 2001), children are in a sense caught in and in between grand narratives – empirical studies seem to show that school education within traditions is not as effective in developing worldview as might be expected, that children in open, democratic societies are not neatly enwrapped within one worldview but caught between many – religious and secular, and a wide variety of these too. Even more recent work (Erricker, Ota, and Erricker 2001) has usefully re-emphasized what the great traditions have always realized: the importance not only of the personal search but also of the *community* dimension of any shared construction of ethical value and spiritual/existential meaning.

Yet, ironically, in a context for which spirituality, especially secular models, have broadened to incorporate the search for worldview and for meaning as defining features, spirituality in education has seemingly turned away from the world. This is the great failing of secular spirituality, devoid of strong ideology or theology. Even if systems may themselves be consciously rejected in a context in which personal search is emphasized, it is difficult to construct systems that have a sense of ethical direction when your worldview remains ambiguously open. One of the results of this, apart from an overemphasis on the personal and the experiential, is that while models of secular spirituality may emphasize relationality, community, and so forth, ethical conceptualizations and frameworks for action are less easy to define. This is troubling in a global context in which worldview has become even more contested. Indeed, studies of conflicts after World War II have shown that *ethnic* conflicts – conflicts in which one worldview takes violent action against another worldview – are as prevalent as ever, if not more so (Ryan 2000). This, of course, is another demonstration of why Lyotard's definition (1984) of the postmodern condition as the ending of all grand narrative is open to challenge. People do not die in such conflicts if the notion of all-encompassing worldview or grand narrative has disappeared from their lives. Religious, ethnic, and cultural identity in many situations is arguably as important today as ever, and the ethical implications – continuing ethnic and political violence – perhaps more so.

The question becomes here a historical one. How do we explain the pattern of history, the collectivity of human action, in terms of the grand narrative of the human species? In 1992 Francis Fukuyama published an ambitious book entitled *The End of History*. His thesis suggested that there is global realization of a collective moral and political consciousness, nothing short of a universally accepted liberal and democratic model of governance based upon a value system of shared human rights. Fukuyama traced the notion of an end to history to Kant's 1794 paper "An Idea for a Universal History From a Cosmopolitan Point of View." What Kant described here as "this idiotic course of things human" seemed to show no particular pattern on its surface and implied that human history is filled with constant warfare and cruelty (Fukuyama 1992: 28). Kant nonetheless wondered, as Fukuyama suggested, "whether there was not a regular movement to human history such that what seemed chaotic of a single individual might not reveal a sole and progressive evolution over a long period of time," or in other words, he considered the notion of a universal history (Fukuyama 1992: 32). Fukuyama has had his critics, and rightly so. His agenda presented a Western-centered, even American-centered, notion of liberal and democratic rights as the inspiration and model for all, not only for today but for the future. The American model is, after all, according to Fukuyama, the end of history. But Fukuyama, for all his overstated polemic about the end of history, is also to an extent correct, for in a crowded world, any notion that radically different standards of the most basic ethical values can be applied in different geographical territories poses certain difficulties. However flawed, the Universal Declaration of Human Rights and subsequent conventions remain, albeit contested, as global benchmarks for behavior. For all the nuances of different religious and cultural systems, universal human rights, arguably and albeit defined by an inefficient and often ineffective global bureaucracy, are the new morality. The UN itself recognizes immense limitations and failings in implementation (Ayton-Shenker 1996); international tensions over cultural norms versus universal rights were highlighted most recently in the discussions about human rights in connection with the International

Olympic Committee's decision to allow China to host the 2008 Olympic Games.

Children's Spirituality and Human-Rights Education

In a talk last year I examined the United Nations Convention on the Rights of the Child (adopted in 1989), looking at selected articles from this convention in the wider context of children's rights. In particular, as a result of a recommendation of the United Nations Committee on the Rights of the Child, the General Assembly in 1993 requested that the Secretary-General appoint an authority to study the impact of armed conflict on children. Graca Machel, the Secretary-General's appointed expert on the subject and a former minister of education in Mozambique, submitted a report, "The Impact of Armed Conflict on Children," to the 1996 session of the General Assembly. The report suggests that armed conflict "more than any other force, has transformed the lives of millions of children and women" and that far from simply being caught in the crossfire, many women and children are actually being specifically targeted. Here, the report chillingly suggests, "Nothing is spared, held sacred or protected."

At the First International Conference on Children's Spirituality in Chichester, England, I argued that it is the power struggles of empires, imperialism, and colonialism – historical and contemporary – often by countries that support grand ideals of spirituality in education, that contribute to the greatest abuse of those ideals. In this context I have presented a notional spirituality of dissent, arguing for an increased politicization of spirituality in education and a greater call for spirituality's ethical engagement (cf. Gearon 2001; 2001a; 2001b; 2002, 2002a, forthcoming). Yet I was struck by Hanan Alexander's comment that the analysis might be fine, but where was the positive agenda? Despite all this, there is "hope against devastation" for there are signs of optimism; and I believe that human-rights education can contribute to and enhance this sense of progress and that our debates on spirituality in education can benefit too. According to Human Rights Watch:

> Every recognized country in the world, except for the United States and the collapsed state of Somalia, has ratified the Convention on the Rights of the Child, pledging to uphold its protections for children. Today the convention stands as the single most widely ratified treaty in existence. Adopted by the United Nations General Assembly on November 20, 1989, the promises of this historic document include children's rights to life; to be free from discrimination; to be protected in armed conflicts; to be protected from torture or cruel, inhuman, or degrading treatment or punishment; to be free from arbitrary deprivation of liberty; to special

treatment within the justice system; and the rights to education, health care, an adequate standard of living, and freedom from economic exploitation and other abuse. (HRW 2001)

Indeed, the years following the adoption of the Convention on the Rights of the Child have been marked by some significant advances on behalf of children:

> Many countries have used the convention as the basis to revise domestic legislation and improve protections for children, or have appointed special ombudspersons or envoys for children. As the Committee on the Rights of the Child, the body that monitors compliance of states parties to the convention, has evaluated country reports under the convention, it has developed new standards of protection and pressed governments for specific reforms. (HRW 2001)

Further signs of hope amid the tragedy are that the number of children killed annually by antipersonnel mines has declined since the adoption of the 1997 Mine Ban Treaty; the adoption of the statute for the International Criminal Court holds out some hope of ending the impunity of those who recruit children in armed conflicts and target schools for attack.

Yet even if there have been positive developments arising from the Convention, for countless children around the world, the promises inherent in it have been broken:

> The armed conflicts that rage in all quarters of the world have produced appalling abuses of children's rights. Hundreds of thousands of children have been pressed into service as soldiers. Millions have become refugees – displaced from their homes, often separated from their families, their future and safety uncertain. Children living outside war zones may also be subjected to routine violence. Street children on every continent endure harassment and physical abuse by police. . . . Millions of children have no access to education, work long hours under hazardous conditions, or languish in orphanages or detention centres where they endure inhumane conditions and daily assaults on their dignity, in violation of the rights guaranteed to them under the Convention. (HRW 2001: 3)

Every anniversary of the Convention marks an important milestone. The rights of children are recognized as never before but, again to cite Human Rights Watch, the Convention "also poses a challenge: for governments and civil society to take stronger action to implement its provisions, strengthen protections, and fulfil the promises made to the children of the world" (HRW 2001: 3).

By way of a caveat to our discussion, we should be aware that notions of supposedly international human rights and the so-called human-rights agenda are often hijacked by economically and politically powerful vested interests that can make implementation difficult. In Bell's *Teaching Human Rights* (1999), principally used for legal education, Wade Mansell's contribution highlights contested issues since the 1948 Universal Declaration:

- A study of the discourse of human rights since the World War II suggests that the rhetoric of human rights has been determined most clearly by the propaganda value it represented.
- The difference in the sort of human rights different states proclaimed was dictated by the political ideology of each state.
- International institutions with power tend to reflect the interests of powerful states.
- International financial institutions have, by their operation, made the protection of economic rights almost impossible for poor states.
- The economic interests of wealthy states have led indirectly but regularly to human rights abuse whether, for instance, through the export of tobacco, the export of pesticides or the export of subsidised food.
- The aftermath of colonialism continues to bedevil former colonial peoples in their attempts to promote and secure self-determination.
- Finally, regardless of proclaimed international standards on human rights, there are some states that may regularly, persistently and blatantly ignore world opinion if their strategic or emotional importance is exceptional. (Mansell 1999: 53)

These reservations about the manipulation of human-rights language aside, spirituality in education must here make a difference to political consciousness. The basic validity of spirituality in education, if it wishes to move beyond self-indulgence and narcissism, must be tested in the world, as I suggested earlier in relation to William James. We need a bridge, conceptual and practical, between children's spirituality and human-rights education – in academic study, in theoretical and empirical research, and in the realities of practical teaching within schools and initial teacher education. A human-rights education agenda for spirituality in education, following from the Universal Declaration, might usefully focus on three articles from the Convention on the Rights of the Child, Articles 27, 28, and 29. The language of spirituality coincides directly with that of human rights in the opening line of Article 27 when it declares that "States Parties recognize the right of every child to a standard of living adequate for the child's physical, mental, spiritual, moral and social development."

Conclusion

The thoughts I have presented elsewhere on a spirituality of dissent (Gearon 2001; 2001a) are not meant to promote a purely destructive, revolutionary force but are offered as a balance between the search for personal meaning and collective responsibility, personal transformation and political change, contemplation and action. And in this context we are inevitably drawn, and rightly so, into the obvious inequalities of rights, and especially children's rights, the world over. Our models of spirituality then inevitably become associated with dissent. Indeed, as Camus famously commented, "The spirit of revolt can only exist where a theoretic equality conceals great factual inequalities."

Spirituality ranges thus into social justice, as it has always done in the religious traditions of the world. And in this context the universal human-rights agenda is one on which there is at least nominal consensus. It can help transform action-neutral models of children's spirituality into systems of and for change. In England a conference in 2001 on children's spirituality entitled The Right to Be sponsored by the children's charity Barnardos was the first conference on spirituality held by a secular U.K. charity. If we have seen time and time again that the high ideals of the United Nations Convention on the Rights of the Child are hardly a reality, this, I think, is where our discussions on children's spirituality must increasingly focus. For children's spirituality is so vulnerably dependent upon the material, physical, social, and cultural conditions of their existence that the basic rights, and the security of these rights, should be used to enable spirituality to exist and develop. In this sense too, children's spirituality cannot even be contemplated without an assessment of human-rights education. This path, a spirituality religiously interpreted or secular, reflective upon existential questions but outwardly engaged in the world, can offer at least some slim hope against the devastation faced by many young lives.

References

Ayton-Shenker, D. 1996: The Challenge of Human Rights and Cultural Diversity. Geneva: United Nations.

Bell, C. et al. 1999: *Teaching Human Rights*. Warwick: Centre for Legal Education.

Camus, A. 1942, 1982: *The Outsider*. Harmondsworth: Penguin.

Carr, D. 1996: Rival conception of spiritual education. *Journal of Philosophy of Education* 30 (2): 159–78.

Coles, R. 1992: *The Spiritual Life of Children*. London: HarperCollins.

Copley, T. 1997: *Teaching Religion: Fifty Years of Religious Education in England and Wales*. Exeter: Exeter University Press.

—— 2000: *Spiritual Development in the State School*. Exeter: Exeter University Press.

Erricker, C., Erricker, J., and Ota, C. (eds.) 2001: *Spiritual Education: Cultural, Religious and Social Differences – New Perspectives for the 21st Century*. Brighton & Portland: Sussex Academic Press.

Fukuyama, F. 1992: *The End of History and the Last Man*. Harmondsworth: Penguin.

Gearon, L. 2001: The imagined other: postcolonial theory and religious education. *British Journal of Religious Education* 23 (2): 98–106.

—— 2001a: The Corruption of Innocence and a Spirituality of Dissent: Some Postcolonial Perspectives on Children's Spirituality in a World of Violence. In Erricker et al. (eds.), *Spiritual Education: Cultural, Religious and Social Differences – New Perspectives for the 21st Century*, Brighton & Portland: Sussex Academic Press.

—— 2001b: A spirituality of dissent: religion, culture and postcolonial criticism. *International Journal of Children's Spirituality* 7 (1): 289–98.

—— 2002: Religious education and human rights: some postcolonial perspectives. *British Journal of Religious Education* 24 (2): 140–50.

—— (ed.) 2002a: *Human Rights and Religion*. Brighton & Portland: Sussex Academic Press.

Hammond, J., Hay, D. et al. 1990: *New Methods in Religious Education: An Experiential Approach*. Harlow, England: Longman.

Hay, D. and Nye, R. 1998: *The Spirit of the Child*. London: Fount.

Hay, D. 2001: Spirituality Versus Individualism: The Challenge of Relational Consciousness. In Erricker et al., *Spiritual Education: Cultural, Religious and Social Differences – New Perspectives for the 21st Century*, Brighton & Portland: Sussex Academic Press.

Human Rights Watch 2001: *Children's Rights*. New York: HRW.

James, W. 1902/1925: *The Varieties of Religious Experience*. London: Longmans, Green.

Lyotard, J.-F. 1984: *The Postmodern Condition*. Manchester: Manchester University Press.

Machel, G. 1996: *The Impact of Armed Conflict on Children*. Geneva: United Nations.

Mansell, W. 1999: A Human Rights Course. In Bell et al. (eds.), *Teaching Human Rights*, Warwick: Centre for Legal Education.

Otto, R. 1950: *The Idea of the Holy*. J. W. Harvey, tr. London: Oxford University Press.

Qualifications and Curriculum Authority (QCA) 1998: "Faith Communities Working Group Reports." London: QCA.

—— 1998a: "Model Syllabus for Religious Education 1." London: QCA.

—— 1998b: "Model Syllabus for Religious Education 2." London: QCA.

Ryan, S. 2000: *The United Nations*. London: Macmillan.

Said, E. 1994: *Culture and Imperialism*. London: Vintage.

Smart, N. 1969: *The Religious Experience of Mankind*. London: Macmillan.

—— 1989: *The World's Religions*. Cambridge: Cambridge University Press.

Thatcher, A. 1991: A critique of inwardness in religious education. *British Journal of Religious Education* 14 (1): 22–7.

Wright, Andrew 1998: *Spiritual Pedagogy*. Oxford: Culham.

—— 2001: *Spiritual Education*. London: Routledge.

Chapter 16

Acts of Courage: Reshaping Tradition in Palestinian–Jewish School Ceremonies

Zvi Bekerman

"Avoiding war is the work of politics; establishing peace is the work of education." *Maria Montessori*

THOSE WHO RESIDE within the physical borders of Israel are continually confined and defined by national, religious, and ethnic boundaries. Although arguably imaginary, these boundaries often become inescapably real in Israel. People are perpetually occupied with the work of marking them, wielding them like weapons, including and excluding, acknowledging or rejecting values and ways of life, even denying the Other the right to exist.

In recent years, a new educational bilingual and binational initiative has been instituted in Israel. Its main purpose is to offer dignity and equality to the two Israeli groups who for the last 100 years have denied each other's humanity: Palestinians and Jews.

Our research examines one organization's attempt at bilingual and binational education in which each group is encouraged to take pride in its own cultural heritage while respecting and experiencing the heritage of the other. This chapter is a qualitative analysis of data gathered on the joint Hanukkah/Eid al Fitr/Christmas celebration held at the bilingual/binational school in Jerusalem. We expect this research to shed some light on identity construction in conflict-ridden environments and the possibility of social healing through educational efforts.

Bilingual Education in the Context of Israel's Binational Conflict

The State of Israel is as much a product of an invented tradition (Hobsbawm 1983) as any other modern nation-state. As such, it has institutionalized itself through the establishment of public education, the standardization of law, the development of a secular equivalent to the church, and by inventing public ceremonies and producing public monuments that mold a unifying history (Ben-Amos and Bet-El 1999; Handelman 1990).

Palestinian presence and the awakening of its national consciousness have caused problems for the seemingly natural construct of the Israeli nation. The Jewish–Arab conflict remains perhaps the most potentially explosive of conflicts in Israel, placing the Jewish majority (80 percent) and the Arab (primarily Moslem) minority (20 percent) at perpetual odds. The two peoples have been plagued with tragedy and suffering, and political efforts to overcome their conflict have been unsuccessful to date. For the most part, Israel as an ethnic democracy has not welcomed the active participation in political, cultural, or social spheres of any other than its legitimate invented community of Jews. Israeli Palestinians, though officially offered full rights as citizens, have chronically suffered as a putatively hostile minority with little political representation and a debilitated social, economic, and educational infrastructure (Ghanem 1998, Smooha 1996).

Though riddled with conflict and social cleavages, Israel must attempt to meet the often competing requirements of a multiethnic national-religious society. The sociopolitical conflicts are reflected in the Israeli educational system, which is divided into separate educational sectors: nonreligious Jewish, religious national Jewish, Orthodox Jewish, and Arab, all under the umbrella of the Israeli Ministry of Education.

Considering the sociopolitical context in Israel, the idea of creating Arab–Jewish coeducation is in and of itself a daring enterprise. It is within the framework of these realities that the recent creation of two bilingual Arabic–Hebrew schools should be considered. The Center for Bilingual Education in Israel (CBE) was established in 1997 with the aim of initiating and fostering egalitarian Arab–Jewish cooperation in education, mainly through the development of bilingual, binational, and multicultural cooperative educational institutions. Since 1997 the Center has been involved in the establishment of two schools guided by these principles, one in Jerusalem and one in Misgav, in the northern Galilee.

The schools at the time of the study include up to the third grade and are recognized as nonreligious schools supported by the Israeli Ministry of Education. Their curriculum is the regular curriculum of the state nonreligious school system, with the difference that both Hebrew and Arabic are used as languages of instruction. The schools employ what has been characterized as a strong additive bilingual approach, which emphasizes symmetry between both languages in all aspects of instruction (Skutnabb-Kangas and Garcia 1995).

Parents who send their children to these schools could be characterized as belonging to an upper middle socioeconomic class in Israeli society. Jewish parents first list ideological reasons for sending their children to the bilingual school; their second reason is that they believe the education to be equal to if not better than what their children would receive in a regular secular Israeli school. Palestinian parents, on the other hand, first mention their expectation of safeguarding their children from the putatively backward and unpromising education offered by regular Arab schools, and only then list ideological reasons.

These schools, still considered a curiosity in the Israeli educational system, must pioneer solutions to the multiple curricular problems raised by mixing these two populations. These problems have to do with cultural and identity borders and with historical discourse and interpretations, including the ones that enable the Jewish population to justify the constitution of Israel as a sovereign state, and to have a "natural" sense of peoplehood through the construction of collective memory.

On the Transformative Potential of Ritual

This chapter focuses on the creation of a new syncretic commemorative event. It is a public ritual, a story enacted by the participating community telling themselves about themselves (Geertz 1973). It is syncretic since it combines fragments of existing stories from three different heritages to create a new tradition. Yet it is new since it can rely upon few or no traditional sources for joint (Jewish, Moslem, and Christian) religious celebrations. As is the case with many other ritual commemorative events, the one under consideration addresses and redresses (Ortner 1978) contemporary conflicts embedded in the social relationships of the participating communities, while at the same time mediating a cognitive and emotional experience through its enactment. Drawing upon fragments of texts and selected symbols, it weaves a narrative that both remembers and transforms.

National rituals and memorial ceremonies are quite common in Israel's education system. These ceremonies have been incorporated into the school curriculum (Ben-Amos and Bet-El 1999) as central tools in the construction and mobilization of the ideology that sustains the state collective. Handelman rightfully notes (Handelman 1990) that schools construct more than reflect the ideological bases of Israeli society, contributing to the development of a well adapted and identified citizenry. In the early years of school, this socialization is for the most part achieved through the development of a complex net of commemorations enacted throughout the school year. In one way or another all these events reflect the national effort to establish the mythical foundations of the imagined community. In the Israeli case, these commemorations form a well-knit texture of revised Jewish narratives that serve the national needs of cohesion and endurance for confronting the political reality in which Israel has lived since its inception.

As prime tools of normative socialization into contemporary paradigmatic thinking, commemorations, therefore, become one of the most problematic elements in the bilingual school curriculum. It is only natural that commemorative acts are considered to be risky moments at the bilingual schools and are widely discussed and planned for by the steering committee and the parent-teacher association. If bilingual educators wish to challenge and adapt Israeli narratives to include the Palestinian experience and to promote peaceful coexistence, then bilingually teaching the standard materials is not enough. The educational texts themselves must be challenged. The most effective and politically expedient way to begin is through the revision of ritual, thereby avoiding a massive curriculum overhaul while effectively moving mountains.

We seek to glean the particular cultural meanings and logic that order both this specific event and the worlds of the participants. In a sense we will be looking at a political event designed to involve the participating children, parents, and educators. Through symbolic activity, the event attempts to draw the attention of its participants to new objects of thought and emotion held to be of special significance in order to transform both the actors and the audience (Lukes 1975). We seek to uncover the possible meanings created through this new ritual event and consider how these meanings can mediate anew the rather painful realities of Palestinian–Jewish coexistence in Israel.

The Festivals of Light:
Revising the Zionist Master Narrative

The Israeli secular curriculum in Jewish schools commemorates four central events connected to the national spirit of Israel: Hanukkah, Passover, Holocaust Day, and Remembrance/Independence Day.

Together they form the basis of the Zionist master commemorative narrative (Young 1993; Zeruvabel 1995).

The Zionist master text begins with the liberation from Egypt in the biblical period, which is celebrated by Passover, and continues with the Maccabean revolt represented by Hanukkah, expressing the heroism of the few fighting the many Syrian-Greek conquerors who destroyed the Temple, the symbol of national pride. It then attends to the victims and heroes of the Holocaust and ends with the Day of Remembrance for those soldiers who sacrificed their lives for the creation of the State of Israel and its continued survival.

Hanukkah, the Festival of Lights, commemorates the victory of the Maccabees over the Seleucids and the rededication of the Temple in 165 BCE. The Talmudic tradition emphasizes the miraculous aspect of the festival. It fails to mention the military victory and subsequent rule of the Hasmonean (Maccabean) Dynasty, which was seen as usurping the authority of the House of David (Kolatch 1981). According to the Talmudic rendition, when the Hasmoneans liberated the Temple, only one flask of oil, enough for one day, was found to fuel the eternal light. This oil miraculously burned for eight days of worship in the Temple until new oil became available.

Hanukkah is celebrated accordingly for eight days. In Israel it coincides with the two-week winter school vacation. Hanukkah celebrates the liberation of the Jews from the foreign conquering Seleucid power, and the triumph of the faith of the few over the many. Within the evolving Zionist ideology and in present-day Israel, the celebration of Hanukkah reflects the contemporary struggle of the Jewish people to create and sustain a national homeland.

Jewish schools celebrate Hanukkah annually. The ceremony, to which parents are invited in lower grades, usually includes an enactment of the heroic stand of Judah Maccabee and his brothers against the sacrilegious demands of the Syrian-Greek conqueror. The short enactment complements the national master narrative mentioned above and stands in contradiction to the traditional Diaspora narrative that emphasizes the miraculous aspect of the festival.

Arab schools in the Israeli educational system follow a very similar pattern. Though not all Jewish religious festivals are part of the Arab schools' yearly schedule, Zionist narratives are to be found in the other curricular disciplines such as history and literature. The Jewish calendar is full of commemorative days and festive opportunities, while the Palestinian Moslem and Christian calendars contain far fewer commemorative opportunities, leaving the Arab students with the sense that their traditions are poorly represented. No place at all is allocated for Palestinian national expressions (Abu-Nimer 1999; Rouhana 1997).

In the specific case of the bilingual/binational schools, the challenge is to create a common Israeli narrative and annual cycle of holiday celebrations that actively includes the two national-ethnic groups. Not only does the meaning of the Israeli national Jewish holidays have to be reconsidered but also the ways in which the other participating religious traditions may be equally represented. For example in the case of Hanukkah, it was determined that as a holiday that traditionally takes place near the winter equinox like many other celebrations of light, it can easily be combined with Christmas in the Christian tradition and Eid al Fitr, the Moslem festival that concludes the Ramadan fast. Light was chosen as the unifying theme: Hanukkah celebrates the miracle of light in the religious tradition, Christmas heralds a new dawn, and the Ramadan month of fasting depends upon the light of the moon for its cessation. Since the children take vacation during the actual holidays, the date of the school celebrations had to be scheduled beforehand, easily allowing the combination of all three traditions into one central ceremony. When considering that the Moslem calendar is purely lunar, it is yet to be seen whether Ramadan will always be able to join the other two festivals (Ramadan could fall in midsummer).

By calling the joint celebration "The Festivals of Light," the organizers are verbally challenging the standard hegemonic celebration of Hanukkah, which carries a similar name, with a revised pluralistic alternative. "Festival" turns inclusively plural, and "Light" turns into an abstract singular, no longer referring solely to the Hanukkah candles. The celebration of this new syncretic ritual attempts to enlighten its participants and cast out the darkness of a present and longstanding conflict.

Description of the Celebration

A week before the festival, the school organizes much activity related to the forthcoming celebration. Class time is allotted for rehearsals of the different sections to be enacted by each grade in the evening event to which all parents will be invited. The walls are adorned with decorations representing the three traditions. Candles and *hanukkiot* (the eight-branched Hannukah lamps, one branch for each night of the festival), stars, Christmas trees, cutouts of mosques, and small Moslem prayer carpets can be spotted in the corridors of the school or hanging from the ceiling. Considering Israel's rather strict segregationist educational policy, the sight in the school is truly surprising. The children, as a rule, seem to take it all in stride, enjoying special days partially dedicated to festive activities. During the breaks you can see them playing as usual. They run and play ball, but these days you can also spot them pretending to ride in Santa's sleigh. The day of the main event is mostly dedicated to rehearsals. They begin rehearsing in each classroom and toward midday move to the central gymnasium where a general rehearsal with the participation of all students takes place.

The festive night of the celebration takes place in the central room of a neighboring community center because the school lacks a space large enough to welcome all parents attending the evening, and indeed all parents, the children, and other invitees fill in the room with more than 200 excited spectators. The rather small entrance hall and the central room have been decorated with posters representing *hannukiot*, mosques, crescent moons, and Christmas trees.

Parents entering the hall are asked to ascend to the second floor where the ceremony will take place. Upstairs, in a large rectangular room, rows of chairs have been prepared for the parents and the pupils, and a high ramp has been erected on the right side of the room that will serve as the stage. Parents sit in the rows in what generally appears to be separate groups of Arabs and Jews. The children start getting organized in the first rows, and the teachers are busy giving out the traditional Hanukkah crowns with the candle that is commonly used in Jewish schools for the festival. All children, Jews and Arabs, are given one, and they all seem to wear it happily. On stage there are three equally large displays: a Christmas tree, a *hanukkia*, and a replica of a mosque. In front of the display ten chairs have been prepared for the actors participating in the presentation. Eight of the chairs are decorated with a big cardboard candle. The air is buzzing with excitement. All teachers, parents, and children are dressed festively. On center stage, a big poster in Hebrew and Arabic reads "Welcome," preserving the school's principle of total symmetry between the two languages. Children are still running around checking on their parents sitting in back rows or talking with one another. For the most part, they too sit according to nationality, though couples of mixed friends can be spotted. Arab children speak Arabic among themselves while Jewish children speak Hebrew. When cross interaction takes place, the lingua franca is Hebrew.

The first to come onstage is the school principal who, speaking in Hebrew, greets all those coming to the Festivals of Light commemorating the three festivals of Hanukkah, Ramadan, and Christmas. Second to the stage is the codirector of the CBE. A Moslem Arab, he gives his opening words of welcome in Arabic, and then, surprisingly, he moves into Hebrew and speaks about the sense of fulfillment he has from participating in this event that represents the success of something believed impossible: a school where both Arabs and Jews are equally represented and work together for a better world. He emphasizes that the success of the school is even greater when considering that all present have been able to overcome the many problems "our society has gone through in the last month," a clear reference to the clashes that took place in October 2000 between the Israeli police and the Palestinian Israeli community in which 13 Palestinians were killed.

The teacher in charge of the event now invites a Jewish parent to light the first Hanukkah candle. The father of one of the second-grade students, wearing a traditional skullcap, ascends to the stage and rather abruptly explains that he is not religious. He then lights the candles, saying the first blessing and leaving out, for no explicit reason, two additional customary blessings said on the first night of Hanukkah. After the lighting of the candles, a handful of parents join him in singing one of the traditional Hanukkah songs. A second parent is now invited to the stage, an Arab dressed in traditional Arabic attire, who tells a short account of the meaning of Ramadan and Eid al Fitr. He is lively, and his presentation in Arabic is received with much laughter. Lastly, four mothers are invited to the stage, two of them Arab, a Jew, and a German Christian immigrant married to an Arab. They form a choir singing Christmas songs, and part of the audience joins in. All Christmas carols are sung in English except the last one, which is sung in German.

After the parent presentations, the students' presentations commence. These are framed as a television program. The first to come on stage are second graders carrying a cardboard construction resembling a television set. They introduce "The Program of the Month" in Arabic and Hebrew. The first scene of the program relates to Ramadan. In Arabic one of the children says, "Black clouds, stars, and moon, from the first sunlight Ramadan starts and with dusk it ends," after which a song praising the month of Ramadan is sung by all children in Arabic. The second scene of the program is introduced by the first two children, one Arab and one Jew, saying, "And now a word from our sponsors." In the corner of the stage two girls, an Arab and a Jew, each holding baskets with olives, say to each other, "I make the best olive oil." The other responds, "No, I make the best oil," after which they both say in unison, "Together we make the best oil." After this short scene in both Hebrew and Arabic, all the kindergarten children take the stage and dance in a big circle singing a Hebrew Hanukkah song about the little flask of oil (*"Kad Katan"*). This is followed by all children singing two more Hanukkah songs, "A Great Miracle Happened Here" (*Nes Gadol Haya Po*) and "Happy Days of Hanukkah" (*Yemi HaHanukkah*). The two children appearing in the television now announce the forecast for snow, and at this point, children who had been waiting at the side of the stage with boxes full of white styrofoam start throwing it in the air, imitating snow. Then Santa, a child in costume, comes in ringing a bell and carrying a sack of sweets. He approaches the children and offers gifts to them all. Santa's gifts to each child are a spinning top (dreidel, *sevivon*) representing Hanukkah, a chocolate representing Christmas, and dates for Ramadan.

Meanwhile the children sing a Christmas carol in Arabic. With this the presentation has come to an end, and all parents are invited to go down to the entrance hall for refreshments.

Discussion

Our interviews uncovered a common discourse among parents, teachers, and NGO functionaries concerning their expectations on issues of identity and culture in the school curriculum, and in the children as a result of their participation in the school. They spoke about the need to find a way to strengthen each group's national-religious identity while furthering tolerance and understanding toward the other groups. Both Arab and Jewish parents are united in their expectation that the school curriculum, though bilingual – and encouraging tolerance between the three national-religious groups, will in no way damage or diminish the sense of pride in the identity of members of any of the groups. The school is expected to strengthen the sense of identity in each student toward his or her assumed group of attachment. According to parents this aim has been very successfully achieved within the school activities.

The adults' perspectives seemed to imply that they had become involved in the bilingual educational initiative because they ideologically believed in the need to coexist and that true coexistence implied first and foremost in-group recognition. They all wanted to recognize the others' identities and assumed such a recognition was possible only after each individual was secure in his or her own identity. Many times in the interviews the parents seemed to be arguing with imaginary adversaries who might doubt the correctness of the initiative and accuse them of betraying their own identity group. Their emphasis on strengthening the children's own particular identity could then be understood to be either a result of a personal conviction or a reaction to the implied accusations of betrayal.

Yet there is a seeming paradox in this reasoning. If the reasons for the historical conflict are related to national or ethnic attachments, then strengthening in-group identity is a way to sustain the conflict. This is clearly an undesirable outcome. So what has to change in the way they perceive national–ethnic identity for the conflict to be resolved? To this they have no clear answer. Maybe the answer is to be found in the way they have chosen to organize the ritual events we have described.

It becomes apparent from the events described that a great effort is being made first and foremost to offer to all involved a sense that all religious traditions are respected equally. There is an effort to create symmetry between the traditions that is expressed in the way the stage and the decorations are constructed and presented. This symmetry is also apparent in the amount of time allotted to the different contents of each festival to be represented; for each there are traditional songs and a short skit, regardless of the numbers of children represented from each group. In fact, the number of Christians represented in the school's Arab population is small, yet Christmas is offered the same status as the other festivals.

Despite the apparent symmetry, one must note that two of the festivals, Christmas and Hanukkah, have been diluted in their symbolic messages. For example, in regular Jewish schools it is customary to see the figure of Judah the Maccabee, dressed in old Roman-style attire and armed with a sword, as part of the theatrical presentation for Hanukkah. This figure is not present at the bilingual school, an apparent attempt to neutralize any conflictual nationalistic aspects related to the Zionist Hanukkah tradition. Instead, the religious version of Hanukkah is favored as in the Diaspora Jewish narrative, without emphasizing the Macabbean military victory; Christmas heralds the New Year, without making any allusions to the Messiah's birth.

Choosing to emphasize the miraculous religious aspects of Hanukkah helps overcome the nationalist Zionist overtones of the holiday that could be offensive to the other populations at the school. Thus the militaristic Judah Maccabee is absent from the stage. The rededication of the Temple, which is made possible by the miracle of the oil, is also left untold, presumably to avoid allusions to the disputed sovereignty over Jerusalem and the restoration of the Third Temple in place of the present Dome of the Rock on the Temple Mount, as promulgated by certain extreme right-wing religious Jewish groups.

As for Christmas, in spite of it being a fully religious festival with no national overtones, for Jews it represents a long and problematic historical relationship between Christians and Jews, particularly of European descent, whose Diasporic collective memory still dominates Israeli culture today. Christianity in the West, which began as one of a number of Jewish traditions, became a competing tradition that was historically identified by Jews as the reason for anti-Semitic persecutions culminating in the Nazi Holocaust. In this sense, Jesus, the Christian Messiah figure, could be seen as a threat to Jews and should be neutralized. Thus in the school event Christmas is represented as heralding the New Year and not as the birthdate of the Messiah.

Ramadan seems to be less of a problem. For the most part, the Israeli–Palestinian conflict is presented as a national, not a religious, conflict. Moreover, the Moslem religion has traditionally not been perceived as competing with Judaism and is known to recognize its debt to Judaism.

Historically, Ashkenazi Jews in Europe lacked exposure to Islam, so it did not carry negative associations for them. However, from the start,

Arab uprisings against Jews in Palestine, and later in the State of Israel, have been associated with Muslim religious leaders and fervent, religiously indignant mobs pouring out of mosques. Yet the secular Israeli Jewish majority continues to read the Palestinian struggle as a national one, without emphasizing the central role of Islamic leaders. Christianity, therefore, remains the historic enemy religion, though its effect on the Israeli experience is minuscule in comparison to the role of Islam. Therefore, the Christmas celebration at the school undergoes a radical revision while the Eid al Fitr remains intact. Paradoxically, the tiny Christian minority is the perceived threat rather than the Moslem Arabs, who Jewish Israelis more strongly associate with the Arab–Jewish conflict. One may observe that at the religious level, there seems to be a reversal of the role of enemy. While nationally Arabs (mostly considered to be Moslems) are the enemy, religiously Christianity, not Islam, represents the greater threat to the Jews.

We conclude that the school's goals of strengthening in-group identity, toleration, and understanding apparently require the revision of identity markers. Both Jews and Christians forfeit central symbols in the public presentation – Judah and Jesus. Yet all parties seem satisfied as the somewhat diluted religious emphasis seems to achieve their higher aim of mutual recognition.

Only at the start of the Hanukkah skit can hints of the national conflict be found. It is here where the two girls say, first separately in the two languages (Arabic and Hebrew), "I make the best oil" and only later say together, "Together we make the best oil." Yet a careful choice of gendered play, that is, the choice of two girls to enact the conflict, helps mitigate the militant aspects of the regional nationalism, reducing the conflict to a seemingly simple, symmetrical, domestic competition. The word from the sponsors implies that despite their differences, the two peoples share the fruits of their common land. They can choose partnership, rebuilding trust by beginning with the most basic day-to-day elements of life.

It is not surprising, therefore, that the only text addressing the national conflict is situated as a word from the program sponsors, after the Moslem presentation, at the start of the Hanukkah narrative of the miraculous oil. Read in the context of both the national conflict and the Hanukkah story, the olive-oil skit sums up the common vision of the school. The oil helps stretch the Zionist narrative to encompass two peoples and three heritages. No longer solely consigned to the *hanukkiah*, oil becomes a symbol for the distinctiveness and commonality of Jews and Arabs. The fact that an Arab and a Jew are standing on stage and enacting such a text engenders hope in the face of terrible odds, conjures up potent images of unity and healing, and, for a moment, makes the miraculous seem within reach.

Clearly any human activity is much more complex than social scientific analysis can render. The people participating in these events are also much more complex than the "natural" categories that define them. It is within this context that I want to add one more item to my present description. The Christmas carol segment of the ceremony was organized by the German Christian mother of an Arab child (counted as Moslem in the school since his father is Moslem). As mentioned above, all carols were sung in English except for the last, which was sung in German. At the end of the German carol, the mother chose to ask the audience from the stage, "Do you know in which language I sang the last carol?" to which the audience answered, "German." At this she smiled and left the stage.

It is rather surprising that this question was raised at all. Yet let us consider for a moment: she is a German married to a Moslem living in Israel, which is no easy thing to be. As such she is assigned to more than one conflict: the Palestinian–Jewish one and the historical German (Nazi)–Jewish one. The evening event was a dedicated attempt to overcome conflicts and to foster tolerance, recognition, and mutual respect. The conflict was diffused by placing emphasis on less problematic aspects of the various traditions, though the national conflict was clearly present in all that was left unsaid or unrepresented and found its expression most clearly in the olive-oil skit. The German woman, locked into the same historical conflicts represented that evening, felt the need to give voice to her attempt at reconciliation between Germans and Jews by asking the audience to recognize her nationality as part of the reconciliation process.

The bilingual school allows those with a previous ideological commitment and a need for good education to meet in the seemingly serene waters of cultural traditions. The holiday event carries the symbolic representation of who we are separately and the seeds of who we can be together in the future. For Palestinian Israelis, it says stick to your religious tradition and forget nationalism. If your tradition is Islam, keep your faith; the Jewish majority has no problem with you. For the Christian Palestinians, the message seems to be: you can be Christian if you publicly disguise those elements that are anathema to Jews: specifically, Jesus and Christian anti-Semitism. For the Zionist Jews, it points at the need to review some of their "natural" connections between religion and nation-state. In a sense it is a call to find solace in the Diaspora, where Hanukkah was about a supernatural miracle rather than a national victory, and Jews were proponents of monotheism rather than violent military conquerers. It is in the Zionist arena where the conflict takes place and to overcome it, the religious tradition has to be separated from the national one. Zionism and Judaism must in some way be kept distinct in Israel.

We remain tentative concerning the possible meanings of the event for Jews. This is not at all the same message reflected in the school's Remembrance Day celebrations (Bekerman, in press). There we see a radically different structure that, while recognizing both national traditions, keeps them apart as separate commemorations.

With the Zionist master narrative challenged, the imagination is freed to explore possibilities outside the present conflict. Hanukkah might be a national event, but it is also originally a religious one in the Jewish collective memory. Sacrificing its national overtones is not too threatening, as this does not require a wholly new search for meaning and identity. How much more can be sacrificed is yet to be seen.

Conclusion

This ritual, like all others, is in the business of "bringing out of the possible might-have-beens a firm social reality" (Douglas 1982: 36). In the words of Don Handelman, "Public events are locations of communication that convey participants into versions of social worlds in relatively coherent ways. . . . Not only may they affect social life, they may also effect it" (Handelman 1990: 15). The public event with which we are dealing and its reshaping of conflictual situations is geared toward effecting a new social order. By mediating people into collective abstractions (togetherness, peace, multiculturalism, toleration of difference, overcoming hatred), by inducing actions (each of us can partake in the religious experience of the other, each of us can reshape our own tradition when necessary), by reconstructing knowledge and experience (Judah Maccabee and the Temple disappear, Jesus and the cross disappear; the miracle of the oil recalls images of reconciliation and cooperation rather than of war; Christmas introduces the New Year rather than the Messiah), this public event is a construct dedicated to the making of a new order. It is yet to be seen whether the foundational ideology of the event can survive the present escalating conflict and achieve its goal.

Note

This study is part of a larger two-year research project supported by the Ford Foundation (Grant No. 990-1558); the study is based on the partial analysis of data collected, using a variety of ethnographic methods, during a two-year research effort conducted from August 1999 to July 2001.

Acknowledgements

The research project is jointly directed with my colleague Gabriel Horenczyk and carried out in close collaboration with our research assistant Nader Schade.

I want to thank Keri Warshawsky and Vivienne Burstein for their critical insights and assistance when editing this manuscript.

References

Abu-Nimer, M. 1999: *Dialogue, Conflict, Resolution, and Change: Arab-Jewish Encounters in Israel*. Albany, NY: SUNY.

Ben-Amos, A., and Bet-El, I. 1999: Holocaust Day and Memorial Day in Israeli Schools: Ceremonies, Education and History. *Israel Studies* 4 (1): 258–84.

Bekerman, Z. (in press): Can Education Contribute to Coexistence and Reconciliation? Religious and National Ceremonies in Bilingual Palestinian–Jewish Schools in Israel. *Peace and Conflict: Journal of Peace Psychology*.

Douglas, M. 1982: *In the Active Voice*. London: Routledge & Kegan.

Geertz, C. 1973: *The Interpretation of Cultures*. New York: Basic Books.

Ghanem, A. 1998: State and Minority in Israel: The Case of Ethnic State and the Predicament of its Minority. *Ethnic and Racial Studies* 21 (3): 428–48.

Handelman, D. 1990: *Models and Mirrors: Towards an Anthropology of Public Events*. Cambridge: Cambridge University Press.

Hobsbawm, E. J. 1983: The Invention of Tradition. In E. J. Hobsbawm and T. Ranger (eds.), *The Invention of Tradition*. Cambridge: Cambridge University Press.

Kolatch, A. J. 1981: *The Jewish Book of Why*. New York: Jonathan David.

Lukes, S. 1975: Political Ritual and Social Integration. *Sociology* 9: 289–308.

Ortner, S. 1978: *Sherpas Through Their Rituals*. Cambridge: Cambridge University Press.

Rouhana, N. N. 1997: *Palestinian Citizens in an Ethnic Jewish State*. New Haven: Yale University Press.

Skutnabb-Kangas, T., and Garcia, O. 1995: Multilingualism for All? General Principles. In T. Skutnabb-Kangas (ed.), *Multilingualism for All*. Lisse: Swets and Zeitlinger.

Smooha, S. 1996: Ethno-Democracy: Israel as an Archetype. In P. Ginosar and A. Bareli (eds.), *Zionism: A Contemporary Polemic*. Jerusalem: Ben-Gurion University (Hebrew).

Young, J. E. 1993: *The Texture of Memory*. New Haven: Yale University Press.

Zeruvabel, Y. 1995: *Recovered Roots: Collective Memory and the Making of Israeli National Tradition*. Chicago: University of Chicago Press.

Chapter 17

Religion, Spirituality and Authoritative Discourse

MOSHE RE'EM

ALF a century ago the distinguished Jewish philosopher Abraham Joshua Heschel observed, "We worry a great deal about the problem of church and state. Now what about the church and God? Sometimes there seems to be a greater separation between the church and God than between the church and state" (Heschel 1987: 57). This chapter focuses on the separation between church and God, the detachment of spirituality from religion that has taken place in religious institutions in general, and in religious schools in particular. It argues that a pedagogy founded on a philosophy of dialogue that views truth as polyphonic and that is based on principles of religious pluralism is morally superior to an authoritarian form of religious instruction. My claim is that an exclusivist approach to the plurality of religions sets the authority of tradition over and above the religious experience of the individual, resulting in a separation of spirituality (or what Dewey called "*the religious*") from religion. Engaging in multiple forms of discourse, I believe, is critical for developing an authoritative model of religious education in which the still small inner voice of the child is allowed to blend in with the authoritative voice of Tradition.

Numerous studies have examined classroom discourse in order to better understand and improve classroom instruction and student learning (Gee and Green 1998). None, however, have considered the spiritual side of classroom discourse. Missing is an examination of how different forms of discourse impact on the child's sense of the divine as it unfolds in interhuman exchange. While the role of language in giving meaning to, and getting meaning from, social activity is surely important, within the context of the religious school the spiritual meaning that students experience in relation to each other and to their teachers is of equal, if not greater, importance. If there is to be any hope in establishing what Hanan Alexander and Miriam Ben-Peretz (2001) call "a pedagogy of the sacred," religious educators must carefully consider the role of discourse in classroom practice. This chapter draws on a philosophy of dialogue with its roots in the writings of Martin Buber and Mikhail Bakhtin in order to claim that a polyphonic approach to religious truth is not only compatible with traditional Jewish sources, but also morally superior to a "coercive" or monological approach. I argue that experiencing multiple forms of discourse is necessary if the religious-school child is to come to know the sacred in an environment that is respectful of his or her well-being.

On the Separation of Church and God

The separation of church from God has taken place on both theoretical and practical grounds. Recent calls to teach about religion and spirituality in public-school classrooms carefully distinguish between "religion" and "spirituality" (Beck 1990; Noddings 1993). Nel Noddings, for example, views spirituality as "an attitude or a way of life that recognizes something we might call spirit," while religion is defined by her as "a specific way of exercising that spirituality" that "usually requires an institutional affiliation" (Halford 1998/1999: 29). Although spirituality can be found within the walls of the church, synagogue, or mosque, it need not be limited by those structures. Indeed, Philip H. Phenix defined spirituality as transcending physical and mental confines:

> Spirit is the name given to the property of limitless going beyond. To have a spiritual nature is to participate in infinitude. Reason refers to the capacity for the rational ordering of experience through categories of finitude. Spirit makes one aware of the finiteness of the structures imposed by reason. To say that persons are beings with spirit is to point to their perennial discontent and dissatisfaction with any and every finite realization. Thus it is sometimes said that spirit finds its exemplification more in yearning impulses of feeling and the innovative projects of will than in the settled conclusions of intellect. (Phenix 1971/1974: 119)

Spirituality, according to Phenix, stands in stark contrast to reason. Although it may be consonant with religious practice, the boundaries set by religious law and dogma hinder rather than advance spirituality. The distinction between religion and spirituality made by Noddings and Phenix continues a line of reasoning first established by Martin Buber and John Dewey.

Throughout the twentieth century, philosophers have repeatedly distinguished between spirituality and religion, viewing the spiritual as transcending the structure of institutionalized religion. Both Martin Buber and John Dewey differentiated between "religiosity" and "religion." Religiosity, according to Buber, describes the human "urge to establish a living communion with the unconditioned; it is man's will to realize the unconditioned through deed, and to establish it in the world" (Buber 1967: 93). Religion, by contrast, is composed of customs and teachings that may have their origin in religiosity, but "its prescriptions and dogmas are rigidly determined and handed down as unalterably binding to all future generations, without regard for their newly developed religiosity, which seeks new forms." When religion's rites and dogmas become "so rigid that religiosity cannot move them or no longer wants to comply with them, religion becomes uncreative and therefore untrue" (Buber 1967: 80). One of the key roles of religiosity for religion, therefore, according to Buber, is to inspire constant renewal.

John Dewey also distinguishes between what he called "religion" and "the religious," but his purpose in making the distinction differs markedly from Buber's. Like Buber, Dewey maintained that the term religion "always signifies a special body of beliefs and practices having some kind of institutional organization, loose or tight" (Dewey 1962: 9). "The religious," or what we might today call "the spiritual," refers to "experiences having the force of bringing about a better, deeper and enduring adjustment in life." The religious, says Dewey, "takes place in different persons in a multitude of ways. It is sometimes brought about by devotion to a cause; sometimes by a passage of poetry that opens a new perspective; sometimes as was the case with Spinoza – deemed an atheist in his day – through philosophical reflection" (Dewey 1962: 14). Though they both distinguish between spirituality and religion, an important difference exists between the approaches of Buber and Dewey. While Dewey sought to emancipate the religious from religion so that "the religious aspect of experience will be free to develop freely on its own account" (Dewey 1962: 2), Buber saw religiosity as a means of revitalizing the Jewish religion (Buber 1967). Following Buber, I too see spirituality as a means of revitalizing Judaism. Why is Judaism in need of revitalization? Because the separation of spirituality from religion is not only a theoretical issue. On a practical level, the separation of church from God is commonly experienced by American Jews.

Recent evidence, based on qualitative research on both moderately affiliated and more committed American Jews, suggests that for many there is no straightforward connection between God and the synagogue. Steven Cohen and Arnold Eisen conclude that "God is simply not what draws those we interviewed to synagogue, or keeps them away" (Cohen and Eisen 2000: 168), while Riv-Ellen Prell notes how her "study revealed that across the spectrum of education and knowledge, committed Jews find prayer a difficult and even confounding aspect of Jewish life" (Prell 2000: 348).

Although the evidence seems to be mixed, the experience of Jewish children in religious schools also seems to be devoid of spirituality. Kathy Simon's case study of a Jewish day school may, indeed, be the exception to the rule. Unlike other religious schools where "teachers of religion do not necessarily welcome moral or spiritual *questioning*," at Agnon School the religion teachers "regularly gave the impression that a meaningful and moral existence required of them as well as of their students an ongoing search, rather than an easy acceptance of given truths" (Simon 1998: 34). I would like to suggest that the nature of one's spiritual experience in religious schools depends greatly on the forms of discourse employed in the classroom.

Between Dialogue and Discourse

What do I have in mind when I use the terms "dialogue" and "discourse"? Alexander M. Sidorkin has noted that when communicative dialogue is investigated, researchers often focus "on the linguistic properties of dialogue at the expense of its more fundamental ontological understanding" (Sidorkin 1999: 76). Following Burbules, Sidorkin, McHenry, and others, I use the term dialogue in its ontological sense, "not as something we *do* or *use*," but as a relationship we *"enter into"* (Burbules 1993: xii). For Mikhail Bakhtin, unlike the Socratic dialogue, which was "little more than an external form of dialogism" (Bakhtin 1984: 294), true "dialogism will incarnate a world whose unity is essentially one of multiple voices, whose conversations never reach finality and cannot be transcribed in monologic form. The unity of the world will then appear as it really is: polyphonic" (Morson and Emerson 1990: 61). Viewed ontologically, dialogue is prior to human being. It is what makes us human. We are human as a result of dialogue. As Sidorkin puts it, "The ontological concept of dialogue explores the place of dialogue in the human way of being" (Sidorkin 1999: 7). As an experience, dialogue is "beyond discourse" since it is more universal than discourse.

Bakhtin distinguishes between two modes of ideological discourse: the authoritative and the internally persuasive. In "Discourse in the Novel" Bakhtin characterizes the authoritative as follows:

> The authoritative word demands that we acknowledge it, that we make it our own; it binds us, quite independent of any power it might have to persuade us internally; we encounter it with its authority already fused to it. The authoritative word is located in a distanced zone, organically

connected with a past that is felt to be hierarchically higher. It is, so to speak, the word of the fathers (sic). Its authority was already acknowledged in the past. It is a prior discourse. (Bakhtin 1981: 342)

Among the examples that Bakhtin provides of authoritative discourse are religious, political, and moral texts. In the classroom the form of transmission that best characterizes the authoritative mode of discourse is "reciting by heart." The main feature of this form of discourse, according to Sidorkin, "is the totality of the message." Authoritative discourse is monological and is characterized by "direct instruction" or "didactic question-and-answer types of interaction" (Sidorkin 1999: 79). The fact that students ask questions does not change the nature of the discourse since the point of the interaction is to receive static knowledge, a tradition that is being passed on. It is quite literally the "word of the fathers." The role of the student is to serve as a "distant descendent" of the tradition (Sidorkin 1999: 344). We can easily see how religious authoritarianism fits neatly into this form of ideological discourse. Although an exchange takes place between teacher and students, ultimately it is the monological voice of the teacher/tradition that is heard.

Internally persuasive discourse, according to Bakhtin, involves a "retelling in one's own words" (Bakhtin 1981: 341). It is "half-ours and half-someone else's" (Bakhtin 1981: 345). Retelling in one's own words is a more flexible and creative process. As the Bakhtin scholar Caryl Emerson describes it, internally persuasive discourse "is the only way we can *originate* anything verbally." It "is as close as anything can come to being totally our own" (Emerson 1996: 133). Unlike the monological authoritative discourse, internally persuasive discourse involves "a double-voiced narration of another's words" (Bakhtin 1981: 341). This form of discourse is characterized by disruption, talking out, and voicing disagreement. When the authoritative discourse of the classroom is interrupted by internally persuasive discourse, it can lead to greater intellectual creativity and consequently a re-imagining of the Other. Bakhtin writes, "Another's discourse performs here no longer as information, directions, rules, models and so forth – but strives rather to determine the very bases of our ideological interrelations with the world, the very basis of our behavior; it performs here as *authoritative discourse,* and an *internally persuasive discourse*" (Bakhtin 1981: 342). The point that Bakhtin makes here is critical, for it means that despite the great differences that exist between the two forms of discourse, in order for the spirit of the individual to unfold, both forms of discourse – authoritative and internally persuasive – must be present. Why is authoritative discourse necessary? Because it allows "for shared knowledge to be established, for shared experience to occur"

(Sidorkin 1999: 105). On its own, however, authoritative discourse remains on the monological plane.

Authoritative discourse is the voice of the fictitious character Rabbi Binder in Philip Roth's wonderful short story "The Conversion of the Jews." There, in a pre-Bar Mitzvah religious-school classroom, Rabbi Binder binds his students to the tradition of the fathers. Although he allows for "free-discussion time," the discourse in the afternoon-school classroom is primarily authoritative. In response to his student Ozzie's question, "Why couldn't God let a woman have a baby without having intercourse?" Rabbi Binder offers an answer, but it is not in response to what Ozzie wants to know. What he wanted to know was "different." Rabbi Binder never engages Ozzie or the rest of the class in true dialogue. Ozzie's theologically challenging question is perceived by Rabbi Binder as a threat to the authority of tradition/teacher. Classroom discourse is thus dominated by the authoritative voice.

In Ozzie's retelling of the events to his friend Itzie, however, we see an example of the double-voiced nature of discourse that occurs in everyday speech. It is this internally persuasive discourse that contributes to the ideological becoming of the human being. In the exchange between Ozzie and Itzie true dialogue unfolds. Ozzie recounts the events leading up to his argument in class with Rabbi Binder:

> "I asked the question about God, how if He could create the heaven and earth in six days, and make all the animals and the fish and the light in six days – the light especially, that's what always gets me, that He could make the light. Making fish and animals, that's pretty good."
>
> "That's damn good." Itzie's appreciation was honest but unimaginative; it was as though God had just pitched a one-hitter.
>
> "But making light . . . I mean when you think about it, it's really something," Ozzie said. "Anyway I asked Binder if He could make all that in six days, and He could pick the six days He wanted right out of nowhere, why couldn't He let a woman have a baby without having intercourse." (Roth 1969: 101)

Rabbi Binder offered no meaningful response to Ozzie's theologically difficult question. He is bound by the tradition and can merely explain over and over how Jesus was a "historical" figure, but not God. Ozzie's reported speech contains within it Rabbi Binder's authoritative discourse, but it is retold in Ozzie's own words. Ozzie and Itzie have an open-ended conversation about God that approaches the dialogical. Each is empowered to express himself freely, without mental or physical constraints. The two boys stand in relation to each other as equal partners in dialogue. It is significant that in the context of mixed discourse spirituality unfolds. Ozzie expresses wonder and amazement at God's ability to create light and the world in six days. As I have argued elsewhere (Re'em 2001), in an educational environment that is saturated with the monological, exposure to diverse discourses in supplementary learning contexts is needed in order to release the child's still small inner voice. (In the Roth story that happens in the informal conversation between the two boys.) But if spirituality can also result from contexts that are primarily monological and authoritarian, albeit outside of the classroom, why advocate exposure to multiple discourses in the religious-school classroom?

Parker Palmer has noted how "the marriage of education and the sacred has not always been a happy one. . . . There are real dangers in this enterprise when the sacred gets attached to the wrong things. There are real dangers when the sacred gets institutionalized and imposed on people as one more weapon among the objectifying forces of society" (Palmer 1999: 19). The dangers that exist come not only in the form of acts of evil committed in the name of God but in the harm that is done to the child. George Lakoff has argued, on moral grounds, that an *authoritative* model of childrearing, what he calls the "nurturant parent approach," is superior to an *authoritarian* model of childrearing, the "strict parent approach." The authoritarian model of childrearing:

- Attempts to shape, control, and evaluate the behavior and attitudes of one's children in accordance with an absolute set of standards.
- Values obedience, respect for authority, work, tradition, and preservation of order.
- Discourages verbal give-and-take between parent and child. (Lakoff 1996: 352)

As opposed to the above model of childrearing, Diana Baumrind offers the more liberal *authoritative* model. Authoritative childrearing:

- Expects mature behavior from the child and sets clear standards.
- Firmly enforces rules and standards using commands and sanctions when necessary.
- Encourages the child's independence and individuality.
- Involves open communication between parents and children, with parents listening to children's point of view, as well as parents expressing their own, encouraging verbal give-and-take.
- Recognizes the rights of both parents and children. "'Firm enforcement' and 'sanctions' do not include painful corporal punishment" (Lakoff 1996: 353).

As Ozzie says at the end of "The Conversion of the Jews," "You should never hit anybody about God." Repeated studies that have shown the physical and emotional harm done to the child raised in an authoritarian environment lead Lakoff to conclude that authoritative childrearing is morally superior.

Bakhtin's authoritative discourse clearly supports an authoritarian approach to childrearing or teaching. In contrast authoritative teaching would encourage the student's independence and individuality and would welcome open communication between teacher and student in the pursuit of truth. It would combine discourses and would offer an authentic form of spirituality. Openness to the pursuit of truth is critical for authoritative teaching.

Polyphonic Truth and Religious Pluralism

Parker Palmer has written, "Authentic spirituality wants to open us to truth – whatever truth may be, wherever truth may take us. Such a spirituality does not dictate where we must go, but trusts that any path walked with integrity will take us to a place of knowledge. Such a spirituality encourages us to welcome diversity and conflict, to tolerate ambiguity, and to embrace paradox" (Palmer 1993: xi). Unlike Buber who maintained the oneness of truth, Bakhtin conceptualized truth as polyphonic, requiring "a multitude of bearers" (Sidorkin 1999: 29). Summarizing Bakhtin's position on truth, Sidorkin writes:

> Truth reveals when one can hear and comprehend both or all voices simultaneously, and more than that, when one's voice joins in and creates something similar to a musical chord. In a chord, voices remain different, but they form a different type of music, which is in principle unachievable by a single voice. . . . In the monological world there exists a singular truth, a singular ownership over meaning there, either by an individual, by a group, or by no one (God). (Sidorkin 1999: 30)

Bakhtin describes "truth" metaphorically as a "chord," "chorus," and "polyphony." The notion of polyphonic truth holds tremendous potential for religious pluralism. Moreover, within Jewish sources one could find ample support for religious truth being polyphonic. Take, for example, the rabbinic reconciliation of the discrepancy between the two versions of the Decalogue that appear in Exodus and Deuteronomy, where one verse states, "Remember (*zachor*) the Sabbath day and keep it holy" (Exod. 20: 8), and the other verse reads, "Observe (*shamor*) the Sabbath day to keep it holy" (Deut. 5: 12). The rabbis maintain that the two verses "*remember* and *observe* were both spoken at one utterance." The same exegetical text continues with a list of contradictory biblical verses concluding that although "this is a manner of speech impossible for creatures of flesh and blood" (Lauterbach 1976: 252), it is not impossible for the divine. Polyphony is part of the divine word. Moreover, this idea is not limited to homiletic literature (*aggadic*), but lies at the heart of the Jewish legal tradition (*Halakhah*). Take the famous statement in the Babylonian Talmud (Tract. Eruvin 13b) where in response to the arguments and disagreements between the school of Shammai and the school of Hillel a heavenly voice proclaimed, "These as well as those [both opinions] are words of the living God." Commenting on this statement the 11th-century Talmud scholar, Rabbi Shlomo ben Yiszhaki (Rashi) writes:

> When two Amoraim (rabbinic authorities from the Talmudic period) disagree with each other about the law . . . there is no untruth there. Each of them justifies his opinion. One gives a reason to permit, the other, reason to forbid. One compares the case before him to one precedent; the other compares it to something different. It is possible to say, "both speak the words of the living God." At times, one reason is valid; at other times, another reason. For reasons change in the wake of even only small changes in the situation. (Quoted in Berkovits 1983: 53)

Polyphony allows for contradictory voices and attributes them both to the same divine source. David Hartman, in fact, cites Halakhah as the source of his religious pluralism. In addressing "spiritual pluralism" Hartman writes:

> The ugly discussions of who has the "truth," of whom does the Father (sic) love, who is the chosen child, and who is the elect and who is the true Israel – those discussions which led to the most violent acts in history – have to be thrown out. We cannot build a spiritual life indifferent to what this type of discussion and this type of concern has led to. We must completely, radically, give up this notion that eschatologically the "truth" will be shown. . . . We have to recognize that ultimately spiritual monism is a disease. It leads to the type of spiritual arrogance that has brought bloodshed to history. Therefore we have to rethink our eschatology, and rethink the notion of multiple spiritual communities and their relationship to a monotheistic faith. (Hartman 1976: 79)

On moral grounds Hartman rejects what Diana Eck has called theological exclusivism, "insistence upon the exclusive and sole truth of one's own religious tradition, excluding all others" (Eck 1993: xiii). Instead, Hartman endorses a form of Jewish pluralism.

Conclusion

The journey to truth is a spiritual one, with many paths, none of which are worn by fear but by freely addressing the questions of life's ultimate meaning. The separation of church and faith may, in part, be due to the fact that "too often, would-be educators who profess religious faith turn out to fear truth, rather than welcome it in all its forms." "Too often," writes Parker Palmer, "spiritual traditions have been used to obstruct inquiry rather than to encourage it" (Palmer 1993: xi). Consequently, religion has developed the bad reputation of being "coercive" or mono-logical, as opposed to being dialogical. What would happen if we developed a pedagogy of the sacred based on a philosophy of dialogue that employs multiple discourses and welcomes a cacophony of sound? What would happen if we paid closer attention to student "disrup-tions," to talking out, disagreement, or chatter? As Sidorkin correctly notes, not all disruptions are bad. Were we to be truly open to multiple forms of student discourse, perhaps then student voices engaged in conversation would not be perceived as extraneous "noise," but as attempts to grasp that which is beyond human comprehension, in a search for life's greater meaning.

References

Alexander, H. A. and Ben-Peretz, M. 2001: Toward a Pedagogy of the Sacred: Transcendence, Ethics and the Curriculum. In C. Erricker, J. Erricker, and C. Ota (eds.), *Spiritual Education: Cultural, Religious and Social Differences – New Perspectives for the 21st Century*. Brighton & Portland: Sussex Academic Press.

Bakhtin, M. 1981: Discourse in the Novel. In M. Holquist (ed.), *The Dialogic Imagination*. Austin, TX: University of Texas Press.

—— 1984: *Problems of Dostoevsky's Poetics*. Caryl Emerson (trans.). Minneapolis: University of Minnesota Press.

Baumrind, D. 1991: Parenting Styles and Adolescent Development. In R. Lerner, A. C. Petersen, and J. Brooks-Gunn (eds.), *The Encyclopedia of Adolescence*. New York: Garland.

Beck, C. 1990: *Better Schools: A Values Perspective*. New York: Falmer Press.

Berkovits, E. 1983: *Not in Heaven: The Nature and Function of Halakha*. New York: Ktav.

Buber, M. 1967: *On Judaism*. N. Glazer (ed. and trans.). New York: Schocken.

Burbules, N. C. 1993: *Dialogue in Teaching: Theory and Practice*. New York: Teachers College Press.

Cohen, S. M. and Eisen, A. M. 2000: *The Jew Within: Self, Family, and Community in America*. Bloomington: Indiana University Press.

Dewey, J. 1934/1962: *A Common Faith*. New Haven: Yale University Press.

Eck, D. 1993: *Encountering God: A Spiritual Journey from Bozeman to Banaras*. Boston: Beacon Press.

Emerson, C. 1996: The Outer Word and Inner Speech: Bakhtin, Vygotsky, and the Internalization of Language. In H. Daniels (ed.), *An Introduction to Vygotsky*. New York: Routledge.

Gee, J. P. and Green, J. L. 1998: Discourse analysis, learning, and social practice: a methodological study. *Review of Research in Education* 23: 119–69.

Halford, J. M. 1998/1999: Longing for the sacred in schools: a conversation with Nel Noddings. *Educational Leadership* (Dec.–Jan.): 28–32.

Hartman, D. 1976: Jews and Christians in the World of Tomorrow. *Immanuel*, 6: 70–81.

Heschel, A. J. 1954/1987: *Quest for God: Studies in Prayer and Symbolism*. New York: Crossroad.

Lakoff, G. 1996: *Moral Politics: What Conservatives Know That Liberals Don't*. Chicago: The University of Chicago Press.

Lauterbach, J. Z. (trans.) 1933/1976: *Mekilta De-Rabbi Ishmael* Vol. 2. Philadelphia: Jewish Publication Society of America.

McHenry, H. 1997: Education as encounter: Buber's pragmatic ontology. *Educational Theory* 47 (3): 341–57.

Morson, G. and Emerson, C. 1990: *Mikhail Bakhtin: Creation of a Prosaics*. Stanford, CA: Stanford University Press.

Noddings, N. 1993: *Educating for Intelligent Belief or Unbelief*. New York: Teachers College Press.

Palmer, P. 1993: *To Know As We Are Known: Education as a Spiritual Journey*. New York: HarperCollins.

—— 1999: The Grace of Great Things: Reclaiming the Sacred in Knowing, Teaching, and Learning. In S. Glazer (ed.), *The Heart of Learning: Spirituality in Education*. New York: Jeremy P. Tarcher/Putnam.

Phenix, P. 1971/1974: Transcendence and the Curriculum. In E. Eisner and E. Vallance (eds.), *Conflicting Conceptions of Curriculum*. Berkeley, CA: McCutchan. Reprinted from *Teachers College Record* 73 (2).

Prell, R.-E. 2000: Communities of Choice and Memory: Conservative Synagogues in the Late Twentieth Century. In J. Wertheimer (ed.), *Jews in the Center: Conservative Synagogues and Their Members*. New Brunswick, NJ: Rutgers University Press.

Re'em, M. 2001: Young minds in motion: interactive pedagogy in non-formal settings. *Teaching and Teacher Education* 17 (3): 291–305.

Roth, P. 1969: The Conversion of the Jews. In P. Roth (ed.), *Goodbye Columbus* 2nd edn. New York: Bantam Books.

Schoem, D. 1989: *Ethnic Survival in America: An Ethnography of a Jewish Afternoon School*. Atlanta: Scholars Press.

Sidorkin, A. 1999: *Beyond Discourse: Education, the Self, and Dialogue*. Albany: State University of New York Press.

Simon, K. 1998: Bring it up with the Rabbi: the specialization of moral and spiritual education in a Jewish high school. *Journal of Jewish Education*, 64 (1 and 2): 33–43.

Chapter 18

Contra Spiritual Education

ILAN GUR-ZE'EV

What is Spirituality?

SPIRITUALITY IS A SPECIAL kind of readiness. It is a unique human quality of openness. Spirituality symbolizes the special human readiness to be called upon. As such, spirituality is the presence of Spirit in the human soul and body. It signifies the possibility of the human dwelling in the nearness of its essence, its telos, as one can see in the writings of St. Augustine, or the entrance into union with it, as one is shown in the 11th chapter of Plotinus's Sixth Anead (Plotinus 1981). It is a special kind of readiness to accept the absence of Spirit, or the presence of that which calls upon us (Heidegger 1996: 125).

Human beings, according to St. Augustine, have a body and soul, as do other creatures. However, they have a special soul, *anima*, *neshama*, in the words of the Holy Scripture. But even the *neshama* in itself does not constitute human uniqueness. It is that touch of godly spirit in the path for union with the One, with the holy totality, that enables or creates the uniqueness of the human soul (St. Augustine 1984). The transcending readiness of spirituality enables one to overcome mere living as the aim of life. It is a special becoming of the human being as open, creative, overcoming its godly *arche*, immanence and telos.

This concept of spirituality was central to Judeo-Christian cultural history, and it effectively enslaved people to what it promised to free the disciples from. Within the framework of normalizing education (Foucault 1980: 137), it enslaved human beings to abstract beliefs and concrete practices that imprisoned them in dogmas and ways of life that avoided contemplating life as an abyss. Within this "spiritual" way of life, a special place was reserved for "love of God" and even for "love of your neighbor," where there is no room for the transcendent moment of nothingness or the sudden appearance of the wordless voice of the burning bush.

Currently, spiritual education is committed to imposing a strong illusion and forgetfulness of the love of life. It enables us to avoid facing the wordless and contributes to the subjectification of the human subject. It is especially good at helping people avoid transcendence by teaching a domesticated transcendence under conditions that will enslave the human being to the governing violence, and thus ensures a person's invisibility or "thingness." By drawing on dichotomies such as Christ vs. anti-Christ, meaningful vs. meaningless, and body vs. spirit, it avoids accepting meaninglessness as the source of "worthy" values and "valid" meanings and reaffirms forgetfulness of the love of life. As it is currently taught spiritual education engenders a false readiness, a domesticated transcendence, and anti-Dionysian love. As such it gives humans a dogmatic home and avoids facing homelessness, the absence of God, and the productivity of educational violence, as the blocks and cement of the Tower of Babel of spiritual life (Gur-Ze'ev 2000b). Normalizing education has played a special role in this subjectification process (Foucault 1980: 156), which ensures a successful dehumanization of people. Understanding education for spirituality as a special version of normalizing education, however, requires some clarifications concerning the essence of education itself.

What Is Education?

Education is the production of the human subject as an object of normalization (Gur-Ze'ev 2002b). It is a special kind of metaphysical violence. A rich and essential connection links violence, spiritual education, and normalization (Gur-Ze'ev 2002b).

Normalizing education is violent in the sense that it produces a human being who is detached from his or her responsibility to become someone. Normalizing education creates the human as something. It constitutes the knowledge, the values, the consciousness, the self, and the Other. This creativity unfolds in a way that guarantees the invisibility of the violence that creates, maintains, and reproduces the governing realm of self-evidence and the invisibility of the absence of nothingness, of meaninglessness, and of the Same, which surrounds, empowers, incubates the human and his or her immanence and his or her exterior horizons. Under the naturalized, unchallenged tyranny of normalizing education, the "I" and its self-evidence become the manifestation of the "not-I" of the system. Only as such it is dressed as the "I," it is being naturalized, signified, and the success of this violence is ensured as invisible and nameless. Spiritual education is committed to camouflaging its violent essence and presents it as "spiritual quests."

Within the process of subjectification the very presence of transcendence is nothing but the manifestation of the closure of the system and its productive subjectification processes. The violence of normalizing education at its most extreme ensures its invisibility.

This process of subjectification, however, is also where the potentials of joy, rational investigation, categorization, evaluation, work and cooperation with the Other dwell. This is also where normalizing education and the governing disciplining practices are facing resistance. A successful subjectification of the student as an object of manipulation is also the foundation of normal intersubjectivity and even a gate for caring for the Other. It is the precondition for the normal facing of "spirituality."

The question that arises, however, is what kind of spirituality should we prefer? Is a spirituality of resistance and repositioning in the cultural or psychological arenas a manifestation of the Totally Other, and as such does it offer transcendence from the violence of normalizing education? Or is real transcendence only possible outside of the various arenas of normalizing education? And, even when normalizing education praises "spirituality" and "transcendence" over the governing cultural, political, or psychological realities, does this praise not remain part and parcel of the governing system? This is where we should say more on the nature of normalizing education.

What Is Normalizing Education?

Normalizing education is responsible for the creation of "relevant" knowledge as opposed to "irrelevant" knowledge, "true" as opposed to "false" knowledge, "truly human" as contrasted with bestiality, "merely natural" or "inhumane." At the same time, however, it is positioned to reproduce the self-evidence of the self and the naturalization of "his" or "her" apparatuses of evaluation of rival values, identities, and agendas, both collective and individual. The constitution of the "real" – of the self-evidence of which the evaluative apparatus is a central element – ensures, or is meant to ensure, that the human being will be deprived of his or her otherness, that the human subject will remain an object of the manipulations that created him or her as a thing, as part of the "thingness" of "reality" which veils what Heidegger called the question of "the truth of Being" (Heidegger 1996: 44). It guarantees, or is meant to guarantee, that you and I will remain silent in the sense of what Cavell describes as having/creating/calling for our own voice (Cavell 1995), that we will be powerless to challenge "our" selves as part of the realm of self-evidence that produces the "I" and its relation to "his," "her," or "our" resistance/critique of the self-evidence and its educational apparatuses. It is neither the structure nor the functioning of normalizing education but its essence and telos that enable this kind of creativity, this manifestation of violence as spirituality. And as such it works in many dimensions and levels of education as "spiritual" or as a call for "spiritual" emancipation, even in the most remote and supposedly "non-spiritual" arenas such as physical education (Gur-Ze'ev 2002a) or cyberspace (Gur-Ze'ev 2000a). The calls for reestablishing "our own voice," such as in Cavell's educational project, normally hesitate to address this challenge and are part of normalizing education.

Normalizing education shields you from the kind of openness that will really endanger your potential by addressing the question of the entrance into the void created by the exile of the gods. As such it protects you from facing that you are not-you in a world where there is no one and nothing that will redeem you from the false quest for redemption that hides the abyss of Life from your life. Normalizing education must lull to sleep that dimension of Being that enhances the living creative power that ensures that there is not even an authentic "you" to return to or to retreat into. Normalizing education ensures in countless ways that you will not face the awakening of the responsibility to overcome "your" forgetfulness; that you will not look for transcendence other then the one that puts you to sleep as a normalized disciple of the given order of things; that you will not be able to transcend "your" forgetfulness of life and of "your" "own" view and voice. There are many keys to this cave but no genuine way for "departure" or "emancipation." One of its most effective keys is the evaluation apparatus, which matches the lock of the gate of the "thingness" of self-evidence. But the absence of the "key" or of "our authentic voice" is already an outcome, an effect of which normalizing education is devoted to veil or "unveil" in a safe, appeasing manner.

By its essence counter-education is committed to challenge the historical triumph of the violence of normalizing education (Gur-Ze'ev, Masschelein and Blake 2001). It is the imperative of counter-education, not its open possibility, to unveil the Same. Its responsibility is to address mere "thingness" as its true nature.

The Enlightenment allowed and promoted the courageous resistance to the tyranny of "external" authority and its forms of violence (Horkheimer 1985: 357). The thinkers of the Enlightenment introduced the imperative of critique as the main way to overcome self-evidence and the false promises of its future pleasures. The critical tradition challenged not only the traditional promises for union with God, the end of dialectics, the end of history, and the dwelling in an harmonic rational totality that historical progress will lead us into (Condorcet 1955: 4). It challenged even its own premises and the foundations of humanistic-oriented education. The dialectics of the Enlightenment rebelled against the critical rebellion itself while being part of it within such manifestations as Hegelian synthesis, Marxist communist utopias, Freudian understanding of the self, and Marcusian stilled redemption (Gur-Ze'ev 1996).

Simultaneously, however, it contained other quests and conflicting possibilities. These challenged the traditional achievements of spiritual education of enslaving humans within new myths, pushing them into newly invented bestialities. The Enlightenment was instrumental in dismantling the foundations of anti-critical versions of normalizing education. It deconstructed simultaneously the foundations of the arena where Spirit could dwell and where the human subject could attune himself or herself to the messianic moment, emancipatory ethos, or rational critique (Horkheimer 1985: 26). It problematized humanistic education itself as a new platonic cave to be deciphered, enlightened, and emancipated. Rational critique itself was challenged as were the presumptions about the foundation of rational humanistic investigation and arguments that rational consensus constituted a gate to more humane conditions of life. These were exposed as dangerous fantasies, or as nothing but a new, especially effective, version of normalizing education. At its best the anti-spiritual alternative did not rest on negative dialectic (Adorno 2000: 54–78); did not consume itself even on the edge of the exile with the quest for Spirit or the responsibility for entering into dwelling in the nearness of Being (Heidegger 1996: 245) and developed a diasporic perspective, called for the edification of a diasporic personality, and opened itself to a non-dogmatic, diasporic, redemptive impulse that negated all versions of normalizing religions.

The Tower of Babel and Education for Spirituality

The anti-authoritative, anti-dogmatic, anti-violent elements of humanistic education are distorted continuations of the project of the first humanists, who had built the Tower of Babel in a pre-philosophical era when they still had one language and no estrangement from life with no genuine/false historical consciousness.

Utopia was a past human condition when subject and object, spirituality and material immanence, mystery and humans were not yet separated. The utopians of the Tower of Babel were united by their human characteristics. For them transcendence was threatened only by divine violence, which destroyed utopia and transformed it into a future "utopia," enslaving them with dogmatic religious consensus and redemptive "education for spirituality." The defeat of the human remnants of the Tower of Babel has been imprinted, along with the Godly anti-human violence, in spiritual education since the fall of the pre-philosophical, pre-"spiritual" language of the early builders who were defeated, forgotten, and overtaken. Yet despite the prolonged triumph of the language of spiritual education and the undisputable hegemony of the essence of its logos, the ghost of the alternative that the Tower of Babel referred to is still very much alive.

Humanistic counter-education acknowledges that there is no way back to the utopia of the Tower of Babel. It accepts that counter-education is only possible within a post monolingual philosophical world, within homelessness and from it, with no God, authority, appeasing consensus or other inhuman manifestations of normalizing education. It is an open possibility not only as a challenge of the Same within consensus, dogma, and pleasure. It is also possible against and within rational emancipatory projects that historically promised more than life as abyss, meaninglessness, and homelessness. It promised consensus, pleasure, and eternal peace as future possibilities that are not endangered by old-style traditions threatened by "spirituality" and other manifestations of myth and pre-cultural dimensions of life. The Same, which benefited from the Fall of the Tower of Babel and its pre-"spiritual" language, is flourishing within the history of spiritual education. While being part of this tradition the Enlightenment rebelled against it in a manner that is still relevant to us today.

Modernity, Postmodernity, and Education for Spirituality

This anti-spiritual promise of the Enlightenment and its humanistic education did not overcome the fruits of the violence of traditional normalizing education. It claimed to be rational, scientific, and practical, but it introduced a new version of enslavement to the Same, to "thingness," to avoiding life in its full dangerousness, endless sufferings, meaninglessness, and homelessness. At the same time, as noticed by Pascal (1958), the anti-spiritual promise of the Enlightenment deprived modern, normalized humans of the possibility of transcending the given facts, overcoming mere life as the aim of Life, and overcoming mere pleasure with worthy suffering and love as elements of dialogical life that continues what the builders of the Tower of Babel began to create: transcendence that overcomes spirituality as set by God or by those violent enough to speak in His name or in the name of the truths about His absence.

The victory of modernity and its technological-scientific-capitalistic culture-industry introduces plenty of new pleasures, even if unequally, joined with new pains, disillusionment, and restrictions. These were justified and enhanced by the new historical forms of normalizing education developed by mass media and the general McDonaldization of reality within a process that was thrown into the sole role of capitalistic globalization logic and practices.

The void left by the disappearance of the gods, the demolition of the traditional holiness, and the cynicism of rational production of endless fashions of production, representation, and consumption of pleasures created a special place, a postmodern arena, for normalizing education. It was the last, most advanced version of anti-spirituality, and it created a place for the return of reinvented versions of Spirituality. This kind of spirituality, while containing some of the marks of the presence of the pre-modern Spirit, fundamentally incubates divine violence that triumphs in so many languages, agendas, and rebellions since the destruction of the utopia of the Tower of Babel.

Today's Education for Spirituality

The hegemonic version of today's Western call for "spirituality," "spiritual therapy," "spiritual consulting," "spiritual experiences" for "improving your quality of life," and the calls for "education for spirituality" are all today's fashion. They are part of the logic of the capitalistic production and consumption industry. In a postmodern society these new-age spiritual options become reified as a commodity that has a special role in the fabrication of human quests – their satisfaction and representation as a manifestation of "the good life."

While using the language of critique and the voice of the culture industry, the culture of "spirituality" reflects and serves the logos of the postmodern era. It is more tempting and dangerous than "merely" another manifestation of new-age cultural fashion. As such it makes a special contribution to the de-politicization of potential resistance to the present order of things and is a vital element of post-ideological normalizing education.

The current versions of normalizing education are domesticating, sometime even castrating, traditional calls for transcendence and resistance to the triumph of normalizing education that appease it within the common postmodern order. Postmodern culture has no problem with the new call for "spirituality," and "education for spirituality" threatens neither its logic nor its practices. The capitalistic modes of production, representation, and consumption here are essentially unchallenged. Here the inhuman condition or the omnipotent process of subjectification becomes not only bearable but also celebrated; the antagonistic potentials of the mystery and the danger of spirit are being dissolved. It has been reduced to "spirituality" and has become domesticated, ornamented, glorified.

Within education for spirituality the quest for transcendence and the presence of the holy becomes a commodity. As a commodity, education for spirituality is reified and obeys the laws of the capitalistic market, and it upgrades the efficiency of the violence of its normalizing education. With each achievement of this order the one-dimensionality of the rich, fluid, and hybrid postmodern culture industry becomes more secure, and the postmodern pleasure-machine drives humans further away from the spirit that was central to the utopia of the builders of the Tower of Babel who in refusing the divine imperative and the logos of the Garden of Eden, aligned themselves with a deeper and more "spiritual" attitude. This is the starting point of the postmodern alternative to the violence of normalizing education as manifested by education for spirituality.

The Violence of the Postmodern "Genuine" Educator

The postmodern educator of this arena calls for overcoming the quest for overcoming violence:

> The decision is not between the ego and the other, not between the self and the absolute other, but between the self and his ego: what kinds of violence should I and must I love, and what kinds should I and must I detest? There is no concept waiting at the telos, nor an absolute singularity at the arche. The sorts of violence associated with history demand merely to make the proper decisions proper to them: to continue history, to continue the logos of violence and the violence of the logos, to learn the enhancement of strengths and of the sensitivities (to history, to violence, to reason). (Tenenbaum 2000: 21)

He or she refuses to accept the division between "thingness," "sameness" and "Totally Other." He or she is committed to being positioned beyond good and evil, overcoming the division between violence, its objects, and its goals/rivals/disciples. Such a postmodern educational voice claims to transcend the quest for meaning, for "true" meaning, or the longing for a return to a pure language, or to overcome the distorted discourse in an ideal speech situation, an emancipated society, or for a redeemed human soul. It is anti-utopian, anti-transcendental, and totally disillusioned about the possibilities of overcoming normalizing education of any kind. This is accepted on faith, as a mission – "the call of the truth of Being," which is not to be resisted but loved, swallowed-by, united-with.

As a committed anti-Levinasian, such an educator surrenders and identifies himself or herself not with God or with the love of God, not with the utopian rebellion against divine violence and its history (whose positive conception/quest/God will eternally be veiled for us), not with prayer to be able to pray in a Godless world; but with pure, aimless violence, to the endlessness of total meaninglessness. Such an educator is much closer to Battille than to Stirner or Nietzsche and the Dionysian violence. As a manifestation of the logic of the historical moment, such a voice educates for total adjustment to the logic and practices of the postmodern pleasure machine, not solely in the level of representations, of the consciousness, but also into its soul, as it were a total unification with the One, with the holiest of holiest, with pure violence. It is only within the infinity of its aimlessness and meaninglessness that he or she finds the possible union with the One, with the omnipotent, with the power that calls upon us to respond, to approach the truth of Being, while refusing the question of truth and the abyss of transcendence from meaninglessness. Only as such it creates (the illusions of) meanings, transcendence, and worthy death.

In its peaceful manner this kind of normalizing education calls for responsibility that is totally different from the striving propelled by the postmodern culture industry. It calls for responsibility toward the nothingness of pure violence as that which will free some of us from the illusions of the "petty" and "low" sorts of violence, which call for the triumph of this or that class, ethnicity, claim, value, discourse, drive, or pleasure.

This kind of postmodern education is not so different from the other postmodern alternatives to the modern, rationalistic, and humanistic normalizing education. Actually, this postmodern education is not to be separated from the violence of the normalization processes as realized in educational sites of normalization such as CNN, MTV, commercial centers. What we are challenged with here is the same logic of spirituality, even if turned on its head. We are faced here with the educational call to do away with the moral dilemma and the dangers of worthy/unworthy life. It is a voice that presents us with nothingness as an ontological question with no ethical implications. It is a drive that calls us to surrender to the imperative of avoiding the question of whether to eat the apple of the knowledge of good and evil. The abyss between meaninglessness and the hegemonic-contingent truths and meanings of today is here bridged by the concept of violence. Counter-education will acknowledge it but will introduce love. But this is why normalizing will secure the impotence of counter-education and will quit its call for the human to become something and not someone.

The celebrated violence of the postmodern educator is an echo and a manifestation of the postmodern condition. This sort of violence has a special voice that calls us to commit ourselves to the absolute, to totality, to that which is beyond words, time, and individual existence. It promises to disconnect us from our "human potential," to enable us to become different from what we have been directed to become. It promises, again, a true Garden of Eden, to be liberated from the burden of the *principium individiationis*, from responsibility, and from uncertainty. Contrary to its will and pride, actually, this kind of postmodern education is nothing more than a supplement to the powers of traditional education for spirituality. As such it is committed to make the burning bush of counter-education irrelevant, invisible, or part of a "multitude of differences." In such a context counter-education becomes impossible or still worse, nothing but another version of normalizing education. In other words, this last version of the triumph of the Same, of pure violence, is not only a supplement of the logic of the other less-sophisticated forms of postmodern culture industry. But as such it is also the first challenge of present-day counter-education. But what is counter-education? And where are we to go to meet its truths, quests, or masters? Here I will end by saying something about the locus where it is impossible for counter-education to dwell: it is education for spirituality. And we should not underestimate education for spirituality even for giving us that much.

References

Adorno, T. 2000: *Negative Dialectics and the Possibility of Philosophy.* Oxford: Blackwell.

Augustine 1984: *The City of God*, H. Bettenson (trans.). London: Penguin.

Cavell, S. 1995: *Philosophical Passages: Wittgenstein, Emerson, Austin, and Derrida.* Oxford: Blackwell.

Condorcet, A. N. de 1955: *Sketch for a Historical Picture of the Progress of the Human Mind*, J. Barraclough (trans.) London: Weidenfeld and Nicolson.

Foucault, M. 1980: *Power/Knowledge – Selected Interviews and Other Writings 1972–1977*, C. Gordon et al. (trans.) New York: Harvester Wheatsheaf.

Gur-Ze'ev, I. 1996: *The Frankfurt School and the History of Pessimism.* Jerusalem: Magnes Press (Hebrew).

—— 2000b: The tower of the University of Haifa, the Tower of Babylon, and western halogocentris. *Theory and Critique*, 16: 239–43 (Hebrew).

——. 2000a: Critical Education in Cyberspace? *Educational Philosophy and Theory*, 32 (2): 209–31.

——, Masschelein, J. and Blake, N. 2001: Reflectivity, Reflection, and Counter-Education. *Studies in Philosophy and Education*, 20 (2) 93–106.

—— 2002b: *Destroying the Other's Collective Memory.* New York: Peter Lang.

—— 2002a: Counter Philosophy of Sport Education. In R. Lidor (ed.) *It is not Solely Sport.* Tel Aviv: Ramot (forthcoming).

Heidegger, M. 1996: *Basic Writings.* London: Routledge.

Horkheimer, M. 1985: *Gesammelte Schriften, VII.* Frankfurt a. Main: Fischer.

Pascal, B. 1958: *Pascal's Pensees.* New York: E.P. Dutton.

Plotinus 1981: *Aneads 11*, pp. 415–17. N. Spigel (trans.). Jerusalem: Mosad Bialik (Hebrew).

Tenenbaum, A. 2000: Anti-Human Responsibilities for a Postmodern Educator. In I. Gur-Ze'ev (ed.) *Conflicting Philosophies of Education in Israel/Palestine.* Dordrecht: Kluwer.

Contributors

Hanan A. Alexander is Associate Professor in the Faculty of Education at the University of Haifa where he heads the Center for Jewish Education and the Department of Overseas Studies.

Iraj Ayman is on the faculty of the School of Education at Capella University and a member of the Board of the Wilmette Institute, USA.

Nicholas C. Burbules is Gauthrier Professor in the Department of Educational Policy Studies at the University of Illinois, Urbana-Champaign, USA and editor of *Educational Theory*.

Ari Bursztein is Rabbi of the Moriah Congregation in Haifa, Israel and Research Fellow at the Center for Jewish Education, University of Haifa.

Zvi Bekerman is Senior Lecturer in the School of Education and the Melton Center for Jewish Education at the Hebrew University of Jerusalem.

Jane Buckley teaches Religious Studies and Citizenship at Tomas Hardye School in Dorchester, UK.

Howard Deitcher directs the Melton Center for Jewish Education at the Hebrew University of Jerusalem.

Claudia Eppert is Assistant Professor in the Department of Curriculum and Instruction at Louisiana State University.

Clive Erricker co-directs the Children and Worldviews Project and is a joint editor of *The International Journal of Children's Spirituality*. He also serves as County Inspector for Religious Education in Hampshire, UK.

Jane Erricker is Principal Lecturer in Education at King Alfred's College

Winchester, UK, co-director of the Children and Worldviews Project and a joint editor of *The International Journal of Children's Spirituality.*

Liam Gearon is Professorial Reader in Education at the University of Surrey Roehampton, UK, where he directs the Centre for Research in Human Rights.

Amihud Gilead is Professor in the Department of Philosophy at the University of Haifa.

Jen Glaser teaches in the Mandel School for Educational Leadership and the Melton Center for Jewish Education.

Ilan Gur-Ze'ev is Senior Lecturer in the Faculty of Education at the University of Haifa and editor of *Issues in Education.*

Pamela Ebstyne King is Research Assistant Professor at Fuller Theological Seminary, Pasadena, California.

Terence H. McLaughlin is Professor of Philosophy of Education at the Institute of Education, University of London and a Fellow of St. Edmund's College, Cambridge.

Mary Elizabeth Mullino Moore is Professor of Religion and Education at the Candler School of Theology, Emory University, Atlanta, Georgia, where she directs the Program for Women in Theology and Ministry.

Moshe Re'em is Rabbi of Temple Beth-El, Allentown, Pennsylvania.

Friedrich Schweitzer is Professor of Religious Education and Practical Theology at the Evangelisch-Theologiches Seminar, University of Tübingen, Germany.

Inna Semetsky tutors in Philosophy and Bioethics at Monash University, Melbourne, Australia, and is a recipient of the Kevelson Memorial Award from the Semiotic Society of America.

Ann M. Trousdale is Associate Professor in the Department of Curriculum and Instruction at Louisiana State University.

Index